FILIPINO AMERICAN SPORTING CULTURES

Filipino American Sporting Cultures

The Racial Politics of Play

Constancio R. Arnaldo, Jr.

NEW YORK UNIVERSITY PRESS

New York

NEW YORK UNIVERSITY PRESS
New York
www.nyupress.org

© 2024 by New York University
All rights reserved

Library of Congress Cataloging-in-Publication Data
Names: Arnaldo, Constancio R. Jr., author.
Title: Filipino American sporting cultures : the racial politics of play /
Constancio R. Arnaldo, Jr.
Description: New York : New York University Press, [2024] |
Includes bibliographical references and index.
Identifiers: LCCN 2023057124 (print) | LCCN 2023057125 (ebook) |
ISBN 9781479820900 (hardback) | ISBN 9781479820917 (paperback) |
ISBN 9781479820924 (ebook) | ISBN 9781479820931 (ebook other)
Subjects: LCSH: Minorities in sports—United States. | Filipino Americans—
Social conditions. | Pacquiao, Manny, 1978– | Identity (Psychology) |
Racism in sports—United States.
Classification: LCC GV709.5 .A76 2024 (print) | LCC GV709.5 (ebook) |
DDC 306.4830973—dc23/eng/20240105
LC record available at https://lccn.loc.gov/2023057124
LC ebook record available at https://lccn.loc.gov/2023057125

This book is printed on acid-free paper, and its binding materials are chosen for strength and durability. We strive to use environmentally responsible suppliers and materials to the greatest extent possible in publishing our books.

Manufactured in the United States of America

10 9 8 7 6 5 4 3 2 1

Also available as an ebook

This book is dedicated to my mother,
Beulah Arnaldo-Dionson,

my brothers,
Nathaniel and Christopher Arnaldo,

and my partner, Norma A. Marrun.

CONTENTS

Introduction

The Crossover

A Filipina[1] American named Jenilyn and I met inside a Coffee Bean Tea & Leaf in Torrance,[2] California, during a chilly early January evening. Born in the Philippines, Jenilyn was six years old when she migrated to the United States in 1988 with her father and sister, settling in Lawndale, California, a relatively diverse lower-to-middle-class city in Los Angeles County. As I learned about her love for sports, our conversation took off around all things concerning sporting cultures, including basketball, softball, volleyball, track and field, and cheering with her family and friends for Philippine-born boxer Manny "Pac-Man" Pacquiao.

During our interview, Jenilyn communicated how her various challenges stymied certain aspects of her love of sports. In telling me about her basketball experiences, especially playing against some of her male Filipino American church friends as an adult, she recounted how she felt they did not take her basketball ability seriously: "I didn't like it whenever they would pass me the ball and all the guys just stood there and [did] not play defense against me. I wanted a challenge [and] I didn't want to be treated like, 'She's a girl, I can't touch her.'"

An admitted competitor, Jenilyn shared that she played with the same intensity and competitive drive against men as against women. When I asked whether she would rather that men compete hard against her, she responded with self-assuredness, laughing, "Of course! Yeah, I definitely want to. I love it when I cross them over." Jenilyn emphasized that this particular move, essentially a fake-out, always captured the attention of her Filipino American friends: "Whenever I would play in the league, or pickup games, whenever I would cross over a guy, . . . everybody would just go, 'Ooh, she crossed you over!,' [and] they would make a big deal out of it. That would be the general reaction." I was interested in what she thought about these comments and reactions: "I just laugh. I mean,

I could see how it could be a bit sexist. It's like, why can't I cross them over? Because I'm a girl? They highlight the fact that I'm a girl. But I mean, I grew up with these guys, so I don't really take it personal[ly]."

The *crossover* is a vernacular term and move in basketball that entails an offensive player using fakery to fool their defender by forcing them into a bodily imbalance. At times, this imbalance leads to the defender stumbling or falling to the ground. When the defender falls, the audience and other players typically respond with astonishment and surprise and colloquially refer to this effective move as an "ankle breaker" or "breaking someone's ankles." The *crossover* in basketball settings is a kind of trickery. When executed correctly, it enables the offensive player to manipulate their body, their opponent's body, the space, and the basketball to move past the defender in order to shoot and score. It requires not only an acute understanding of timing and spatial awareness but also creativity and basketball skill. It is considered a particularly noteworthy move because of its high degree of difficulty. In gendered (masculine) terms, for South Asian American *ballers*—the slang term for skilled basketball players—the move also involves "crossing over" into normative masculinity.[3] In this example, Jenilyn routinely performed the crossover on the basketball courts. It is a move that many athletes practice repeatedly, honing their skill. Crossing someone over is a desirable practice that evokes pleasurable reactions and celebratory narratives from ordinary people in their everyday lives. The move, as we know it today, owes much of its stylistic flair and evolution to 1970s African American working-class communities who played in parks and playgrounds. It was in these spaces where creativity, imagination, and improvisation—like the crossover—flourished outside of the rigid playing style of the National Basketball Association (NBA).[4]

Jenilyn's experiences illuminate the everyday, taken-for-granted nature of (certain) sports as a masculine domain. She did not seem to find her friends' comments egregiously sexist, given her ambivalence to their reaction. Her embodied memory of performing the crossover is a nod to athletic performance that traverses time and space. Her recollections also tell us that there is a clearly gendered realm of sporting ability and of how sporting achievements are read: her male teammates evidently perceived her femininity as incompatible with the broadly masculinized reading of sports in the American nation or in the Filipina/o American diaspora—a perception that prompted the highly affective and somewhat surprised responses to her athletic performance vis-à-vis her opponent of "Ooh, she crossed you over!" Although her crossover was a part of her self-expression, pleasure, and repertoire of basketball creativity, that response in itself shows that others did not commonly associate it with Filipina Americans. Jenilyn was keenly aware of the gendered contours of sports, the negative perceptions of women's abilities, and the types of activities they are expected to do and enjoy. Performing the crossover was not one of them.

Jenilyn's love of sports, it became clear through our conversations, was not just as a fan but as an athletic participant who enjoyed sports as physical practice, pleasure, and play. This vignette challenges the idea of meritocracy in sports. It offers a window into the practices of gendered, sexualized, and raced citizenship in sport, in the diaspora, and in the nation(s). We see here how certain sporting practices, such as the crossover, are gendered and raced in relation to longer histories that transcend this moment. In other words, these practices exceed the realms of pleasure and desire generally associated with Asian America and Asian American women's lives.

The reaction to Jenilyn's crossover is not unique to her experience, nor does it happen only in Filipina/o communities. In mixed-gender basketball settings, I have witnessed countless instances in which (cisgender) men and women have played against each other, and I have noted the kinds of competitive, athletic, and gendered expectations they are scripted to perform. In these settings, I have observed how race, gender, and sexuality collide in particular interpellations of women on the sporting court and playing field that result in "patriarchal dividends."[5] Still, Jenilyn's sporting experiences invite a wider exploration of Filipina/o Americans' relationship to nation, diaspora, race, class, gender, and sexuality. What does it mean for Filipina Americans like Jenilyn to play a sport that many in the community consider an arena of masculinity? How is her crossover also a crossing over of various desirable, policed, and pleasurable realms of identity formation? And how do Filipina Americans in particular, through their play and competitive desires, destabilize the diaspora's highly masculine boundaries and forms of ethno-nationalism? It was clear that Jenilyn's friends regarded her gender as a point of rupture rather than seeing

her crossover as a normative performance of basketball culture. Jenilyn crossed over into gendered and racial identities. By performing the
crossover, a move that is largely associated with maleness and masculinity, she rejected and reconfigured stereotypical projections of Asian
American female bodies as demure, submissive, and passive. It was
her way of challenging the historical racializations and connections
between "race and ability."[6] This dissonant reality invites us to rethink
how basketball is imagined as a quintessentially American sport that
both restricts and expands forms of belonging to both the American
nation and the diaspora.

In this book I demonstrate how Filipina/o Americans engage with
sports to reveal the shifting nature of Filipina/o Americanness, and in the
process, understand how Filipina/o Americans have negotiated US racial,
class, gender, and colonial processes. The majority of the research for this
book occurred in Southern California, as the Filipina/o American community constitutes one of the largest Asian ethnic groups in California, as
well as in the United States as a whole (over four million in total), and has
a rich history of sporting participation that has been largely overlooked.[7]
In this book, I highlight issues of Filipina/o American identity formation through the popular cultural realm of sport and its consumption in
order to understand Filipina/o American desires, their relations to colonialism and postcolonialism, the various kinds of racialization of Asian
Americans, and the local, national, and transnational scales of sporting
engagement and resistance that extend and exceed white normative citizenship. I document how American sports, once a US colonial institution
in the Philippines, in the twenty-first century remain an integral, but differently conceptualized and consumed, social institution through which
Filipina/o Americans engage questions of US and Philippine nationhood,
respectively, as well as of belonging and identity formation. In short, I investigate and come to understand the crossover as a metaphorical, symbolic, and corporeal practice of engaging and disrupting stereotypes and
racializations that bind certain communities to certain locations, certain
nations, and certain leisure spaces. I resist the dominance of a singular
nation in understanding (Asian and Asian American) identities, and I
cross over or obfuscate the minimal attention paid to race, sports, and
women in Asian and Asian American diasporic contexts.

By incorporating both everyday sporting engagements and spectator sport settings, I illuminate how Filipina/o American identity crosses over (as verb) multiple histories, nations, and locations, refusing to be bounded by fixed ideas of space, time, and territory that dominate earlier academic considerations of diasporas. Furthermore, I show how crossovers (as noun) are a transnational, transhistorical measure of analysis and ethnography that centers movement and mobility while attending to the material realities of colonialism, imperialism, and race. Crossing over is not a simple movement across terrains, but rather can be a set of lenses by which to investigate the dis-easing of normative conceptions of Filipina/o American identities, desires, and pleasures.

Filipina/o Americans' engagement with games, sport, and leisure is evident prior to and during US colonialism. Indeed, their participation in sports has been and is varied, whether as amateur athletes playing on club teams, in leagues, and in tournaments, or as avid supporters of their favorite collegiate teams, professional teams, and favorite athletes from a variety of sports. Moreover, professional sports teams intentionally market to the Filipina/o community. Major League Baseball (MLB) teams, like the Oakland Athletics, San Francisco Giants, San Diego Padres, Los Angeles Dodgers, and Seattle Mariners, have all identified Asian Americans as an important consumer base, and they have dedicated Filipino Heritage Nights to celebrate and cater to their large Filipina/o American fan populations.[8] In the NBA, the Golden State Warriors and Los Angeles Clippers also designate a Filipino Heritage Night.[9] The fact that these professional sporting institutions cater to the Filipina/o American community indicates an emerging but already substantial Asian American presence in the larger sports world. Yet, to assume that access to these sporting spaces is available to all members of the community ignores how patriarchal privilege and middle-class resources shape who can access these spaces.

Although the US sporting industry recognizes and targets Filipina/o Americans as key consumers, scholarship about their sporting participation largely fails to take into account how sports are critical arenas in and through which to understand larger questions of Filipina/o identity formations, racialization, diasporic contours, and postcolonial sporting cultures. One exception is *Desi Hoop Dreams* by anthropologist Stanley

Thangaraj. In it, Thangaraj shows how basketball and performances of masculinity are simultaneously inclusionary and exclusionary. He illustrates how practices of masculinity among South Asian American men offer examples of basketball crossovers that challenge Asian American masculine lack and thus offer different readings and performances of their racialized masculinity.[10] I, by contrast, examine and employ the crossover that implicates women like Jenilyn—a crossover that also crosses transnational realms in order to make sense of the local.

Crossover as Analytic and Theoretical Optic

Inspired by Jenilyn's sporting practices, this book takes seriously the instructive possibilities of the multiple applications of crossing over—as an embodied practice across the intersection of gender, race, sexuality, class, and ability and also as a form of trickery. In much the same way that the physical act of the basketball crossover destabilizes the defender by suddenly moving in an unexpected direction, this book takes sudden turns to illuminate new and unexpected directions of thought, both theoretically and methodologically. Thus, in unexpected ways, I interrogate the practices of race, gender, and sexuality in nationalist and ethnonationalist spaces of sport and leisure. I chart the movement of Filipina/o American communities through leisure spaces in a transnational context in sudden and destabilizing ways that go beyond and transgress territorially bound notions of self and identity. Crossing over is thus literally and symbolically a traversing, challenging, and rewriting of diasporic identities in a hypermobile, highly mediated, and global world. It fakes us out and moves us in unfamiliar directions that lead to new pathways and new interventions. In thus engaging and charting such understandings, I emphasize how the theoretical contributions of queer of color critique and women of color feminism animate the crossover.[11] I investigate how this conceptualization offers a window into understanding the tactics through which Filipina/o American communities affirm and challenge racial and gendered norms that govern their experiences in the United States and their imaginations of the Philippines.

The crossover is a challenge to the expected, normative, racialized, and heteropatriarchal understandings of diaspora, "home," and the nation. It insists upon social formations of difference coconstituted through race, gender, class, sexuality, and nation.[12] In order to make sense of this type of movement and to highlight instability, I underscore a reading practice that honors and critically engages with these social categories to undermine "universal" readings of subjecthood and national belonging. As scholars Grace Hong and Roderick Ferguson note, social formations refuse equivalence because lived experiences for people of color are heterogeneous across different spaces, places, and times.[13] Thus, rather than a single way forward, these disruptions and crossings break singular, essentialized readings of identity and reveal multiple directions. Race, gender, sexuality, ability, ethnicity, and class intertwine in shifting and unexpected ways; they move differently based on social context and the canon used to describe various spaces. As evident in my interview with Jenilyn, Filipina Americans in the diaspora engage with the contours of diaspora in ways that unsettle its masculine borders and reconfigure the perception that its boundaries are immutably gendered.[14] Jenilyn, along with other Filipina/o Americans highlighted in this book, "play[s] with the world," to borrow from the anthropologist Martin Manalansan's seminal work on Filipino gay men in the diaspora. Manalansan alludes to the politics of everyday life and how queer Filipino men mobilize ritual performances of self and identity to articulate resistant identities. In his book, participants "played with the world" not only to "confuse, distract, and fool the public" but to fake out dominant notions of diasporic Filipina and Filipino Americanness.[15]

I likewise create distance from normative understandings of Filipina/o America in this book while underscoring new subjectivities, possibilities, desires, and dreams. Some of the Filipina Americans I highlight in this book, for example, reimagine what we have long conceptualized as femininity and masculinity. Jenilyn's crossover highlighted practices of sporting masculinity that were not solely relevant to men. Her crossover becomes recognizable when done *to* men. It is a crossover informed by female masculinity that tricks, disrupts, and breaks the normative gendered (male-bodied, men-centered) conceptions of sporting masculinity. This book refuses to acquiesce to binary categories. Masculinity, as queer theorist J. Jack Halberstam notes, cannot solely be ascribed to "the male body and its effects."[16]

Why the focus on Filipina/os? Contemporary Filipina/o immigrants navigate various national borders as laborers to fill the needs of the global capitalist economy.[17] They are, as the sociologist Robyn Rodriguez reminds us, "migrants for export" whose labor generates almost thirty billion dollars in remittances,[18] which crucially become a way in which overseas Filipino workers (OFWs) sustain the Philippines economy.[19] Thus, moving back and forth literally and figuratively, Filipinos have always crossed boundaries and seas—within and outside Philippine and US borders—demonstrating the elasticity of their movement in the form of labor and cultural cross-pollination.[20] It is in this crossover/cross over spirit that I decenter and disrupt social and national formations as discrete, coherent, and singular. In this book, I build on scholarly conversations with Filipina/o American studies scholars in particular and Asian American studies and American studies scholars in general who critically engage with the promises and possibilities that transnational and transhistorical cultural forms afford Filipina/o Americans.[21] Refusing to believe that culture is static or that it is *always* an avenue of resistance, I confront the messiness, the in-betweenness, and ambivalence of sporting cultures as a metaphor for understanding such people and ideas that move and theorize in unexpected, sudden, and necessary ways.

Filipina/o American studies scholarship on leisure, for example, has focused on expressive forms of culture, including Pilipino Culture Nights music, DJing, taxi dance halls, and contemporary dance forms like hip-hop.[22] Largely absent from that focus is knowledge about and scholarship on the enduring legacy of sports to Filipina/o American life in the contemporary period, despite US colonialism's role in institutionalizing sports in the Philippines. However, two notable publications on basketball cultures do demonstrate how sports are constitutive of Filipina/o diasporic formations—albeit in Canada and Australia. The critical geographer May Farrales notes how Filipino Canadian men negotiate identities that are intimately tied to the Canadian colonial project. She illustrates how Filipino Canadian men perform heteronormative and virile masculinities through basketball that allow them to invert their racializations, but she focuses only on how they do this within settler colonial logics in Canada.[23]

Traveling west across the Pacific, sociologist Kristine Aquino observes how Filipino Australian basketball players embody everyday resistance to combat a hegemonic national identity of Australian whiteness.[24] The dominant white society, Aquino argues, deems Filipinos' basketball style of play to be "uncontrollable." From Filipinos' perspectives, however, their styles of *streetball basketball* and bodily habitus are modes through which they negotiate and resist the whitened boundaries of Australian national belonging. In these spaces in Canada and Australia, basketball not only governs how Filipino men negotiate their identities, but how they do so in ways that reflect their particular locales and histories.

In contrast to Farrales and Aquino, I perceive and apply the crossover as an appropriation of pathways and improvisations that lead to other diasporic possibilities. For example, while Farrales and Aquino analyze Filipino diasporic masculinity, my interlocutors' actions and embodiment, including those of Filipina American athletes, like Jenilyn, and queer Filipina/o Americans, dissipate the heteropatriarchal rigidity of seemingly fixed gendered diasporic boundaries. While the crossover can further disrupt perceived immutable boundaries of diaspora, it also, through the racial signifier of "brown" intervenes in and reconfigures the Black-white racial paradigm.

Crossing Over the Racial Parameters of Brown Bodies at Play

Sport is deeply connected to the outside world. At the same time, it maintains its own distinctiveness from other social institutions.[25] Sporting cultures are tied to notions of what it means to claim the American and (at times) the Philippine nations simultaneously. For some Filipina/o Americans, cheering on boxer Manny "Pac-Man" Pacquiao is more than about his wins and losses. How they interpret his muscular brown body has as much to do with how they feel *seen* and *represented* in the local and global popular imagination and how he serves as a metaphor for diasporic and national identification. My analysis builds on existing scholarship by the relatively small, but growing, cohort of scholars who critically center not only Asian Americans' sporting cultures but also the diverse ways that these communities negotiate different relationships to the nation, their community, and society.[26] I underscore the dynamic between transnational and local processes that inform Filipina/o American identities by ethnographically capturing everyday embodied encounters of leisure and play. In this way, I engage with the messy and contradictory processes of diaspora, transnationalism, masculinity, and heteropatriarchy, showing that Filipina/o Americans both reaffirm the masculine borders of diaspora and, at other times, challenge it.

I use *brown* as a historical and contemporary racial lens of Filipina/o Americans' lived racial realities across social, political, and legal realms.[27] Brown, as a racial signifier, interrogates how Filipinos have negotiated racial meanings throughout different historical and contemporary moments in US society.[28] Filipina/o Americans' racial legibility has at times been ambiguous;[29] Americans often imagined them as "shape shifters," according to literary scholar Allan Punzalan Isaac, because the US imperial past renders Filipino racialized bodies incommensurable within the dominant US racial classification system of Black and white. During US colonialism, *brown* signified colonized Filipinos' "Little Brown Brother" status within the racial (and gendered) hierarchy, a perceived term of colonial endearment and yet one already structured through domination and power.[30] The "Little Brown Brother" trope crossed the Pacific when working-class immigrant Filipinos arrived on US shores in the early twentieth century. "Brown" thus became a racial descriptor and intersected with Filipino masculinity and sexuality. Americans used it as a pejorative and racist term to describe Filipino male laborers variously as "little brown monkeys,"[31] "brown hordes,"[32] a "brown peril,"[33] a "brown menace,"[34] and a "brown-skinned servant force."[35] White society, and in particular white femininity, perceived them as threats. Despite these racist classifications, some Filipino immigrant men saw the potential of the brown body through boxers like Pancho Villa and Ceferino Garcia, whose skills, boxing prowess, and brown masculine performances inverted stereotypes of the meek, emasculated, and feminine Filipino man. Instead, Villa and Garcia embodied Filipino virility, power, and possibility.[36] Indeed, in everyday life, early twentieth-century Filipina/o Americans created sporting spaces precisely because they were excluded from white sporting spaces.[37] Their brownness reflected their liminal state, the in-between, and the ambiguity through which they, via sports, sought to make claims to belonging.[38]

Thus, my application of *brown* undermines the dominant Black-white racial logic in the United States. As a racially liminal term grounded in the afterlives of Spanish and US imperialisms, *brown* notes the limits of the Black-white racial paradigm and US colonial amnesia. It shifts and moves within the paradigm—never bound to either Black or white—to highlight sociocultural, national, and historical mixing that produces brown Filipinos.

In the 1960s, Filipino Americans reclaimed and reappropriated the term "brown." "Brown," as second-generation Filipino American Peter Jamero asserts, claims difference from East Asian Americans. Jamero notes how the civil rights movement enabled Filipino Americans to claim their brownness in a more affirmative manner. Intentionally using the term "brown" marks a refusal to see a homogeneous "Asian America," and instead embraces the "heterogeneity and multiplicity" that Filipina/o Americans experience as brown Asian Americans.[39] The Filipina/o American community I describe in this book thus, intentionally or not, creates brown communal spaces of belonging in a number of sporting spaces including boxing fandom settings, basketball leagues, and flag football tournaments. These communal spaces are akin to Thangaraj's notion of "brown out spaces" which South Asian American male basketball players create. Paradoxically, these spaces are inclusive of the community and yet exclusive to "various Others."[40] Moreover, brown, as Thangaraj asserts, is a flexible racial category that gives South Asian American men some social mobility while underscoring that the category also comes with its own contours of racial ambiguity, resulting in racial illegibility. Similarly, Filipina/o Americans' production of brown communal spaces fittingly demonstrates the shifting nature of racial belonging, citizenship, and sports.

My conceptual framing of the crossover does not aim to recreate racially stark or gendered divisions of Black and white or male and female but instead aims to analyze the in-betweenness, the ambiguous and ambivalent renderings of Filipina/o American subjectivity that harken back to how they have occupied a liminal national space, while also taking us through the unexpected ways in which these communities speak with and against nationalist and ethno-nationalist projects.[41] Because historically race in the United States has been grounded in the Black-white racial binary, it ignores Asian Americans' racialized experiences and obscures how they have used sports to navigate their own understandings of the racially inflected contours of national belonging.[42] As Thangaraj importantly reminds us, the Black-white racial paradigm is both "insufficient and critical to"[43] Asian American communities.

Crossing over is consequently about how Filipina/o Americans negotiate the Black and white racial binary in ways that disrupt and exceed the dominant political and social discourses of Black or white. In particular, by bringing in queer diasporic critique and queer of color critique,[44] we can see how Filipina/o Americans' negotiations of racial logics always work through gender and sexuality to clarify how they are always outsiders to the normative sporting logic of the United States.[45]

Filipina/o Americans fake, challenge, and escape simple or easy racial classifications. In being racialized through a particular brownness, Filipina/o Americans have toggled in and out of racial categories in their claims to whiteness, Latinoness, and Mongolianness, while also being racialized alongside Blackness.[46] Through the spontaneity of the basketball crossover, the theoretical crossovers in this book engage with ethnography and history to shift and move in similar ways to destabilize hegemonic understandings of sport, race, and diasporic identity. If we align ourselves with hegemonic examinations of sports, we not only privilege sporting performances as a male preserve,[47] we also ignore the different ways in which Filipina Americans challenge existing stereotypes of Asian American women as "fragile," "sexually exotic," or "passive."[48] As an act of transgression narrated in the opening vignette, Jenilyn's crossover prompted her male counterparts to reflect upon what a Filipina American body *can do, mean,* and *index.* In this instance, sport not only generates pleasures for Filipino Americans, it also enables some of my research participants—particularly Filipina Americans—to use their embodied athletic performances to reconfigure perceived limitations of what racialized and gendered bodies can and cannot do while also critiquing and expanding the contours of belonging within the diaspora, within nation(s), and within transnational circuits of popular culture, labor, commodities, and desire.[49] Crossovers illustrate the possibilities that were always in these multiple spaces, but were typically erased, silenced, and elided.

Filipina/o Americans' "critical muscle memories"[50]—to borrow a term from media studies scholar Samantha Sheppard—remind us that the invention of the sporting Filipino body is historical, a "kinesthetic metaphor" that remembers US colonial imperatives of social control in the embodied form of discipline, routinization, and Christianized training along with Filipina/o resistance and interjection of their own particular sports and forms of leisure. In this way, twenty-first-century Filipina/o Americans' sporting performances in arenas and on fields cross over time, space, and memory and are thus always transhistorical and transnational.[51] Whether they know it or not, when they cheer on Pacquiao, or engage in forms of *play*, Filipina/o Americans summon and communicate longer histories of immigration, labor, leisure, pleasure, and power that are tied to postcolonial, global rankings of nation, US empire, and their lived experiences of race.

US Colonialism, Expansion, and Sports

Filipina/o Americans and their participation with quintessentially American pastimes such as basketball, football, and baseball, did not begin *in* the United States. A more critical account identifies that sporting institutions were a fundamental part of US colonial rule in the Philippines starting in 1898. At the turn of the twentieth century, Filipina/o revolutionaries, who were already fighting against their Spanish colonizers and had declared their independence from Spain, were then forced to turn their attention to invading US colonizing forces in what became the Philippine-American War. The historian Luzviminda Francisco notes that the Philippine-American War was the "first Vietnam,"[52] a genocidal campaign in which up to one million Philippine civilians were killed through isolation, starvation, and "scorched earth" practices, among other tactics.[53] The Philippine-American War quelled the Philippine nationalist movement. Once US colonial forces wrested control of their new territory and its subjects, they implemented a "benevolent assimilation" policy, putting in place an education system modeled after the US public school system as English became the primary language of instruction. The earliest colonial teachers were soldiers of the invading US army and, thereafter, American missionaries, followed by American teachers. Colonized Filipinos were taught US history and the United States' lofty ideals of "freedom" and "democracy." The schools ostensibly sought to "build character" through education and, to that end, encouraged Filipina/os to embrace notions of honesty, industry, and sportsmanship.

Following a dogmatic belief in "manifest destiny" and ideologies of racial superiority over Filipinos, US colonial administrators and organizations like the Young Men's Christian Association (YMCA) ushered in American sports. The idea that sport would "civilize" the racially "inferior" Filipinos drove this collaboration. Under the aegis of the US education system (primarily through the category of physical education), sport and recreation were part and parcel of the US educational, colonial process.

Indeed, promoting sports and physical education was hardly a benevolent endeavor. Sports, at one point, were a disciplining tool to promote and perpetuate ideas about Filipino bodies as inferior, uncivilized, and savage, in need of sports to "assimilate" them by transforming their bodies into "'good' colonial subjects."[54] The US colonial state regarded sports as key to training their "Little Brown Brothers." Coined by William H. Taft, first general governor of the Philippines, the phrase "Little Brown Brothers" connoted the US state's desire to exacerbate a perceived Filipino familial (colonized) intimacy—one that was already embedded in unequal relations of power—by symbolically and physically placing colonized Filipinos in a racially subordinated position.[55]

Indeed, Filipinos crossed over from being racialized as Black (they were called the n-word[56]) by US military forces during the Philippine-American War into the "softer 'brown'"[57] Little Brown Brother. These dynamics involved comparative racializations that framed Black communities in certain ways and subsequently to interpolate the Filipina/o as little, as brown, and as family in need of older brotherly, paternalistic guidance. Framing Filipinos as diminutive, in other words, had much to do with asserting colonial hierarchies and developing the Filipino under US tutelary knowledge; sports and physical education became one of the vehicles through which this assertion was carried out. Furthermore, tropes of Filipinos as Little Brown Brothers flowed from one part of the Pacific to the US mainland, popularized by American newspapers that informed how early twentieth-century Filipino boxers were represented as "Little Brown Dolls," or "little, brown-skinned boxer[s]" who drew a big crowd.[58] Yet with their fistic success, boxers like Ceferino "the Bolo Puncher" Garcia and Pancho Villa challenged assumptions of Filipino athletic inferiority. This, however, did not free them from the white supremacist racial logics that imposed diminutive markers upon them.[59]

One of the ways in which the United States used white supremacist logic to show "progress" was through the medium of photography. Images captured from the *Philippine Exposition Souvenir Booklet* show a picture of the Igorot Ball Players,[60] which not only displayed the white American public's panoptic power of *looking* but was also used as empirical evidence of sports' assimilative promise.[61] The linguistic anthropologist Angela Reyes asserts how photography, as a colonial state technology, calcified an *image sequence* of Filipinos, noting evolutionary logics of "before and after," and "wild and civilized," which carried symbolic import through a "transformability of personhood across the lifespan."[62]

In one cartoon in the *Boston Sunday Globe* titled "Expansion, Before and After" depicted Filipinos as animals, savages, and barbarians prior to expansion (see figure 1.1). On the left side of the panel, a Filipino baseball player is dressed up in a standard baseball uniform holding a bat. The caption below reads, "He could exchange the war club for the baseball readily." On the right side, another panel reads, "His old habit of running amuck will aid greatly on the football field."[63] In the foreground of both panels, Filipinos are literally blackened—wearing nothing but grass skirts, holding "war clubs," and showing their uncontrollable dispositions to run amuck and chase each other. Here, the uncivilized constitution of Filipinos is hypermarked in conjunction with the civilizing promise of American sport.[64]

Indeed, the *Boston Globe* was communicating that US expansion and Filipino involvement with sports would facilitate a transformation of savage Filipinos into subjects who would eventually transform into civilized beings with civilized ways of knowing and acting. This was the normative understanding of crossover that Filipina/os had to negotiate. Thus, the United States regarded sports like baseball and football—two quintessentially American sporting pastimes—as vehicles by which not only to train Filipino bodies to become civilized subjects but also to inculcate US-centric notions of loyalty to the nation and to performances of masculinity.

But there were always other possibilities and, thus, other crossovers. As dance studies scholar J. Lorenzo Perillo astutely notes, analyzing the same image in the context of dance, "The caption and other 'before and after' scenes depicting sports, transportation, and a beaming native pri-

Figure 1.1. "Expansion, Before and After," *Boston Sunday Globe*, March 5, 1899.

marily serve to caricature Filipinos as hostile and uncivilized, naturalize these traits as 'well-suited' for colonization, and minimize the violence of war and subsequent 'benevolent assimilation' to 'but a step.'"[65]

Filipinos also became subjects of racial derision and were racialized alongside African Americans.[66] Rather than isolate race-making as distinct and singular, it is critical to underscore how civilizational imperatives, like African American enslavement and US colonialism in the Philippines, worked as racial projects. These racial projects, as American studies scholars Grace Hong and Roderick Ferguson stress, benefit from a comparative racialization framework to animate the overlapping configurations of power that inform relationality and the intersectional nature of racializations.[67]

Although Filipina/os learned sports through US empire, this does not mean that the colonial process was smooth, linear, and seamless, or that Filipina/os simply reinforced colonial sports' intended goals.[68] There were particular Filipina/o consumption patterns and reconfigurations of sport both in the Philippines and in the diaspora. As we see next, once immigrants and their second-generation children settled in the United States, sports were one arena through which they negotiated their racially subordinated status, all while confronting various anti-Filipino sentiments apparent in the immigration policies, racist sporting spaces, and various laws that targeted them.

Filipina/o Immigration, Exclusion, Sports, and Community Formations

Significant waves of Filipino immigration occurred in the early twentieth century.[69] The damaging and devastating effects brought on by the Philippine-American War left colonized Filipinos with little to no sense of financial security on the islands. This, coupled with the fact that the US implemented a public education system that taught US ideals of "liberty," "democracy," and "freedom," influenced Filipinos' desires to migrate to the United States. The US colonial government sent a smaller number of Filipino students—known as *pensionado/as*, or children of wealthy families—to study in elite universities. As part of the US colonial government's "benevolent assimilation" decree, pensionado/as were expected to complete their studies and return to the Philippines, take up political positions, and influence the trajectory of the Philippine nation (to the benefit of the United States' interests, of course). According to *the Filipino Student Bulletin*[70] (which was part of the Filipino Students Christian Movement), some of these students immersed themselves in sports through intramural activities, competed against other Filipino student organizations, and subscribed to the US goal for colonized Filipinos to perpetuate its Christian ethos.[71]

United States colonialism also structured immigration patterns to occupied Hawai'i, the West Coast, the Pacific Northwest, and the Midwest.[72] Many of these immigrants were working-class Filipino men, and a smaller number of immigrants were Filipina. In the post–World War II period, an increasing number of Filipinas came as a result of the War Brides Act, which allowed the Filipina wives of US military men who had served during World War II to join their spouses in the United States.[73]

Upon arriving on US shores, Filipino immigrants, considered "cheap and exploitable laborers," filled labor needs in agricultural, cannery, and domestic work sectors. Once the Great Depression hit in the late 1920s and early 1930s, their small but significant population experienced white racist, anti-Filipino sentiment, hostility that both expressed and shaped how white society perceived Filipinos.

A number of factors related to decreasing labor opportunities for the white population, subsequent anti-immigrant, and thus anti-Filipino policies, myths about Filipino sexuality, and political motivations contributed to a movement to expel Filipinos from the United States.[74] During the Great Depression, in Los Angeles, immigrant Filipino working-class men constituted a largely young, single, bachelor population. As urban domestic workers (for example, as houseboys or chauffeurs) or as rural laborers in California's agricultural fields, they were considered an exploitable labor force. During this moment of economic strife and labor competition, Filipino men became easy scapegoats and, therefore, targets of violence. Because Filipinos were considered cheaper labor, farm owners preferred hiring them over their white, working-class male counterparts. As a result, white people viewed them as both labor and sexual competition. For example, Filipino men frequented leisure spaces as a reprieve from the everyday backbreaking work in California's agricultural fields, and in doing so, they sought company with white working-class women in taxi dance halls, among other spaces. Transforming their bodies from stoop laborers into sites of sensuality, pleasure, and objects of desire, working-class Filipino immigrant men formed intimate connections with white women. These interactions led to stereotypes of Filipino men as sexual deviants. Because white women supposedly embodied white "morality" and "purity," white men's racial animus toward Filipino men culminated in a series of white vigilante mobs targeting Filipinos. In 1930, one of the major anti-Filipino events, known as the Watsonville Riots, occurred in Watsonville, California. Armed with guns, a group of white men fired upon Filipino farmworkers, killing Fermin Tobera, one of the laborers.[75] The Watsonville Riots spilled over into other areas, with anti-Filipino violence spreading to other parts of California including San Francisco, Stockton, and San Jose.

But violence was not always physical. White supremacist policies through antimiscegenation laws in California also prevented Filipino men from marrying white and Mexican women. To circumvent these laws, some Filipino men, white women, and other women of color, traveled to other states to get married.[76] Nonetheless, prevailing themes of anti-Filipino sentiment and everyday racial violence culminated in the US government's passage of the Tydings-McDuffie Act of 1934. Prior to the act, colonized Filipinos had been classified as US nationals and had been exempt from immigration exclusion that targeted their Asian ethnic counterparts (e.g., Chinese, Japanese, and South Asians). However, the Tydings-McDuffie Act reclassified Filipinos as "aliens" and, as a result, they became ineligible for citizenship. The act also slowed Filipino immigration to a trickle and promised Philippine independence after ten years. A year later, Congress approved the Filipino Repatriation Act of 1935, which sought to deport Filipinos living in the United States, offering them a one-way ticket back to the Philippines and ordering them never to return. In these congressional policies, we see how the culminating effects of white nativism and anti-Filipino hostility sought to expel Filipino immigrants and preserve the alleged sanctity of white society.

Despite such white nativist efforts and legislative acts to exclude Filipinos, they and their offspring, the second generation, found ways to participate in American sporting cultures—as we see in the late literary pioneer Carlos Bulosan's canonical text *America Is in the Heart*, in which he contemplates a moment of relaxation with his countrymen and Indigenous women in response to their hard labor of working in the Alaskan canneries: "It was only at night that we felt free, although the sun seemed never to disappear from the sky. It stayed on in the western horizon and its magnificence inflamed the snows on the island, giving us a world of soft, continuous light, until the moon rose at about ten o'clock to take its place. Then trembling shadows began to form on the rise of the brilliant snow in our yard, and we would come out with baseball bats, gloves, and balls, and the Indian girls who worked in the cannery would join us, shouting huskily like men."[77] As this passage shows, sports events were also sites of racial intimacy and connection with other communities of color and Indigenous communities.

For second-generation Filipina/o Americans, sports created an arena in which they could carve out a space for themselves in the face of segregated public leisure spaces and in schools in places like Isleton and Walnut Grove, California. One of the most prominent Filipina/o American athletes to confront these early twentieth-century racist and exclusionary measures was the late Olympic gold medalist diver Victoria Manalo

Draves, the first Asian American to win an Olympic gold medal. Born in 1924 in San Francisco, California, Draves won two Olympic gold medals in the 1948 London Olympics. Draves, whose father was Filipino and whose mother was white (English), recalled in an oral history how she had not been allowed to use San Francisco's Fairmont Hotel swimming pool because of its racist policy excluding people of color like her. In response, Draves's coach, Phil Patterson, circumvented regulations by creating a "special club" for which Draves was the sole member. Patterson also suggested that Draves use her mother's surname (Taylor) in competitions to "pass" as a white competitor. Draves confided, "I think [Patterson] was a prejudiced man. It wasn't special for me. It was his way of separating me from the others."[78] Although Draves could claim citizenship as an American and represent the United States in the Olympics, what she experienced also demonstrates the contradictions and limits of (racial) citizenship and belonging.

Even Filipina/o Americans who were not Olympic-level athletes like Draves were subjected to the same kinds of Jim Crow–era racist policies as she was. Throughout the 1930s, 1940s, and 1950s in the Northwest and on the West Coast in places like Seattle, Stockton, San Francisco, and Salinas, second-generation (also known as the Bridge Generation) Filipina/o American youth organized events for their peer community. Barred from entering mainstream (white) leisure spaces, they created a sense of Filipina/o American belonging informed by their upbringing in the United States—sports tournaments, derbies, youth clubs, and social box dances, all of which were distinctly Filipina/o American cultural productions. In doing so, they engaged with American leisure and reconfigured it to honor their own desires and pleasures. This is not to overstate things—it is important to remember that their activities were a reflection of how they were seen as *racialized* subjects, evident in that sports (unintentionally or not) were part of their desire to claim their place in American society.[79] They always crossed over into Americanness, regardless of whether or not they were granted entry into American national belonging by the dominant white society.

One of the most established Filipina/o American youth clubs in the Bay Area was the Filipino Mango Athletic Club (FMAC). Established in 1939 by five Filipino American boys, members of the FMAC shared a passion for and interest in basketball.[80] And although the club initially started with basketball, it subsequently included other sports, including volleyball, football, and baseball, becoming a touchstone for other Filipina/o American youth to play sports. Yet, the athletic activities were not simply to create a network with other Filipina/o Americans. They also became a "refuge from racism,"[81] with these clubs propelling other Filipina/o American youth to create their own sports networks that lasted for decades. Yet despite performing their Americanness through sports, these youth "were never regarded by their non-Filipino classmates as Americans during the 1940s and '50s."[82]

Origins of the Project

The foundations of this book emerged from my own experiences as a sporting enthusiast, amateur athlete, and fan. I grew up in the Bay Area of California, a son of immigrant parents from the Philippines who migrated to the United States in the 1960s. My mother, a retired nurse, benefited from the nursing shortages in the United States at the time. During this period, the United States recruited foreign-trained nurses to shore up the demand for nurses and nursing services.[83] My late father, a Navy man, came to the United States as a result of US Navy recruitment policies.[84] He fervently enrolled my two older brothers and me on various sports opportunities. Throughout our childhoods and into our young adulthoods, we played soccer, baseball, basketball, football, and volleyball. When my father passed away, my mother took up the task of raising us, shuttling us to and from our games and tournaments and boisterously cheering us on.

However, it was not until graduate school that I began to think about sports as a viable academic topic. As a casual boxing fan, I vividly remember Pacquiao's 2008 fight against then boxing superstar Oscar "Golden Boy" De La Hoya. (Pacquiao defeated the Mexican American superstar by technical knockout.) To all intents and purposes, it seemed that Pacquiao had "arrived" as a global boxing icon. Admittedly, I was not interested in conducting research on him at all. Rather, I entered graduate school at the University of Illinois, Urbana-Champaign, to study Filipino martial arts. It was not until 2009 that I started to consider seriously what Pacquiao meant to diasporic Filipina/os, including my friends and family. This realization was spurred, in part, by many of the people I interviewed during my preliminary research in 2009, who shared enthusiastically how they were inspired by his "rags to riches" story, how he "represented" Philippine fistic success, and the kinds of diasporic familial attachments that he embodied, reflecting their own. Angelica, a second-generation Filipina American, reveled in seeing Pacquiao as part of mainstream popular culture: "It's fabulous, because for us it's like, 'Oh, our uncle is on [TV singing karaoke]. It's interesting, like a cool thing to see you know? He's a part of pop culture, it's great." This example, among many, demonstrates how Pacquiao emerged on the fringes of the Philippines and its diasporas as well as in the global marketplace as a site of consumption and desire.

Like many of my interlocutors, I not only played and watched sports but have had a love affair with sports. I bring to this exploration these experiences playing sports and cheering on teams and athletes. At the same time, I remain critical about sporting meritocracy and ideas of "fair play," and I understand firsthand how sporting cultures are fraught with complexities, paradoxes, and tensions between minoritized communities, sexist ideologies, and heteronormative underpinnings.[85] While not the primary focus of the book, my own sporting experiences, as well as my racialized, gendered, classed, and sexualized identities, serve as an important backdrop and point of comparison to the lived realities of the Filipina/os and Filipina/o Americans I document here.

This book captures the dynamic, contradictory, and promising ways in which Filipina/o Americans participate in sporting cultures—that is, how they not only engage in the joys of physical play and its accompanying pleasures and competitive desires, but also in the exuberance, euphoria, sorrow, and feelings of loss generated in fandom.[86] This book is not exhaustive of all sports; I specifically examine the systems of meaning that take place for fans in Pacquiao-inflected boxing fandom spaces, for Filipino and Filipino American ballers playing in basketball leagues, and for Filipina American and Asian American women playing in flag football tournaments. These sporting cultures in both spectacular settings and everyday encounters provide important vistas to help us understand community formation, diasporic identity through transnational practices, and national belonging to both the United States and the Philippines.

The book is thus a historically situated, multisited ethnography that examines how Filipina/o American sporting cultures and practices are framed within multiple sites of sporting contexts and practices: the transnational, the national, and the local. An intellectual, theoretical, and methodological crossover entails never being bound to only one of these sites. These sites are situated within and connected through the long historical relationship between the United States and the Philippines and what I would call (drawing on Arjun Appadurai) *sportscapes*—the expansive flow of ideas, images, practices, bodies, and institutions in sports in an increasingly global cultural landscape.[87] Focusing on such sportscapes in Southern California and the Midwest, I show how Filipina/o American sports practices are registered, disseminated, and performed through a series of gendered, racialized or ethnicized, sexualized, and class-inflected scripts that shed light on the complexities of Filipina/o American selves and identities. Because participants engaged in a variety of sporting practices whose frames of reference at times stretched beyond the United States, I map their sporting cultures and practices to make sense of their selves in relation to the circulation of ideas, images, and ideologies from the United States to the Philippines and vice versa. Given the diasporic nature of the Filipina/o American communities, conducting ethnographic research is "always and already a multi-sited process," that moves beyond physical spaces.[88]

Juxtaposing the Spectacle with the Everyday

Drawing upon diverse research methods including participant observations (in both public and private spaces), interviews, and media analysis was key to understanding the nature of Pacquiao's reception. I do not follow Pacquiao through a contained ethnographic fieldwork site because conducting research on someone like him cannot be confined to a single ethnographic space. Not only does he literally travel across national borders, boundaries, and boxing venues, but he also metaphorically inhabits virtual arenas like Facebook and Twitter.[89] At the same time, Filipina/o American Pacquiao fandom is spatialized in everyday sites like barbershops, homes, and the virtual arena.[90] Thus, this book's multisited ethnography incorporates the interrogation of the multiple and overlapping ethnographic Pacquiao-inflected fandom spaces.[91]

These spaces include live and closed-circuit boxing matches in Arlington, Texas, and Las Vegas, Nevada,[92] and peoples' homes in the Midwest and Southern California. At these sites, I made observations and wrote field notes, paying particular attention to fan culture. I observed how spectators engaged in fandom and nationalism through their bodily expressions, including clothing styles, cheers, chants, the display of posters featuring Pacquiao and his boxing counterparts, and the national symbols of the Philippines' flag and its colors. In these public spaces, I also held informal conversations with Filipina/o, Filipina/o American, Asian American, Latina/o, and African American spectators and fans. In addition, through the snowball sampling technique, I conducted interviews with fifty first-, 1.5-, second-, and third-generation Filipina/o Americans who were either Pacquiao fans or had strong criticisms of his worldview, in particular, of his homophobic comments in 2012 and 2016. The majority of the interviewees were 1.5- and second-generation Filipina/o Americans (totaling thirty male and twenty female).[93] Because the majority of the participants were 1.5 and second generation, it is difficult to identify differences between the first, 1.5, and second generation and their perspectives on Pacquiao's worldview. That is not to say that the 1.5 or second generation were always overtly critical. Some 1.5-generation Filipina/o Americans were ambivalent, saying, for example, "It's just his opinion" or "It wasn't that big of a deal," while one second-generation Filipina American shared, "He's [Pacquiao] not exactly in line with my political views." In this way, Filipina/o Americans' consciousness about his comments range within the 1.5 and second generation.

If Pacquiao, as a spectacularized body, is a vehicle through which I make sense of how Filipina/o Americans negotiate transnational and local processes, then documenting their everyday engagement with sports is a necessary juxtaposition to understand how Filipina/o Americanness is crafted, negotiated, and managed away from the spectacle. From 2011 to 2012 and in 2015, I immersed myself as an experiential ethnographer in two separate US field sites: one in Orange County, California, in an Asian American basketball league and the other in Champaign, Illinois, in a Filipino American–only basketball league.[94]

I had known some of the Orange County basketball players when, as a college student, we played together in basketball tournaments, leagues, and pickup games. In 2011, they invited me to play on their basketball team and granted me permission to conduct research among them. In 2015 in Champaign, Illinois, I first signed up to play in the basketball league when it was advertised at a local Filipino store. After a few weeks of building rapport with the basketball community, I asked for, and was granted, permission to conduct research. As an experiential ethnographer, I implicated myself and the somatic sensations I experienced with regard to my own sporting pleasures, desires, feelings, and emotions. I observed how Filipino and Filipino American basketball players claimed the basketball space and manipulated their clothing styles to articulate a Filipino and Filipino American masculinity publicly, and I observed how, through their play, they contorted their bodies to demonstrate and draw attention to their athletic feats.

In addition, I conducted interviews with Filipina and Asian American women with whom I practiced when we played in annual flag football tournaments. My playing experiences and interactions with them built a level of trust and facilitated entrée into later asking for permission to conduct interviews. Although my chief engagement with these women was through interviews, I also include in my analysis key moments when I observed them in motion playing against white women in the early 2000s. I have since kept in touch with some of these women and, starting in 2012, asked some of them to participate in my study. I draw upon my own experiences playing, training, and cheering them on when they played. Focusing on such different sporting spaces, athletes, and levels of fandom is important to understand the complexity of Filipina/o American identity formation in the twenty-first century. Each of the chapters in this book tells a different story that highlights the promising and contradictory processes of sports.

The diverse spectrum of lived experiences of Filipina/os and Filipina/o Americans in this book cannot be confined to singular narratives of immigration patterns, gendered lives, or classed backgrounds. Many of the participants were either born in the Philippines and came to the United States as children (the 1.5 generation) or were born in the United States and are children of immigrant parents (the second generation) who migrated to the United States in the post-1965 immigration era. This era was sui generis due to the increased immigration from Asia, the Caribbean, and South America. Whereas late nineteenth- and early twentieth-century immigration policies targeted and excluded Asians, the Immigration Act of 1965 was a watershed moment in US immigration history. With the backdrop of the Cold War shaping geopolitical competition with the former Soviet Union, the United States shifted its immigration policies to recruit a more highly educated class of immigrants, particularly individuals who could augment the US scientific and technological infrastructures. In addition to the major turning point of 1965, the Philippine diaspora is particularly informed by the acts of the late Philippine dictator, Ferdinand Marcos. On September 21, 1972, in order to quell civil unrest and further consolidate his state-level power, the US-supported Marcos declared martial law, subsequently censured the free press, and suspended the writ of habeas corpus. During this period, he also committed thousands of extrajudicial killings and tortures of his opponents and critics. At the same time, he embraced neoliberal policies to entice foreign investment, and implemented a human-labor-for-export policy, which resulted in the Philippines sending millions of Filipina/os to work abroad. Many professionals, or those who were educated with advanced degrees, migrated to the United States and the Middle East, while others who were considered semiskilled and unskilled went to other Asian countries like Japan. This context grounds understandings of the contemporary Philippine diaspora, which comprises over ten million overseas Filipina/os scattered throughout the world, including in the United States, Canada, Saudi Arabia, Australia, Japan, and the United Kingdom.[95]

Still, some of these highly educated Filipino immigrants with ad vanced degrees could not apply their skills to land a job in the United States that was equivalent to theirs in the Philippines. Take, for example, Gabriela, a second-generation Filipina American who works in community finance. She shared that although her father already earned his medical degree in the Philippines, the United States expected him to take and pass a federally mandated medical licensing exam in order to practice in the United States. Gabriela explained, "To practice in the US you need a [score of] 75 and both times he got a 74, so it's kind of a heartbreaking situation for him that he was never able to pass his boards here."[96] Many of the participants featured in chapters 3 and 4 are second-generation Filipina/o Americans whose parents (like Gabriela's) came to the United States in the post-1965 era. They are college-educated, have the disposable income to pay for tournaments and leagues, and regularly travel to the Philippines. However, the participants who are the focus of chapter 2 comprise a more recent wave of working-class Filipino immigrants whom family members petitioned to migrate to the United States or whom a local health care company actively recruited.

Mapping Filipina/o American Sporting Cultures

Like the crossover, this book is about the movement of ideas and brown bodies and how desires, pleasures, and intimacies traverse time and space. Employing the crossover as a metaphor enables us to make sudden shifts and turns to capture both historically, ethnographically, and theoretically the capaciousness not only of the afterlife of US empire, but also of the significance of Filipina/o American social lives in sports. Thus, the chapters in this book move in unexpected ways—from global boxing spectacles to quotidian sporting spaces, from the West Coast to the Midwest and back, and to the diasporic locations (virtual and physical) that enliven spaces where Pacquiao's presence looms.

In chapter 1, I introduce eight-time world boxing champion Manny "Pac-Man" Pacquiao. Many Filipina/o Americans participate in transnational fandom by cheering for him in their homes, at boxing spectacles, and in the virtual arena. I analyze his iconic status to map his diasporic topography and take stock of how Filipina/o Americans "read" him in ways that manifest social critiques not only of the US racial system, but also of the fraught US-Philippine neocolonial relationship. Often represented as the patriarchal "godfather" to the Philippine diasporic "family," Pacquiao's masculine acts of care have enabled diasporic Filipina/o Americans to claim a measure of diasporic belonging. Throughout his career, some Filipinx/a/o American fans of Philippine-born boxer Manny "Pac-Man" Pacquiao have celebrated his philanthropic work, Christianity, and carefully crafted image of respectable politics. This chapter examines how Philippine-born boxer, Manny "Pac-Man" Pacquiao's brown masculinity acts as a signifier of anti-Blackness and sets the conditions of (im)possibility for some diasporic Filipina/o American claims to identity and national belonging. Pacquiao's hypervisibility is but *one* way to understand Filipina/o American sporting cultures. Because he is such a dominant presence in the diaspora and beyond, I use his iconicity as an entry point to discuss how he obscures much more complicated renditions of Filipino and Filipina/o American subjectivity.

In chapter 2, I take the reader to an underexamined Filipina/o community located in Urbana-Champaign, Illinois. Indeed, whereas much of the literature on Filipina/o American communities has discussed diasporic formations in coasts, ports, and waterways, this chapter instead locates an emergent Filipina/o community in the heartland of the US empire: the rural Midwest. I examine how recently arrived working-class Filipino immigrant men cultivate a sense of homosocial intimacy and perform masculinity in everyday spaces like basketball courts, apartments, and homes. As part of a global labor force, many of these men work in "feminized" labor occupations as cooks, factory workers, and caregivers for the local community, what Nayan Shah and David Eng refer to as *queer domesticity*.⁹⁷ To negotiate their working-class status and to recoup masculinity in other arenas, these men organize a Filipino and Filipino American only basketball league. This league allows them to formulate masculinities that are otherwise managed by the United States and Philippines.

Chapter 3 looks at how transnational movement and consumption patterns permeate everyday sporting spaces and inform how Filipino American masculinity is performed. I emphasize how class becomes a way for Filipino Americans to articulate a particular kind of cosmopolitan Filipino American masculinity. I describe how they use their capital to travel to the Philippines, order team uniforms at a local shop, and wear those uniforms in an Asian American–only basketball league and in their everyday lives. Designed by my interlocutors, this ethnically inflected sense of sartorial style is rooted in Philippine national symbols—in particular the Philippine flag, sun, and map—and constitutes the means by which they express a middle-class, Filipino American masculinity. I particularly note how ideas of community and identity are mobile and transnational and in what ways notions of self implicate the Philippines, the United States, and local popular culture practices.

As so much of the literature on sports studies tends to focus on racial relations between Black and white male athletes, and, to a lesser degree, between white and African American female athletes, chapter 4 details how the sport of flag football becomes a crucible of competition between white and (predominantly) Filipina American college-age women in an annual flag football tournament. Filipina American flag football players described how white women perceived them as unathletic and incapable of athletic excellence. Aiming to prove that they belonged, Filipina Americans did not take their exclusion lightly. Using Cheryl Harris's theoretical framework of whiteness as property,[98] I argue that white women drew upon their whiteness as a resource to secure their own pleasures, to exclude Filipina Americans from the annual flag football tournament, and literally to remove Filipina and Asian Americans' team name from the tournament archive. Although Filipina Americans confronted racist attitudes about them through their athleticism, they also negotiated and challenged the normative contours of diaspora as the domain for men. I argue that flag football spaces became an arena to "cross over" expected notions of Filipina American femininity and womanhood that complicate normative familial expectations of Filipina American chastity and demureness.

In the book's conclusion, I argue for a more robust reckoning with the institution of sports and its relationship to US colonialism and what this context can tell us about the lives of diasporic Filipina/o Americans. I do so to highlight how sporting cultures encounter possibilities, ambivalence, and contradiction.

Throughout the book, it is clear that sporting cultures and practices play a profound part in the lives of many Filipina/o Americans. Those cultures and practices have enabled them to craft memories about their lives, connect and sustain familial relations, experience pleasure and joy, and express desire through play and fandom. In the pages that follow, the reader will find a community that is not always in agreement about sports as a system of meritocracy and the ideologies that it uncritically possesses. Some of these narratives offer political critiques about how sports structure their experiences along the axis of race, gender, sexuality, class, and religion. Indeed, those with whom I spoke also have different emotional, physical, and leisurely investments that do not always form a consensus about what sports mean to them. Indeed, they claim different ways of belonging and have a varied set of responses to sports and sporting icons.

For Filipina/o Americans, sports matter because sports allow them to speak to and against dominant narratives that have historically and contemporaneously framed them and their bodies in ways that carry racialized, classed, gendered, and sexualized implications; sports literally allow them to embody something more than just what the historical and contemporary record tells us. They thus use sports as a vehicle to create and imagine alternative pathways of cultural citizenship, ethnic and national identity, and belonging to the American national fabric while also reinforcing power hierarchies. At the heart of this book is a complicated story intricately bound up with power, ideology, discourse, and practice. It is a story of how and why Filipina/o Americans take up sporting cultural practices that traverse time, space, and memory. It demonstrates that seemingly whimsical matters of playing and consuming sports are not inconsequential activities absent of pleasure, joy, pain, legibility, domination, or power. Rather, it documents how engagements with sports reveal the shifting nature of Filipino Americanness and Filipino American subjectivity as well as frustrations, longings, desires, and inchoate feelings for and about America and what Filipina/o Americanness means in all its complexities. Finally, the book suggests that these racializations, desires, and pleasures are unpredictable and can be crossed over at any time, keeping everyone guessing and refusing to make Filipina/o American identity something fixed, static, or motionless.

1

"He's Not Your Champ!"

Complicating Manny "Pac-Man" Pacquiao's Muscular Christianity

But if you know what's poppin' in the Philippines, you know that they got a whole generation of kids in the Philippines, growing up without their mothers! Yes, a lot of women in the Philippines go to the Arabian peninsula, come to the United States, they make all their money here, they send all their money back home, which is still one of the number one staples in the Philippines' economy—money that their expats send back to the Philippines. The men on the other hand, are left rearing children, twiddling their thumbs, waiting on their wives' checks. These men have been fucking emasculated! Then suddenly, a boxer rises from amongst them! And reinstates their manhood with his motherfuckin' fist! This is not the guy you're supposed to ask, "What do you think of homosexuals?" [Audience laughs.] "He's not your champ!"
—Dave Chappelle, *Age of Spin*

The afternoon after Manny "Pac-Man" Pacquiao's 2019 fight against Adrien Broner, I walked into the Mandalay Bay's Michael Jackson ONE theater to attend Pacquiao's Bible study. I had heard from a number of people that the boxer organized Bible studies in his hotel room before and after his fights in Las Vegas. The Bible study was not necessarily open to the public; I found out about this semisecret gathering during the weigh-ins, through one of my Filipina informants, a security guard who knew some members of Team Pacquiao. I had read that in 2011 Pacquiao had converted from being a devout Catholic for most of his life to evangelical Christianity, and this made me particularly eager to attend.

When I arrived at the venue, there were about fifty people inside the auditorium, and it appeared that many in the audience were with their families. By about noon, the theater crowd had swelled and, in my estimation, at least 1,500 people were now gathered, most of them Filipina/o or Filipina/o American, with a handful of people of color and white people.

After choosing our seats, we settled in and engaged in small talk with people seated in our vicinity. I struck up a conversation with Sofia, a second-generation Filipina American who lived in Las Vegas. She was holding a Bible that Pacquiao's team had given her at a previous Bible study. She smiled after I asked her about the classes, and I sensed that she found joy, pride, honor, and pleasure in recalling how she had been gifted the Bible. As she showed me her Bible, I was surprised to see that it had Pacquiao's "MP" logo in black lettering with the Philippine sun, which covered most of the Bible cover. Underneath the logo, "Holy Bible" was written on it in white lettering, followed by "New International Version." According to Sofia, Pacquiao previously held Bible studies inside his hotel room, but because so many people wanted to attend, his team had decided to rent out the theater. People continued to filter in, with many wearing Pacquiao and Philippine-themed T-shirts and hats adorned with the Philippine flag and its colors to express their Pacquiao fandom as well as their national and ethnic identity.[1]

At approximately 12:45 p.m., I heard sounds of people rising from their seats and looking toward the back of the auditorium. Pacquiao, his wife Jinkee, and the rest of Pacquiao's entourage arrived. Sporting a burgundy jacket with sunglasses, a gray and black striped polo shirt, and a pair of black jeans, Pacquiao had gauze covering his left eye from the night before. People used their phones to record or take pictures of him as he gingerly walked down the aisle. With his left arm around Jinkee's shoulder, it appeared he had difficulty navigating the stairs to reach the stage. The theater space had been manipulated to create a sacred space for Pacquiao, the guest of honor. It had already been symbolically saturated as a spectacle of sacrifice in which Pacquiao sacrifices his body for the win and now sacrifices the pain to come to the theater for the devotional time.

The service started with a greeting from one of the pastors, followed by a prayer. Then, a Filipino band led us in a song titled "This Is the Day That the Lord Has Made," a reference to Psalm 118:24. The space, sounds of music, and peoples' energy created a sense of exuberance and an upbeat mood. Speaking in Tagalog, the national language of the Philippines, the band leader encouraged us to be a little louder. Tagalog became part of the performance of ethnic identity. Throughout the song, some of the attendees rhythmically sang and clapped to its beat. There was a palpable fervor felt throughout the service as smiles, clapping, and joyful singing provided the soundtrack to the gathering. After the song, Dudley Rutherford, a white senior pastor at Shepherd of the Hills Church in Porter Ranch, California, gave the sermon titled "A Time for Communion," which was also projected on a small portable screen on stage. In Christian tradition, Communion is a ritual in which its members participate. It symbolizes Jesus's "body" and "blood" by commemorating his death on the cross and resurrection from the grave. As someone who was raised in a Baptist Christian church, I was familiar with the ritual and accompanying effervescence that permeated the Bible study.[2] Communion acted as a catalyst to create an affective and emotional atmosphere for people in the theater. Throughout the Bible study, I heard people's deep and meaningful whispers of "Yes," "Thank you Lord," and "Thank you Jesus"—affirmations of their commitment to God.

Throughout the service, Pastor Rutherford referred to Pacquiao as "the senator," "Senator Pacquiao," or simply "Manny," demonstrating not only a reverence for Pacquiao's role as a government official but also as a friend. Rutherford and Pacquiao had forged a relationship a few years prior when Pacquiao rededicated himself to God and embraced evangelical Christianity. At one point during the sermon, Pastor Rutherford asserted that the Bible study was a "divine appointment," that people in attendance were chosen by God to attend. Our presence, in other words, was no accident. Rutherford then emphasized the importance of Communion and that participating in it was an act of remembrance: "And Jesus knew in his wisdom that after two thousand years that we'd probably forget about what he did for us on that cross so he set up this memorial that we would do this each and every week. I want you to remember this. This is the Lord's table. Everybody say, 'Lord's table.' This is the Lord's table." He then quickly pivoted to Pacquiao.

First time I ever really met Manny Pacquiao he invited me over his house for Bible study. And there was no furniture in the entire living room.

There was some chairs, there was one table. And after the Bible study, Manny went and sat at the head of the table. And there were about three or four of us who sat around the table. Everybody else is standing. But everybody was focused on Manny: it was his house, his Bible study, his table and he was at the head of the table. And we're all just sitting around looking at him. It's Manny's table. When you take this Communion in just a few moments, I want you to picture yourself sitting at a table and then at the head of the table is Jesus Christ.

Approximately fifteen minutes into the sermon, Pastor Rutherford led the group in prayer and again referenced Jesus *and* Pacquiao in the same breath: "Jesus's body was broken upon that cross, the sacrifice." I thought it was curious that the pastor referenced Pacquiao immediately after speaking about Jesus: "I saw a boxer last night in the ring whose face was all bloody from one little cut, just one cut, I saw his face I could hardly look at it." Then, in the next sequence, Pastor Rutherford pivoted back to talking about God. "Yet, God when I see you on the cross and I see the crown of thorns pressed down upon your brow and I see the spear that is thrust into your side, the cat-o'-nine-tails. Your back was beaten and your body is stripped and naked hanging on that cross. God, I can't help but say thank you." The service concluded after the group took Communion. Manny and Jinkee Pacquiao then walked up to the stage, with Manny Pacquiao saying a few words to the audience. "My strength comes from God. I hope you're happy for my performance. I really did my best at age forty." He then took a group selfie—"groufie"— with everyone in attendance.

This chapter begins not at a Pacquiao weigh-in, nor a boxing match in Las Vegas, Nevada, nor even in a home that is a Pacquiao fight night space. Instead, this chapter pairs an epigraph of Dave Chappelle's Pacquiao joke with an ethnographic description of the Bible study to argue that white supremacy, anti-Blackness, masculinity, respectability, and homophobia are enveloped in the US colonial afterlife of muscular Christianity. Muscular Christianity originated in the nineteenth century and is part of a Protestant Christian movement that emphasized physical fitness and morality as an avenue for spiritual development. Using sport to analogize the male body and masculinity, muscular Christianity foregrounds ideas of developing the sporting self in order to remedy society's perceived social ills.

Chappelle accurately joked that Filipinas working abroad send remittances to their families in the Philippines while their husbands stay home and raise their children. An outcome of the complex processes of neoliberalism, globalization, and the late Philippine dictator Ferdinand Marcos's labor for export policy, remittances are one of the primary ways in which the beleaguered Philippine economy is sustained. Linking feminized labor, parenting roles, and masculinity, Chappelle implies that it is Filipino men who should be working abroad rather than their wives. But because their wives assume the role of provider, Filipino men's masculinity becomes emasculated, inverting dominant narratives of *men as providers* who work abroad. Of course, Chappelle's punchline threads gendered labor roles, perceptions of Filipino men's laziness, their emasculation, and heterosexual masculinity. Placing Pacquiao in the same group as these emasculated men, Chappelle refuses to champion Pacquiao when it comes to advocating for gender equity or LGBTQ rights for the Philippines and the diaspora. He is not their champ. Chappelle's joke opens up broader questions of ethno-nationalism, muscular Christianity, and the role that the Young Men's Christian Association, a relic of US colonialism in the Philippines, played by which to understand the contemporary moment.

As a global figure, Pacquiao is a cherished icon whose reach is disseminated across the world. Acting as a connection between "home" and the nation of residence, between "here" and "there," he has become a link or node in the elusive effort of belonging to a nation, whether the Philippines, the United States, or elsewhere. Indeed, he has made a home for himself in the various diasporic communities across the world in physical and virtual realms.

Manny "Pac-Man" Pacquiao and the Rise of a Global Superstar

Born in the Philippines in Kibawe, Bukidnon, Pacquiao is now a retired, eight-time world boxing champion. He has also served as a Philippine politician. He was elected as a congressman, serving from 2010 to 2016 in the Sarangani province, and later took up a position as a senator from 2016 to 2022. He ran for president in 2022 but was soundly defeated, finishing third to then Philippine vice president Leni Robredo and Bongbong Marcos, the son of the deceased dictator Ferdinand Marcos, who eventually became president.

Many Filipina/o American participants celebrated Pacquiao as their national "hero," whose triumphant narrative was linked to how he overcame tremendous personal odds, especially poverty. Pacquiao emphatically announced his arrival in 2008, capturing the imagination of the boxing world when he defeated then boxing superstar Oscar "Golden Boy" De La Hoya to cement his status as one of boxing's greatest. Pacquiao's ascension to this global professional boxing status has been widely celebrated. His ascension has enabled Filipina/o Americans to claim a measure of national belonging to the United States and to the Philippines. Pacquiao's name carries an appeal that is likened to retired African American boxer Muhammad Ali, a kind of cultural cachet that is consonant with star power and success and yet absent of the political resonances for which Ali was known.[3] Part of his cachet derives from his charisma. His personality and way of being in the world inspired a devotion and attraction from fans in ways that moved beyond his boxing prowess. He demonstrates a piety that transcends the material world. "I see him as really spiritual" and "a religious person," shared Manuel, a second-generation Filipino American. One participant described him as an "angelic person," who inspires humility, hard, work, and respectability in and outside of the ring. Although his job in the boxing ring demands that he literally beat up opponents through conventional markers of toughness, aggression, and physical dominance, outside of the ring he constantly smiles, gives thanks to God, and has a quiet demeanor of humility despite both his wins and his losses.

Pacquiao's Bible study that day included the key Christian ritual of Communion. Yet, the ritual did not feel like an ordinary Communion. For many in attendance, it was a chance to see Pacquiao in a realm outside of the boxing ring, and for non-Christian believers, it was a rare opportunity to get his autograph or to show friends and family members that they were there to see Pacquiao. The event offered an intimate connection between fans and Pacquiao, an atmosphere at times akin to a transnational, Philippine-infused, Christian revival. More than a space to celebrate a Filipino boxer, the space was a diasporic, Christian, national space, with Pacquiao and his wife Jinkee signifying its heterosexual dimensions. For me, as someone raised in a Christian household, the Bible study's message stood in stark contrast to the hundreds of Bible studies I had attended as a child. My previous experiences attending Bible studies had never explicitly narrated a secular figure into a Christian ritual. As the ordained authority to speak God's message, Pastor Rutherford merged the sacred and the secular with elements of gendered nationalism by placing Pacquiao in the same spiritual and deified realm as Jesus. It was a process of deity affirmation and worship that bled from the figure of Christ onto the beaten and sacrificial body of Pacquiao.

In situating the longer history of US Christianity and its white supremacist roots,[4] what is revealing is how a white pastor—through an unmarked whiteness—legitimated and affirmed Pacquiao *as the savior* of the Philippines. Thus, rather than viewing Pacquiao as a boxing migrant laborer and global sporting icon, the meanings attached to him through religion and gender demonstrate a twenty-first century version of muscular Christianity, one that is immediately ethnicized, racialized, and sexualized to affirm a desirable and worship-worthy muscular Christianity. As a prizefighter in the global marketplace, Pacquiao depends upon his boxing body to labor physically and manually, engaging in a kind of bodily self-discipline to make a living.[5] Yet, the Christian muscular ethos he performs exceeds the meanings of *body as laborer*. Instead, in this sermon, Pacquiao's body is also imagined as one for "world uplift,"[6] to "evangelize people about morality and Christian values."[7]

When the pastor describes how he first met Pacquiao at his Bible study, he evokes the iconic Last Supper scene where Jesus is sitting with his disciples: "It's Manny's table." Pacquiao literally makes the sign of the cross not only during his boxing matches and in his everyday life, he also analogously crosses over and, applying Christian language, crosses into various forms of masculinity, diasporic belonging, and desire (see figure 1.1). Some diasporic Filipina/o and Filipina/o Americans imagine Pacquiao as constructing a heteropatriarchal, hypermasculine, Christianized Philippines that reverses national narratives of colonial loss.[8] These narratives are inextricably linked to legacies of colonialism that have feminized the Philippine nation and its people; they imagine Pacquiao as the proper masculine subject to reclaim a normative masculine nation that Chapelle, among others, has discounted and mocked.[9]

Figure 1.1. "Give Us This Day." Nike, Inc.

Pacquiao's dominance in boxing helps to fulfill diasporic Filipina/o Americans' hopes, dreams, and aspirations within and beyond US borders. For some of my interlocuters, his athletic, brown body at times becomes a Christian-inflected symbol of a suffering Philippine nation. With each punishing boxing blow, Pacquiao absorbs pain and anguish, akin to Jesus's narrative of pain and suffering. Within the context of the Bible study, he is symbolically granted martyrdom status and becomes the "savior" of the Philippines. A cultural artifact like Sofia's "MP" brand Bible shows how Pacquiao's corporate brand is imposed upon a sacred text, the two folding into one another the seemingly diametrically opposed realms of boxing and religion. Sofia's Bible garners meaning in relation to Pacquiao's iconicity, his devout Christian practices, and what Pacquiao represents to some members of the diaspora. The Bible, in this instance is an object that narrates its significance to her life and an assertion and expression of her spirituality. The Bible, through narrativization, is as sociologist Ian Woodward notes, "a site for articulating an individual's values and beliefs."[10] Because Sofia subscribes to Christianity and sees Pacquiao as a moral authority figure, she not only brought the Bible to affirm her Christian faith, but to express her fandom in a space that is largely imagined as a site of vice, gambling, sex work, and illicit activities.[11] Christianity, through Pacquiao's iconicity, is commodified and deeply embedded within the marketplace. The Bible also becomes part of his iconicity and a symbol of Philippine ethno-nationalism.

In a US context, Pacquiao's life narratives reflect a deeply rooted, immigrant-driven, Horatio Alger story. The story emphasizes how Alger pulled himself up by his bootstraps to "make it" in the face of seemingly insurmountable odds. Pacquiao followed a similar trajectory, and is celebrated by Filipina/os and non-Filipina/os alike. In his youth, Pacquiao lived in abject poverty, and sold *pan de sal* and cigarettes on the streets to survive.[12] He left Mindanao and stowed away on a ship to Manila. At sixteen years old, Pacquiao fought his first professional boxing match. The Bible study, along with fragments of colonial history, demonstrates traces of a palimpsestic past,[13] most notably in how Pacquiao seemingly embodies and instantiates US colonial goals of racial and economic uplift, Christianity, civilization, and heteropatriarchal nationalism.[14] We shall see next how he has this in common with the Young Men's Christian Association in the Philippines.

The Young Men's Christian Association and Muscular Christianity

By 1915, the Young Men's Christian Association (YMCA) had been established in Manila. As a bureaucratic, colonial institution, the YMCA played a key role in framing sport as an important way in which Filipinos could learn "democratic" and modern ideas like self-discipline, rationality, meritocracy, and fair play. Modern sports, colonists believed, were a metric to gauge colonial progress, and "an indication of the success of their 'civilizing mission.'"[15] Institutionalized alongside US-style education and politics,[16] the YMCA and US colonial administrators worked to "train bodies in the service of religion."[17] The result of this training was the development and deployment of a muscular Christian ethos which was antithetical to that of their former Spanish colonial counterparts. Whereas US colonists saw Spanish colonists and Catholicism as backward, muscular Christianity moved colonized Filipinos toward a more liberal and progressive trajectory. Muscular Christianity, in other words, was entangled with the US imperial project, and subsequently imported social ideas about the body in which gender and race were two of the primary means through which this doctrine was linked to colonial ideas of power.

Under the aegis of the US education system—and primarily through the category of "physical education"—sports and recreation were embedded in Filipina/os' everyday lives.[18] Through muscular Christianity as manifested in outdoor activities and the promotion of physicality embodied by white, muscular Christian men, it was believed that sports could enhance colonial progress. Team sports and team activities like scouting often had military overtones including uniforms and hierarchical forms of leadership that perpetuated manliness. To this end, the United States advanced a mix of religious, racial, and gendered ideologies about the cultivation of body and play in the context of Western imperial expansion.[19]

The YMCA in the Philippines sought to provide "wholesome activities" for its colonized wards in the archipelago, merging these with public education and a Christian-inflected religious doctrine to cultivate "moral fiber."[20] First propagated by British public schools for elite young men, muscular Christianity was exported to the United States and its

elite class status was institutionalized in American universities. As a reaction to the marked increase in women in churches, men feared that
Protestantism was "feminizing" society. Once the United States emerged
as an imperial power, it then exported muscular Christian ideology to
the Philippines and it became connected to US colonial goals of "benevolent assimilation." The United States believed that sports would facilitate the disciplining of Filipino boys and men with the goal that they,
too, would embody morality through sport. In the YMCA's understanding, disciplining a sporting body meant that it was being cultivated in
the service of God. Through strenuous activity, "manhood" could be
achieved. We can already see how the figures of boys and men became
embodied sites for the cultivating of modern and suitable colonial subjects. Yet, Jenilyn's twenty-first century embodiment of basketball acumen and skills cross over or transgress US (post)colonial directives that
were originally meant for boys and men.

Filipinos who achieved pugilist success in places like Australia and
the United States challenged ideas about Filipino racial inferiority and
white racial superiority.[21] In this way, Filipino boxers and spectators
engaged with the processes of masculinity learned in the Philippines
and the United States by appropriating the boxing space to affirm their
"manliness" in organized boxing events, while at the same time inverting
their racialization.[22] These boxers, as Linda España-Maram has shown,
were already bending, extending, exceeding, and inverting the racializations of their communities. They challenged the idea of Filipinos as
being always the inferior racial Other, showing that the Filipino body
could be a site of incredible strength, desire, and mimesis.[23]

Pacquiao's Body, Masculinity, and Muscular Christianity

As we have seen, the Bible study was a space for Pacquiao (and attendees) to actualize their Christianity—a Christianity that was also a
performance of gender, class, and race. Yet the Bible study corresponded
with Pacquiao's embodiment and performance of Christianity in the
boxing ring. During his boxing matches, Pacquiao repeatedly performed
the sign of the cross, a relic of his Catholic past.

As noted earlier, Pacquiao grew up practicing Roman Catholicism,
and it was not until 2011 that he converted to evangelical Christianity.[24]

After years of "vices," which included extramarital affairs, gambling, and drinking alcohol, one day he "heard the voice of God" and rededicated his life to him. He was "born again," attesting that "Christ said unless we are born again we cannot enter the kingdom of God."[25] Since then, Christianity has been completely enmeshed in his everyday life. As pastor Rick Warren has observed, Pacquiao is a "Bible quoting maniac."[26] Pacquiao's stances also align with the conservative politics in some white evangelical circles, including his views against same-sex marriage and for the need to police queer desire.

Nevertheless, Pacquiao does not solely perform muscular Christianity through his individual Christian beliefs and practices, though one can find numerous representations of him reading the Bible, clasping hands in prayer, and kneeling before God. There are also Nike-sponsored ads that offer Christ-inspired images evoking a Christian-themed Philippine nation.[27] Besides, the fact is that although relatively short in stature (he stands five feet, six inches tall), Pacquiao is physically muscular. Throughout his career, he employed a strict strength training program that transformed his body from skinny and weak to a powerful and muscular boxer infused with speed and quickness (see figure 1.2).[28]

The result of Pacquiao's training is that he is dynamic, innovative, quick, explosive, and powerful in his motions. There are thousands of images and hundreds of videos of his half-naked body that circulate on the internet demonstrating the kind of self-discipline and endless hours required to build his body and perfect his boxing technique. "His body is frickin' ridiculous," shared Gabriela, a second-generation Filipina American who notes Pacquiao's extraordinary musculature, six-pack abs, and chiseled frame. Gabriela's sentiments about Pacquiao's body are an uncommon take on Asian and Asian American men, who are commonly viewed as racially castrated, emasculated, and incapable of being objects of desire.[29] Similar to the reaction to his Filipino pugilist predecessors, like Ceferino Garcia, Pancho Villa, and other early twentieth-century Filipino boxers, Pacquiao fans celebrate "the potential of the brown body symbolized by the pugilists."[30] Moreover, Pacquiao's persona inside and outside of the ring are central to how his muscular Christianity connotes a respectability that informs how some Filipina/o American participants attach meaning to him. Angelica, a second-

Figure 1.2. Pacquiao poses for photographers. Photo credit: Esther Lin

generation Filipina American, shared that one of the reasons she cheers for Pacquiao is because "he's super humble and he's always praying." His body (as temple) is compatible with notions of morality, Christianity, and piety that signify salvation for the nation.

Negotiating "Pac-Man's" Representation

Pacquiao's iconicity is embedded in a transnational cultural circuit,[31] with his representations traversing various mass-mediated arenas and platforms that make their way onto mobile devices, laptops, and television screens. Filipina/o Americans who watch videos of Pacquiao on YouTube have intense and passionate conversations about him on Twitter and Facebook and, as one participant shared, are inspired by his life in the documentary film, *Manny*. In the mass-media landscape, these repertoires of representation manifest various types of affective desires, pleasures, connections, and ideas about Pacquiao. Representation, as Stuart Hall asserts, involves the production of meaning through language, signs, and concepts, a cultural arena "in which the production of meaning through language—that is[,] representation—takes place."[32]

Furthermore, Filipina/o Americans' strategies of consumption are part of a larger representational system of meanings and are instantiated in the form of codes. These codes convey messages that consumers then interpret, taking in or consuming the intended meaning and customizing them according to their lived realities and desires. Representations of iconic figures—among others—are not passively consumed and accepted. Rather, the process of representation involves transmission and reception of ideas and desires that are then interpreted and negotiated in myriad ways. Media institutions *encode* meanings and people, like Filipina/o Americans, *decode* those meanings, demonstrating that the interpretative strategies of consumption are never seamless, symmetrical, or equivalent.[33]

Consumers draw from their own social lives, lived experiences, and frames of reference, and "make sense" of Pacquiao's iconicity as it is embedded in particular interpellations of Christianity. Within this realm, Filipina/o Americans' senses of identity are "always in process, and always constituted within, not outside, representation."[34] For some Filipina/o Americans, the mass-mediated narratives surrounding Pacquiao broadly encompass themes of the "American Dream," work ethic, immigration, success, failure, and racial legibility that subsequently shape the contours of his reception.

Carlos is one such person. A 1.5-generation Filipino American, he explains that Pacquiao "is my idol." I asked why, and he elaborated: "He's transcended sports himself. I don't know any boxers other than [Muhammad] Ali. It's really big for a Filipino to be so successful in sports 'cause there's no other Filipinos that are successful in sports except Manny."[35] Here, Carlos points to popular culture as a critical site of representation, one that privileges the male athletic body as a site of masculine power and prestige. Pacquiao's successful brown body becomes an accessible medium through which to claim racial legibility and visibility. As Carlos avers, Pacquiao is made particularly meaningful because of the limited amount of Filipina/o American exposure in mainstream sports beyond the Filipino Heritage Nights in professional sports leagues. His world champion success as a boxer heightens his popularity. There are also key elements of his representation that reference his Filipinoness, reifying a certain kind of authenticity, elements that include his religiosity, (sporting) immigrant mobility, work ethic, and Filipino accent. Carlos and other Filipina/o Americans spoke to me of the pleasure they cultivated when they were organizing fight night spaces and of finding joy in reveling in Pacquiao's wins while also reflecting on their extreme disappointment when he lost. At the same time, this ethno-nationalistic desire still unfortunately exists within the norms and narrow boundaries of heteropatriarchy. As a result, diasporic Filipina Americans like retired mixed martial arts (MMA) fighter and world champion boxer Ana Julaton, as well as Filipina Canadian tennis player Leyla Hernandez, do not become part of the conversation of athletic excellence and success.

Pacquiao exerts a powerful influence in the lives of my interlocuters. Although the United States is but one diasporic node in the global circuit, for some Filipina/o Americans, Pacquiao symbolizes cultural, social, and geographical links to the Philippines through which they maintain diasporic intimacy.[36] These linkages enable them to interpret him in ways that facilitate their construction of their own identity and express a sense of belonging—interpretations no doubt aided by the mass-mediated Pacquiao representations that veritably saturate the lives of Filipina/o Americans. Equally significant is *how* Pacquiao's presentation of self resonates with some of my interlocutors.[37] In particular, Christianity becomes a way to "cleanse" imaginings of some members of the diasporic Filipina/o community that (as I will describe) do not fit within the rigid confines of heteropatriarchy.

Pacquiao has effectively crossed over into the US popular culture arena, becoming a major fixture in transnational mass media.[38] He has been referenced in hip-hop songs, was a regular guest on *Jimmy Kimmel Live!*,[39] and was sponsored by a number of corporations related to food, clothing, and alcohol. Perhaps most significant is that Pacquiao was referenced in the movie *Easter Sunday* (2022), which was the first time Filipina/o Americans were represented as the protagonists in a Hollywood film. *Easter Sunday* served as an important cultural production through which Filipina/o Americans could claim their place in popular culture. The film stars Filipino American comedian, Jo Koy (in the film, his name is Joe Valencia), who is the film's protagonist. Valencia struggles to make amends with his immigrant mother and forge more intimate connections with his teenage son. The film is set in Daly City, California, one of the largest Filipina/o communities in the United States. The movie imagines Daly City as what the anthropologist Benito

Vergara terms the "Pinoy Capital."[40] *Easter Sunday*, as the film title in- dicates, is infused with Christian meaning. Of course, Easter is first and foremost a celebration of Jesus's resurrection. In various scenes, the au- dience glimpses the extent to which Christianity is embedded in the diasporic community's mundane rituals and spaces, such as characters attending an Easter Sunday church service, a Santo Nino baby Jesus figu- rine placed in the living room of a home, and a character making the sign of the cross, reinforcing their Catholic identity.

Although Pacquiao does not make even a cameo appearance in the film, his presence looms large, as one of the subplots involves his stolen boxing gloves. The film narrates how Pacquiao's gloves were stolen when he fought and defeated then boxing superstar Oscar "Golden Boy" De La Hoya in 2008. The gloves were first stolen by Dev Deluxe, a South Asian American villain, and then by Eugene, Valencia's cousin. Joe and Eugene were hoping someone would buy the gloves to enable Eugene to pay back the money Eugene had borrowed from Dev Deluxe. Interestingly, Eugene and Joe stipulate that the gloves must be sold to a Filipina/o. Eventually, they find a buyer called the "Jeweler," who turns out to be Lou Diamond Philips. Pacquiao's gloves are a key point in the film, not simply because Pacquiao wore them, but also because the match after which they were stolen was a turning point in his career arc: his victory over the great boxer De La Hoya. That victory propelled Pacquiao from being a well-known fighter to a global superstar. Valencia consequently treats the gloves as if they were holy relics, vowing to retrieve them and keep them within the community. Eugene proclaims, "Can you believe that a non-Filipino had such an important part of the Filipino culture? So I had to liberate them! For our people. Our country!"

The desire to keep the gloves within the community reflects what some of my interlocuters shared when they discussed their Pacquiao fandom. Angelica, a second-generation Filipina American, asserted that Filipina/o Americans have a sense of shared ownership and pride for Pacquiao. "We all have this ownership for him and he represents all of us. And I think as a Filipino American, it's something to be proud of." Moreover, like Sofia's Manny Pacquiao–branded Bible, the gloves are a key way in which diasporic Filipina/o Americans forge connections to a (masculine) material culture artifact that symbolizes success, an object of a prized masculinity, and an avenue through which they maintain diasporic intimacy to Pacquiao, who is imagined as the (masculinized) symbol of the Philippines. Indeed, at the end of the film, Valencia uses the gloves to knock out Dev Deluxe with a left hook, which is one of Pacquiao's signature punches.

For many Filipina/o Americans, one scene in particular depicts the mood and tenor of the aftermath of the Floyd Mayweather vs. Pacquiao fight. When Dev Deluxe holds Joe Valencia's family hostage and demands his money, Joe's mother offers her pin number: "My pin number is 1217." Tita Teresa chimes in, "Also is mine." The rest of the family follows with, "So is mine, mine too, mine, too." With a clearly annoyed look, Dev Deluxe asks, "Why do you all have the same pin number?" In unison, the family enthusiastically replies, "It's Manny Pacquiao's birthday!" After a brief pause, Deluxe replies in a condescending tone, "Oh right, the guy who couldn't beat Mayweather." The family reacts with astonishment and is offended at Deluxe's assessment that Pacquiao could not, in fact, defeat Mayweather. Angered, they crowd Deluxe and his henchmen before Deluxe and his men pull out their guns to keep the family at a distance. This scene was a nod to some Filipina/o Americans' shared diasporic disappointment when Pacquiao lost. Even though the fight took place seven years prior to the events in the film, the fact that it was referenced in *Easter Sunday* tells us of Pacquiao's staying power in the diaspora, his ability to be a transnational symbol to forge connections among Filipina/os and to the Philippines.[41]

It is not just Pacquiao fans who make meaningful interpretations of Pacquiao's representation. Pacquiao himself recognizes his role as the Pambansang Ninong, or "national Godfather." Through self-representation, he willingly participates as the patriarchal authority. In Catholic tradition, for example, male and female godparents act as second parents, and in a national sense, Pacquiao considers himself to be a "parent of the whole Filipino people."[42] Through Christian masculinity, Pacquiao is a "father" to the people, similar to a priest, who then serves as a spiritual guide.

Pacquiao is an omnipresent figure among Filipina/os and diasporic Filipina/os alike, giving aid to the destitute and poor and garnering authority through respectable social politics. Whereas in the United States the godfather figure usually takes on racialized white, ethnic, and violent meanings, Pacquiao's self-constructed godfather identity is celebrated as a benevolent figure who acts beneficently for the people. Although he commits acceptable violence in the ring, he uses this violence to attain riches and help the downtrodden.

During one of his Philippine-based game shows titled *Manny Many Prizes*, Pacquiao invited poor and working-class Filipino men and women to sing karaoke and participate in various trivia games in hopes of winning cash prizes. During one segment, journalist Lawrence Osborne observed how Pacquiao embraced his role as a godfather (and the Godfather): "When he shouted into the microphone to ask what his audience wanted, they cried back 'Transportation money!'—to cover travel costs to come to the show. I heard shouts of 'ninong—godfather' and soon this word became a chant. 'Whatever you need, my people, I am listening,' he responded. 'Just tell me.'"[43]

These stories, and countless others, frame Pacquiao as one of the few voices of the Filipina/o people whose compassion, empathy, and humanitarian efforts are offered in the service of the nation. As a philanthropist, he performs for the needs of the state and endeavors to provide a solution to Philippine societal poverty. Yet his philanthropic deeds are also part of the emerging nonprofit industrial complex.[44] As American studies scholar Karín Aguilar-San Juan reminds us, Pacquiao's celebrity philanthropy, while a noble cause, in fact masks structural inequities brought on by colonial legacies and neoliberal global capitalism.[45] At the same time, Pacquiao is not the paragon of virtue that his framing at the Bible study and broader public persona suggest. His mass-mediated global iconicity operates in a broader cultural and political climate that produces contradictory outcomes in the service of racial heteronormativity and white supremacy. Thus, rather than see his brown heterosexual masculinity and muscular Christian body as an unambiguous tool for social good and moral uplift,[46] his identity forces us to consider the exclusions and marginalizing practices that produce anti-Black and homophobic sentiments.

The Fight of the Century: Mayweather vs. Pacquiao

On Friday, May 1, 2015, I traveled to the MGM hotel to park in time to watch the weigh-ins of Floyd "Money" Mayweather and Manny "Pac-Man" Pacquiao. Driving through the Las Vegas Strip, I saw vinyl billboards featuring the boxing match and hotels, including the MGM, Aria, and Cosmopolitan, showing digital billboards promoting the fight. Inside the MGM lobby, in large orange capital letters, one billboard read "Mayweather Pacquiao: Saturday, May 2," with the half-naked boxers at opposite ends of the billboard, staring at the camera. Inside the hotel, squarely in the center of the lobby, I saw a boxing ring with a lion in the middle of it. All around, people were taking pictures in front of the billboard with this boxing ring in the background. Wrapped around the ring was a skirt branded with a Tecate beer (Tecate is a Mexican beer founded in Tecate, Baja California) promotion featuring Mayweather and Pacquiao. Banners reading "Tecate: Taste of Triumph" were also hanging from the pillars, with Mayweather and Pacquiao as the featured boxers. The fact that Tecate was sponsoring the fight linked corporate branding with boxing and leveraged the practices of masculinity in the boxing ring to encourage fans and spectators to consume beer. As I tried to navigate the crowded lobby, I had to negotiate a mass of Black and brown people, many of whom were expressing their allegiances to—and perhaps their shared identities with—either Mayweather or Pacquiao. Some people, mainly Filipina/os, wore "Team Pacquiao" T-shirts, hats, and Philippine flags draped around their shoulders. One Filipina/o American couple held a sign that read "Pound4Pound King" with Pacquiao sitting on a throne. Another Filipino was wearing a black T-shirt with yellow lettering that, in Tagalog, read "*Putang ina* Floyd," (*Putang ina* means something along the lines of "son of a bitch" or "your mother is a whore.") By contrast, others, mainly African Americans, were wearing hats that read "TBE" (the best ever) or "TMT" (the money team), referencing Mayweather's nickname, "Money." The lobby was spatialized as Black and brown, with auditory cues of English and Tagalog and of other Philippine-based dialects that I could not decipher. As I walked through the hotel to get in line, I was overwhelmed by the number of people waiting to catch a glimpse of the two boxers the day before their "fight of the century."

Boxing fans in general, and Filipina/o American Pacquiao fans in particular, had been waiting anxiously for this fight to happen from well before 2015. As far back as 2011, research participants I interviewed and boxing fans more generally were clamoring for the fight and were frustrated that the two pugilists—who were each at the peak of their boxing careers—had not yet agreed to a match. Some of my Filipina/o American participants wondered whether or not Pacquiao had the skills to defeat Mayweather, whom many boxing experts and pundits considered to be one of the best boxers ever. For Filipina/o Americans, Mayweather, the undefeated boxer, was the antithesis to Pacquiao; he performed a brash, "cocky" and hypermasculine persona. Unlike Pacquiao, he was known for his spectacular speed and movement, never for his punching power.

Pacquiao was seen as the more "respectful," respectable boxing hero. He was humble, did not brag or boast, and was the more "Christian" fighter, despite Mayweather's own devotion to Christianity. The performance scholar Javon Johnson notes that while we must acknowledge Mayweather's sordid past of misogyny (including domestic violence), racially problematic statements about Pacquiao, and homophobia, we must also remember that Mayweather exists in a white supremacist and racial capitalist marketplace that was never designed as a place in which his Black hypermasculinity could flourish.[47] Moreover, Christian discourses are intertwined with notions of value and piety, evident in how Pacquiao fans describe Mayweather's misogyny, with a politics of religious respectability coded through the lexicon of masculinity, race, and heterosexuality.[48]

How do such discourses persist? Some Filipina/o Americans used the virtual arenas of Facebook, Twitter, and Instagram to post about their excitement. Others expressed their anxiety and nervousness about the looming bout. I text messaged some of my interlocutors to see where and with whom they were watching the fight. All of them replied that they were watching with either their friends or family, in homes or bars. Many Filipina/o Americans organized Pacquaio fight nights with other Filipina/os with whom they were close, indicating the extent to which race was one of the organizing markers of group identity and Pacquiao fandom. It was also a way to forge coethnic bonding with their friends and family members. If there were non-Filipina/os in the space, they were often "screened" to ensure they were rooting for Pacquiao and not his competitor, their fandom pleasures involving the regulation of who could and who could not enter the fight night space. For example, one participant admitted, "I make sure that when I invite my friends, they don't cheer for the other guy." This practice replicates how admittance to the Mandalay Bay theater referenced in the opening vignette screened for respectable Filipina/o Americanness.

Later on the day of the weigh-in, I purchased closed-circuit boxing tickets at a bar in the New York-New York hotel casino to watch the following day. Several hours prior to the start of the fight, the bar was already full of boxing fans. As the undercard fights ensued, images showed Mayweather and Pacquiao arriving at the venue. A smattering of cheers and boos rippled through the bar.

After the introductions and the singing of the Philippine and US national anthems, Michael Buffer and Jimmy Lennon, Jr., introduced the two boxers of color. With Pacquiao standing southpaw and Mayweather in an orthodox stance,[49] the two finally met to determine who was the best boxer of their era. After a few rounds, I sensed that the initial excitement of the fight had quickly dissipated. Mayweather's crisp jab to Pacquiao's midsection and head kept the Filipino boxer at bay. Mayweather used his footwork and timing to angle out of the ring's corners and ropes to avoid Pacquiao's power shots. Mayweather's reflexes and defensive prowess matched Pacquiao's patented speed and quickness. With the exception of the fourth round, when Pacquiao countered Mayweather with a hard left hand followed by a flurry of left right combinations to Mayweather's face, head, and body (chants of "Manny, Manny, Manny" erupted during this sequence), the fight seemed rather pedestrian as Mayweather's defensive prowess, ring command, and expertise in anticipating Pacquiao's moves dictated the terms of the fight. One could hear the hopeful cheers as Pacquiao sought to be the aggressor. However, Steve Farhood, one of the fight's commentators, admonished the viewers by warning them, "You have to score with your eyes, not your ears." In between rounds, I text messaged some of the interlocutors to gauge how they felt the fight was unfolding. Some shared that Mayweather was "running," while others texted back, "Dude, Floyd's scared. He won't box Manny." Rather than acknowledge Mayweather's defensive expertise and tactical maneuvering in the ring, participants instead relied on reducing Mayweather's Blackness in ways that harken to parallel discourses of Mayweather as a feminized and queered version of "Gayweather."[50]

In the end, Pacquiao was no match for Mayweather's boxing ability, intelligence, and superior defensive maneuvering. The fight went the full twelve rounds, with Mayweather defeating Pacquiao by unanimous decision. Two of the three judges scored the fight for Mayweather 116 to 112, and the third judge gave Mayweather the nod with a score of 118 to 110. The bout did not live up to what many Filipina/o and Filipina/o American fans had wanted from Pacquiao: for him to knock Mayweather out. It was a disappointing end to a boxing match that had been promoted as a once in a lifetime event.

Manichean Logics of Race-Making and White Supremacist Christianity

Beyond looking at the fight as simply a bout between two men of color, it is crucial to examine how race is made meaningful in the sport, beyond the Black-white binary. One image in particular serves as an interesting way in which to analyze how Pacquiao and Mayweather are imagined by some Filipina/o and Filipina/o Americans. In a blog post from April 2015, titled "Why My God Won't Show Up for Mayweather-Pacquiao," blogger Norman A. Novio wrote about how his Christian God would not be present in the outcome of the Mayweather vs. Pacquiao fight. The reason? Because his God allegedly does not subscribe to a practice where the goal is to hurt the opponent. Novio also included an image of Mayweather and Pacquiao in an arm-wrestling match. Though the image frames the homosocial intimacy (e.g., touching and facing each other in proximity) of the boxers, it simultaneously symbolizes a contest of masculinity.[51] In an arm-wrestling match, the competitors must physically overpower the other by forcing their competitor's hand down onto the table. The image is set in binary terms and infused with Christian messaging, connoting Manichean elements of good vs. evil with a stark spatial demarcation separating the two. Pacquaio seemingly embodies "good," while Mayweather embodies "evil," thereby reducing Mayweather's "blackness itself and black people in general into a semi-humanized category of radical otherness."[52] For example, on the left side, Mayweather embodies devilish characteristics (with pointed ears and horns) as flames and darkness envelop him. In the image, and its interpretation, the element of desire is constantly mediated and repudiated; Christianity becomes the way to repudiate both Blackness and same-sex desire. Conversely, Pacquiao is caricatured in Jesus's likeness, occupies a heaven-like space, and is dressed in nearly all white attire. He wears a white robe with a gold sash placed diagonally across his torso. With a beard and long hair (evoking dominant images of Jesus), Pacquiao has a self-assured smile against the struggling Mayweather, and his Christian faith facilitates his inclusion in an imagined white nation-state.

Pacquiao's Christlike image racially elevates him over Mayweather's Blackness and is positioned closer to whiteness and white supremacy. Regardless of the long histories of Christianity in African American communities, there is a foregrounding of Pacquiao's Christianity that consequently elides Mayweather's.[53] While Mayweather's excessive Blackness and hypermasculinity is racially overdetermined, Pacquiao's racial ambiguity is vital in crossing over as an acceptable (brown) racial figure who does not upend the colonial project of white supremacy. Moreover, dominant discourses of Black athletes are part of a dichotomizing process that depict them as either "good" or "bad," with their Blackness often imagined as dangerous, uncontrollable or out of control, and inherently violent, ignoring the white supremacist ideologies imposed upon them.[54] The image resembles what the sociologist Ben Carrington terms the *white colonial frame.* Adapting Joe Feagin's notion of the white racial frame,[55] Carrington theorizes that the white colonial frame reproduces white supremacy through colonialism and Christianity in ways that result in "anti-black racism, both historically and contemporaneously, even after the formal dismantling of European colonial regimes."[56] Although Carrington is referencing European colonialism, we see how vestiges of American colonialism and racial projects inform racializing processes.[57] Ultimately, the Bible study and the image of Pacquiao and Mayweather secure a certain kind of racial respectability that is intimately tied to the US colonial and postcolonial Philippine nation-state.

"You Know He Called Us Animals": The Limits of Pacquiao's Heterosexual Masculinity and Diasporic Belonging

While Pacquiao seemingly embodies the hopes and dreams of thousands of Filipina/os in the diaspora, we need to trouble the recurring and dominant narrative which celebrates his faith, and his accomplishments and philanthropic activities. Not all Filipina/o Americans feel a sense of belonging and overtly claim Pacquiao as the Philippines' national symbol. Pacquiao's brand of Christianity, masculinity, race, class, and sexuality does not represent all of the Filipina/o American diaspora. In this diasporic context and in the enduring afterlife of US empire, Pacquiao himself aspires to and practices what Black feminist scholar Audre Lorde conceives as the "mythical norm," a "trapping" of power that demands an elision of difference and that prizes Christianity, white masculinity, heterosexuality, and class affluence above all else. Lorde writes, "In america [*sic*], this norm is usually defined as white, thin, male, young, heterosexual, christian [*sic*], and financially secure." As the "good vs. evil" image suggests, the mythical norm is a myopic aspiration toward inhabiting a white racial heteronormative ideal whereby queer people and women are expelled from belonging to the nation and the diaspora.

Pacquiao came under intense criticism and scrutiny amid comments he made about same-sex marriage and the queer community. On February 15, 2016, TV5, a Philippine-based television station, interviewed Pacquiao. During the interview, the anchor asked Pacquiao his views on same-sex marriage. Pacquiao declared, "As a Christian, same-sex marriage is prohibited. Women were created for men, and men were created for women. It's common sense. Do you see animals mating with the same sex? Animals are better because they can distinguish male from female. If men mate with men and women mate with women they are worse than animals." In the wake of an outcry, Pacquiao offered what was meant as an apology on his Instagram account, posting "I['d] rather obey the Lord's command than obey . . . the desires of the flesh. I'm not condemning anyone, but I'm just telling the truth of what the Bible says. The truth from the Bible is what changed me from my old ways."[58] He then used Twitter to post a video stating, "I'm sorry for everyone who got hurt due to my comparison of gay people (homosexuals) to animals. It was my mistake. Please forgive me for those who I've hurt. But this does not change my position against same sex marriage. That's what I believe. My only mistake is comparing gay people to animals." Although he apologized for dehumanizing gay people and placing animals above LGBTQI people and asked for forgiveness, Pacquiao doubled down on his strict, literal biblical reading of same-sex marriage, which, founded in American Protestantism, embraces heterosexual desire as "the natural order of things."[59] We can find connections in these comments to white, mainline evangelical Christians and Donald Trump's national populist politics.[60]

That Pacquiao adheres to heteronormative notions of sexuality, desire, and pleasure aligns with the dominant notions of the nation, obscuring the spectrum of Filipina/o/x gender expressions and sexual desire in the diaspora. Citing the Bible (through a Western-centric, male, and heterosexist lens) as a moral compass and moral authority, Pacquiao, knowingly or not, intentionally or not, expels LGBTQI people from the diaspora and relegates them to the margins. Certain desires, like queer desire and queer sexuality, become "impossible desires" that further substantiate and exacerbate particular racial and gendered identities.[61] As one who embodies the proper patriarchal authority, Pacquiao's voice resonates with, and shapes, conservative ideas of sexuality, masculine visions of the nation, and a hardening of diasporic boundaries of belonging. In a world of global ideas, through transnational linkages, diasporic imaginings, and neoliberal globalization, Pacquiao represents a desire to strengthen heterosexual masculinity by shoring up perceptions of an emasculated Philippine nation.[62] Indeed, as a national trope, Dave Chappelle's joke introduced at the outset of this chapter speaks to nationalist concerns and anxieties about the erosion of the heteronormative family unit.[63]

The response to Pacquiao's homophobic comments was immediate as people took to social media to denounce his worldviews. Other Filipina/o Americans with whom I spoke were ambivalent. "It's his opinion," shared one second-generation Filipino American. Others agreed with his views and did not see his comments as problematic. Celia, a first-generation Filipina American in her fifties shared, "He said something about as far as what I have read, I don't know if it's all that he said. He does not approve of gay marriages because it's against his religion. And then he clarified himself that it doesn't mean he despises or have an aversion for gay people. I share the same view. It's not a big thing." Celia's version of a diasporic Filipino community is likewise demarcated and imagined through heterosexual boundaries. Similarly, with the long history of Filipino American emasculation under American imperialism, some Filipino American men adore Pacquiao and view him as the heterosexual remedy to perceptions of masculine lack. For example, in July 2019, a few hours before Pacquiao and Keith Thurman's weigh-in, I spoke with Rouel, a 1.5-generation Filipino American. Rouel was wearing an "MP" brand black T-shirt depicting Pacquiao wearing a hoodie. He told me that he's been a Pacquiao fan ever since he beat British boxer Ricky "the Hitman" Hatton in 2009. During our conversation, he compared Pacquiao to "the colonized versus colonizer kind of thing." And while he did not mention which of Pacquiao's boxing opponents were the colonizer, he asserted that for him, Pacquiao "represents all those years of struggle." Moreover, Rouel discussed his own struggles as a "smaller person" playing sports, being picked on and feeling inadequate. He reflected, "As a smaller person he [Pacquiao] demonstrates that strength so I feel like that's why [I root for him]."

Struggling to find the words to respond to my question regarding Pacquiao's homophobic comments, Sofia paused a few times before saying, "He doesn't mean to have malice and doesn't try to hurt anyone's feelings. I know his heart. I was a little offended. I 'unfollowed him' on social media. We are human and not perfect. He is a good person and means well. He doesn't hate people living that kind of lifestyle." Yet when I interviewed Everisto, a self-identified queer 1.5-generation Filipino American, he was angry at Pacquiao's homophobic comments and vowed to boycott the rest of his fights. He forcefully asserted, "We can find different heroes. We can find great representatives of the Filipino community beyond him. Yes, he is a great boxer and probably has put the Philippines on the map. [But] all you need to [do is] look around your own family. They represent the community much, much better than having someone who is a boxing champion but has a different view of what equality really means in the Philippines." Rather than embrace the heteronormative construction of Pacquiao's embodied nationalism, Everisto instead asks us to think beyond the global icon and look to our own families and communities for models of behavior. He signals that while Pacquiao has brought global attention to the Philippines because of his athletic success, he fails to recognize the complexity of desires and pleasures of the LGBTQI community. Pacquiao's vision for equality, Everisto asserts, does not consider queer peoples' humanity, an ironic twist given how Pacquiao's philanthropic acts are placed high on the pedestal of giving and care. Moreover, Everisto asks us to expand the contours of diasporic belonging beyond normative constructions that privilege heterosexuality and promote homophobia. Reproducing the diaspora according to this logic leaves little room to account for the heterogeneity of identities in the diaspora.

Annalisa, a second-generation, self-identified, Pilipinx American was angry that Pacquiao called the LGBTQ community "animals":[64]

> He's dehumanizing the community and I felt offended. I understand he's for God, loves God, and the Bible so much. But I'm sure there were those who identified as queer who did support him. And I think he lost a lot of people's respect for saying that. [He's] using [his] own image and reputation to say that. So if [Pacquiao] is allowed to say it, then other people are allowed to say it. He's spearheading that. It wasn't just him who said that, "Ok gay people suck or are like animals." If he's allowed to say it, it enable[s] everyone else to say it.

Annalisa recognizes the religious diversity of the Filipina/o American community and honors Pacquiao's own faith-based beliefs. Yet she critiques his dehumanizing language while also pondering how his voice shapes public perceptions. In other words, she warns of the dangers that Pacquiao's worldview can have for queer people. Equating Filipinos to animals is a rhetorical relic of US colonial discourse in the late nineteenth century. As we saw earlier, already seen as inferior to white America, colonized Filipinos were depicted in popular US newspapers variously as animals and insects in the form of snakes, monkeys, mosquitos, and bees (see figure 1.3).[65]

In Annalisa and Everisto's responses to Pacquiao's homophobic comments, they offer alternative claims to heteronormative ethnic nationalism, causing a rupture in the seemingly fixed imaginings of the nation and diaspora. Rather than align themselves with Pacquiao's brand of conservative nationalism, they instead recognize that sexual differences within the imagined community are fraught with contradiction. Pacquiao, knowingly or not, enlists Christianity, homophobia, and heterosexual masculinity as social forces of exclusion. Moreover, Everisto and Annalisa's observations demonstrate what late theorist Jose Esteban Munoz terms *disidentification*. Disidentifying with Pacquiao's politics means rejecting sentiments of exclusion within the diaspora and from the dominant and normative notions of ethnic and nationalist politics of belonging.[66] Everisto's call to search for models within our commu-

Figure 1.3. UNCLE SAM: "The critter barks and wags at the same time. Which end of him is lyin'?"
The Minneapolis Times, also published in *The Literary Digest*. Vol. XXIV, No. 12, March 22, 1902, p. 386 [artist unknown]

nities outside of Pacquiao's myopic vision of belonging is a powerful rejection of heteropatriarchal nationalism. As their "deviance" already unsettles heterosexist diasporic boundaries, they make claims to a much more expansive form of diaspora that affirms their humanity without feeling like their pleasures and desires are policed, regulated, and under surveillance.

For some Filipina/o Americans, Pacquiao is a symbol of diasporic desires, longings, and pleasures, a heroic figure whose symbolism is as promising as it is paradoxical. He is the embodiment of an affluent and respectable Christian heterosexual man, adored for his boxing success and admired for his generosity to the poor and for bringing attention to a nation which has endured hundreds of years of Western empires and Japanese occupation. His victories inside the boxing ring extend outward, with some of my interlocutors expressing intense emotions about how Pacquiao not only represents the Philippines but their diasporic lives as well. His victories are their victories and his losses are their losses. Of course, obscured in these popular culture representations are issues of race and racism, heterosexual masculine nationalism, the afterlife of US empire, and what it means to belong to a diaspora that isn't always welcoming.

Pacquiao's brown body is a potential antidote to normative white masculinity, built with power, strength, and toughness. These masculine attributes invert and subvert global popular imaginings of the Philippine nation as weak, effeminate, and emasculated. Unfortunately, his muscular Christianity operates in the service of white supremacy. As the Bible study shows and the image highlights, Pacquiao's brownness confers upon him a certain proximity to whiteness that simultaneously repudiates Blackness. Moreover, his muscular Christianity opposes an expansive vision of diasporic belonging, especially in the realm of sexuality, where LGBTQI Filipina/o and Filipina/o Americans are already seen as marginal to national politics of belonging.

Pacquiao is not the only one who crosses borders and boundaries. Although he is a professional athlete, there are also working-class Filipino immigrant men who immigrated to the United States who were recruited to work in health care and educational industries, as well as in other service-sector jobs. Far from simply working to make a living, they also carve out coethnic leisure spaces as a form of pleasure. With this in mind, the next chapter is a misdirection of sorts, a sudden move across sports, landscapes, and regions. It examines how recently arrived Filipino immigrants form community in the Midwest, engaging in the pleasures of basketball play, and negotiating their masculinity through the Black-white racial paradigm in Urbana-Champaign.

2

"Yo, Pogi!"

Basketball, Boodle Fights, and Filipino Masculine Homosocial Intimacies in the Midwest

On a humid mid-August afternoon in 2014, I walked into Soriano's,[1] a local Filipino grocery store in Champaign, Illinois—one of a handful of Asian grocery stores in the area that sell Filipino ingredients. I needed groceries for my vegetable fried lumpia.[2] In this semisuburban, working-class community, which is more than 60 percent white, close to 20 percent African American, 15 percent Asian American, and less than 10 percent Latinx, sits an ethnic store in a hollowed-out parking lot in the middle of America's heartland.[3] After I took a few steps inside the store, Marlon, the owner, asked if I wanted to play basketball and pointed to the brown piece of paper taped to a shelf that read "Filipino-American basketball league." I realized it was a sign-up sheet. Decorating the sign-up sheet were the Philippine sun and stars, along with the familiar Philippine flag's colors of red, blue, and yellow. Underneath, employing national colors, the text stated "committed only," meaning that only people who were serious about playing in the league should sign up. Eager and excited to start playing basketball again, I wrote my name and phone number, making sure my handwriting was legible enough for another person to read.

A few weeks later, I received a text message from Fredrico, one of the league's organizers. He wanted to confirm my interest in playing and invited me to play at the local recreation center in Champaign, where some of the players met every Wednesday and Sunday for games. The invitation to play at the recreation center served as a sort of tryout, as Fredrico wanted to evaluate my basketball skills in order to assign me to the appropriate team. When I walked into the recreation center, Fredrico and I made eye contact and introduced ourselves. He then introduced me to Aldrin and Angelo while we waited for others to arrive. We then started shooting around and engaging in small talk. Angelo, a dark-skinned Filipino with tattoos covering his arms, casually shot three-point shots. I was impressed by his shooting form and the smooth nature with which he dribbled the ball. He was one of the players to whom I paid particular attention because he seemed to have a particular shooting ability and an impressive and broad repertoire of basketball skills. As we shot around, more Filipino men walked in, and after about thirty minutes, we decided that there were enough of us to form teams of five. As we started to play the first game, more men arrived and waited their turn to play. During the first half of the game, players started with a casual nature and it seemed as if the teams were more interested in conversing than actually playing. They were joking around, laughing, and did not seem to worry that they were missing what I deemed to be relatively easy shots. I inaccurately assumed that they were not taking the competition seriously, not realizing until after many more instances of meeting up and playing pickup basketball with them that, apart from playing, they congregated on the court to converse with each other about life's happenings, including managing relationships with girlfriends overseas, their new jobs, or how much their current job tired them out. In other words, playing basketball was the activity through which these men cultivated community.

As the game continued, the intensity escalated, and the playful and jovial nature of the players and playing dissipated. The squeaking of basketball sneakers and the proximate bouncing of basketballs, with distant voices on other courts, replaced conversations. Both teams' defensive intensity picked up, and we started to guard each other with intention. The shift made me realize that these men were indeed serious about playing basketball. I channeled my competitive drive and used my lateral agility and speed to defend Angelo and try to prevent him from shooting. Despite my defensive pressure, he still managed to score over me by using a number of offensive maneuvers. He was a few inches taller and heavier than me, and during one possession he used his thick frame to post me up and shoot a fadeaway shot, which is a shot that involves a high degree of difficulty, using one's body to shield oneself and "fade away" from the hoop, making it difficult to block the shot. During another possession, he used a pump fake (pretending to shoot to force me to react) before sidestepping and shooting a three-pointer. I had been fooled, and we both knew it. He manipulated my body so that he could create space to score using one, among many, of his offensive moves.

During another possession, one of the men who was guarding me said "Dude, *mabilis ka!*" ("Dude, you're fast!") as he was trying to catch his breath. A few possessions later, one of my teammates passed me the ball and I sprinted toward the basket to beat the rest of the team. I knew I was faster than many of the players, so I sought to create a quick offensive tempo to create layups for my team. One of the opposing players recognized my strategy and immediately blurted "*Takbo siya!*" ("He's running!") and implored his teammates to keep up. I realized he was talking about me and I was amused that he recognized my strategy. After we finished playing three more games, I was exhausted and decided to observe the rest of the games. As I was sitting down, Fredrico and Angelo approached me before playing their next game. Fredrico said, "Hey man, thanks for coming out to play. Are you still gonna play in our league?" As I wiped the sweat from my forehead, I immediately said, "Yeah, count me in. This was fun!" He then said he would text me about the team to which I would be drafted. I was interested in learning more about the community, the league, and the stories of some of the Filipino immigrant and Filipino American men. After playing a few more times in pickup basketball and getting to know the players, I asked for, and was granted, permission to conduct fieldwork observations and interviews for a year.

Whereas cultural institutions like ethnic Filipino "Oriental" stores are sites for nostalgia, identity, and place-making politics for Filipino Americans,[4] stores like Soriano's may also serve as an important hub and network, such as, like in this instance, for recruiting Filipino Americans to play sports. Although basketball has a long history in Illinois via the National Basketball Association (NBA) team the Chicago Bulls (particularly popular when led by Michael Jordan), as well as via the basketball success at the University of Illinois, the narrative of this engagement with the sport is often limited to a Black-white account that does not acknowledge the diversity in the region. However, anthropologist Sujey Vega provides an important intervention in studies of the Midwest, drawing attention to a different narrative.[5] Focusing on Indiana, which is home to the Ku Klux Klan, Vega details the much longer history of Latinx communities and enhances our understanding of the expansive racial histories of the region. Similarly, the vignette asks us to reimagine the Midwest and Filipina/o America. Soriano's store served as a means by which Filipina/o and Filipina/o Americans forged community beyond conventional spaces, assisting in interjecting a Filipina/o identity into the Midwestern landscape and into the popular cultural terrain of basketball.

What we witness in this example of the basketball league is the formation of community, the performance of identity, and the management of labor and leisure. Instead of consolidating Filipina/o American identity only through Manny "Pac-Man" Pacquiao or sporting cultures in the Philippines, there is a deep engagement that shifts and breaks the ankles of (e.g., subverts) our intellectual and methodological canons. The basketball league and similar kinds of social networking via the store and the court open up new avenues by which to recognize identity formations in the heartland of the United States. Basketball in this iteration is not a whimsical practice. Rather, it is an important arena in which to manage social life, invert damaging racializations, and sustain a space for pleasures and desires.[6] In a time of late capitalism and post-Fordist strategies, the arrival of the men in Urbana-Champaign and their efforts at sustaining community are examples of how labor and leisure work together to crossover dominant narratives of the Midwest, migration, and masculinity. This chapter delves into racial geographies of play and the spatializing of race, and how they are negotiated through various competing realms of race, gender, sexuality, and migration. It queers our understanding of Midwest male homosociality and intimacy, which are typically reserved for white men. It suggests that in order to understand intimacies, we must understand Filipino immigrant male homosociality and the thoroughly everyday, intimate spaces of playing basketball, eating, and performing other forms of contact that affirm and yet complicate how we understand masculinity.

Destabilizing the American Heartland's Roots and Routes

Analogous to what the anthropologists Britt E. Halvorson and Joshua O. Reno describe as a knot, the Midwest constitutes a series of social, cultural, and political processes that become entangled through power, manifested in "intersecting projects of race, nation, and empire."[7] For

Filipino Americans, their relationship to the Midwest region is fraught with these entanglements as a result of various crossings and connections, which link racial projects, nation, empire, and sport. The Midwest is part of a cultural mythology that often characterizes itself as insular and isolationist and as the "heartland" of America, replete with pastoral settings and idyllic farm life. In this region, working-class labor and whiteness converge to form a prized working-class masculinity and one that projects outward to consolidate an American national identity.[8] Even the story of basketball in the heartland is often whitened and whitewashed. For example, the movie *Hoosiers* has had a far-reaching effect in historicizing and interpellating basketball in the Midwest as white. The very fact of its very white cast erases the stories of communities of color who have a long history in Indiana in particular and the Midwest in general. This depiction of the region belies a much more complicated history of the heartland, obscuring connections between race, masculinity, and US imperial intimacy at the nexus of postindustrialization, migration, and labor. Indeed, this chapter, which focuses on Illinois in particular, and the Midwest region in general, is situated in a larger postindustrial history beginning during World War II and continuing up until the 1950s, when Northeast and Midwestern cities were key sites of a vibrant manufacturing industry. Because of the changing landscape of the labor market caused by the transformation and decline of the manufacturing industry in places like Chicago and Detroit, these industries then shifted, outsourcing their labor into rural locales or even to off-shore sites.[9] In central Illinois, for example, from 2003 to 2010, the health care and social assistance industry witnessed steady growth while jobs in the manufacturing sector declined.[10] Some Filipino immigrant men and second-generation Filipino American men found jobs in these locales, including in Champaign-Urbana, Illinois. Thus, the longer intimacies of US empire are also connected to the marketplace as labor and migration create communal pockets in places where outsourcing is spurred by shifts in the industrial landscape.

If the Midwest is imagined as a white, homogenized space, then it is also imperative to locate how whiteness and masculinity are crucial to its production. The Midwest and sports construct a space where white masculinity—the only typically unmarked and value-free signifier—

takes place. Popular culture films about the Midwest deserve particular attention. In the 1989 Hollywood film *Field of Dreams*, starring white actor Kevin Costner, we see how baseball's pastoral setting in Iowa's cornfields becomes the stage for "America's national pastime" to portray a reconciliation between a deceased white father and his living son.[11] This reconciliation symbolizes a generational transfer of sporting intimacy that consolidates baseball as a white masculine narrative of redemption. The film employs the lone African American character, civil rights activist Terrance Mann, played by James Earl Jones, to legitimate white masculine agency while offering disgraced white baseball players an alternate ending to their World Series scandal. The scandal took place in 1919 when eight Chicago White Sox baseball players were bribed by mobster Arnold Rothstein to throw the World Series against the Cincinnati Reds.[12] Mann's Black masculinity and progressive politics are figuratively depoliticized as the corn "consume[s] a black radical" in its wake.[13] In this way, the Midwest showcases a particular rural and working-class masculinity that is seen as germane, natural, and deeply embedded in the region's landscape. White masculinity becomes a compass to guide the region, a compass that excludes both the "multiplicity of masculinities" and people of color.[14] The reproduction of the mythical narrative of white masculinity in sports in the Midwest leaves little room for exploring the various racialized and gendered entanglements that Halvorson and Reno reference.

Moreover, applying such a queer analytic reveals how the Midwest region is imagined as an "uncontested site of middle-class white American heteronormativity."[15] Although this imagination produces normative representations of whiteness and ideologies of a normative middle, the region itself may be queered by refusing a dominant (white normative) reading and instead underscoring nonnormative paradigmatic readings as a way of knowing.[16] I challenge not only the heteronormativity of the American heartland but also the West-East narrative of Asian American migration. Rather than privilege the origin stories of Filipina/o migration to places like California, Alaska, and Hawai'i, as typically occurs, I instead map alternative routes, trajectories, and narratives to emphasize Asian American "scatterings" across the United States that refuse geographically bounded communities who exist in isolation from larger social, cultural, and economic processes.[17] The "origin" story of Filipina/o America in the heartland reflects this scattering.

To answer historian Kristen Hoganson's question—"What is the nation at heart when we unbind it from myth?"[18]—unbinding the American heartland from its myth reveals histories of Indigenous dispossession, its role as an imperial center, and its global capitalist dimensions through the export of meat production and agriculture. In the context of the Midwest Filipina/o community, taking the call to untangle or unbind the American heartland myth requires us to examine the complicated routes of US empire and sport that historically situate Filipina/o American community formations at the nexus of US colonialism, immigration, and sporting cultures. Thus, for Filipina/os, at heart, the nation is not compatible with the white masculine sporting narrative above.[19] Instead, I point to a historical moment and event involving Indigenous people of the Philippines and Filipina/os that took place in St. Louis—an event called the "Special Olympics"—that shows how white masculinity and white supremacy were bolstered in America's heartland over a century ago.

The St. Louis World's Fair and the Special Olympics

The partial story of Indigenous people of the Philippines and Filipina/os' presence in the Midwest is situated within US imperial intimacies dating back to 1904. The US colonial state and its actors and the academic discipline of anthropology organized a highly regulated and racialized sporting space. Indigenous people of the Philippines were brought to St. Louis in August of 1904 for the St. Louis World's Fair, under the Louisiana Purchase Exposition (LPE), to "celebrate" American progress, innovation, modernity, and civilization. Indigenous people of the Philippines, as well as Native American and central African tribes, came not to be visitors to the fair but rather to be "displayed" in order to help the white American public imagine how US civilizational imperatives materialized through the representation of the "wild" and "savage" other.[20] Although the St. Louis World's Fair is an oft-cited historical event in Filipino and Asian American studies, frequently overlooked is how athletic abilities of Indigenous people of the Philippines, along with those of other people of color, were measured through the Special

Olympics, which also served as a disciplinary apparatus.[21] Race and its biological meanings were most easily located, fixed, and managed through sport and bodily practice. Thus W. J. McGee, the director of the Division of Anthropology's exposition, under the direction of James Sullivan, the head of the World's Fair's Division of Physical Education, sought to evaluate whether people of color, whom many in the West had heretofore regarded as "savages," were capable of usurping the supposed athletic superiority of white men. McGee and Sullivan subscribed to pseudoscientific ideas that white people were the superior race with regard to athletic ability. White men supposedly embodied all of the virtues of athletic ability and were therefore the highest order of masculinity, racial hierarchy, modernity, and rights regimes. During the fair, Indigenous people from the Philippines competed in spear and javelin throwing competitions, tree climbing, pole climbing, archery, and foot races. They were measured according to the "rules" of eugenic science in order, on the one hand, to reaffirm long-held preconceived beliefs about racial hierarchy, in which people of color were supposedly "naturally" inferior, and, on the other, to celebrate white masculinity as particularly suited for athletic prowess.

The enduring legacy of the St. Louis World's Fair and Special Olympics resulted in racist representations of Indigenous peoples of the Philippines coded through honor, nostalgia, and memory.[22] Although nowadays much of the racial discourse in the state of Illinois centers around the racial mascot University of Illinois, Urbana-Champaign, Chief Illiniwek, and the National Hockey League team the Chicago Blackhawks,[23] we also witness problematic racist representations of Indigenous people of the Philippines.[24] During the World's Fair, the exhibit featured Igorots,[25] an Indigenous tribe of the Philippines who were recruited to be a part of the exposition, and a village made to look (theoretically) like a village the tribe would have lived in. The exhibit was located in the area around Clayton, Missouri. After the fair, the village was razed and several schools were built before Wydown Middle School superseded other schools that had been built in the town.

In 1937, Wydown Middle School students launched an "Igorrote yearbook" and "Igorrote football team" to commemorate the tribe,[26] and at one point, their school mascot was an Igorot (see figure 2.1).[27] This moment illustrates how the Midwest imagined its body politic, relying not

Figure 2.1. "Wydown Middle School's Mascot Takes Sixth-Graders Back to 1904." *St. Louis Post-Dispatch*, Thursday, April 20, 2000.

on the space and distance of an "over there" colonial subject but on a much more intimate and proximate Indigenous Philippine subject who is seemingly frozen in time and can be appropriated and consumed.[28] The racial iconography of the Igorot people shows us how the circulation of racial images challenges the whiteness of the Midwest despite the absence of people of color. The Midwest, in other words, is what the literary scholar Thomas Sarmiento posits as the "heartland of US empire."[29] Sports, as a social, cultural, and colonial institution, were not simply carried out in the US imperial outpost of the Philippines but also within the America's imperial heartland. The Special Olympics, organized and led by white men, was a crucial way in which white supremacy was consolidated to cement American (white) athletic superiority and to imagine people of color as athletically "inferior" in America's imperial heartland and beyond.[30] For the Filipino immigrant community in Urbana-Champaign, rather than seeing sport as a (voluntary) way in which intimate connections with the American nation could be forged, events like the Special Olympics were "forced intimacies" by the American empire toward its colonial wards.[31] The Special Olympics, in other words, illustrate alternative Filipina/o routes and pathways and how such pathways are fundamentally tied to the interiority of the heartland of US empire.

As racial spectacles and abject others, Igorot bodies exemplified the proximity of sports and "metroimperial intimacies" of the US empire toward its colonial subjects. Metroimperial intimacies, as literary and gender scholar Victor Mendoza notes, conceptualize US imperial power as a mutually constituting national project, one that places the contiguous US metropole and its overseas colonies, like the Philippines, together. In this instance, the Special Olympics brought the Philippines and its people into an intimate and more proximate view and sutured the colonized Filipino sporting subject to the US nation-building project. This moment in the heartland of American empire reveals a much more complicated understanding of Asian American and Filipina/o "migration" beyond ports, seas, waterways, and coasts.[32]

Locating Filipina/o American Communities in the Heartland

Filipina/os' presence in the Midwest was, however, acknowledged not only through the fair and Special Olympics. Although their numbers were not as significant as their West Coast counterparts, early twentieth-century students had likewise migrated to the US Midwest. They were "earnest, ambitious young men (fewer than 5 percent were women) who liked the adventure of studenthood in a country long dreamed of [and] aspired to a future in the Islands they had only temporarily abandoned."[33] They became "unintentional immigrants," and formed small Filipino community pockets in places like Chicago.[34] Though their aspiration was to achieve social mobility by becoming educated at American universities before returning to the Philippines, they unfortunately encountered the significant hardships of racism and the Great Depression, which severely curtailed their hopes and dreams of returning to the Philippines with a college degree.[35] Their transition from being liminal subjects as students to immigrants reduced their labor opportunities to working in the service industry, at the post office, or for the Pullman railway company. Similar to immigrant men on the West Coast, white people criminalized the sexuality of this predominantly male population of Filipino immigrants by deeming it socially unacceptable for them to date white woman students. To manage their racialization and marginalization, many of these Filipinos turned to Chicago's taxi dance halls as welcome leisure spaces, in which they carved out a sense of pleasure and desire.[36] However, because white people already read their brown masculinities as nonnormative, white men in particular came to view them as sexual predators, ascribing to them a "lascivious" nature and accusing them of ostentatious displays of sexuality with white women. Moreover, white men imagined Filipino men as threats to white masculinity, and this often resulted in violent outcomes.[37] Anti-Filipino violence in this period, and racist ideas about Filipinos' menacing and "perverse" sexuality, illustrate how Filipino racialization was already being queered.[38] It was this racial interstitiality and ambiguity—oscillating between allegations of being hypermasculine and hypomasculine—that was vital to white people's shifting racial depictions of these Filipinos.[39] They couldn't win. The constantly shifting terrain of the racialization of Filipinos made them always nonnormative and always situated in opposition to respectable and heteronormative white masculinity.

In addition to the St. Louis World's Fair and the Special Olympics, a smaller group of Filipinos also came the Midwest at the turn of the twentieth century, this time as *pensionados*. Pensionados were students sponsored by the colonial government; they were children of elite and powerful Filipino families. The pensionados were expected to carry out the US colonial government's policy of benevolent assimilation by attending elite white educational institutions such as the University of Illinois, Urbana-Champaign, and, upon completing their studies, to return to the Philippines and take up influential positions in US colonial institutions, those promoting and enacting US ways of leadership, commerce, and morals. Thus, in the early twentieth century, the Midwest already had global pathways and circuits of exchange and mobility between the United States and the Philippines.

Smaller numbers of Filipina/os arrived in the Urbana-Champaign area in the 1980s.[40] By this point, Urbana-Champaign was already regarded as deeply embedded in histories of migration and was a key area of labor for Filipina/o communities. From the 1980s onward, demographic shifts in immigration included women arriving in the United States in significant numbers, in contrast to earlier migration patterns in which Filipino men, as virtually the only ones immigrating at that point, were seen as key subjects of assimilation and modernization. It was an approach that effectively dismissed women from the narrative.

Among the women who arrived during this time was Tita Lovelynn, an elder and community leader who in 1985 migrated from the Bicol region of the Philippines to Urbana-Champaign as a student. During my interviews with her, she shared that the growing presence of Filipinos in the area really first took root in 1996. During this period, Central Illinois Care Center (a center that cares for patients with severe cognitive disabilities) was having a difficult time finding staff to care for their patients. Tita Lovelynn explained, "There's not a lot of local people who want to work here. It was in bad shape in terms of staffing." The owner was introduced to a lawyer who sent him a letter asking if he would be willing to hire certified nursing assistants (CNAs) from the Philippines. He hired sixteen Filipinas who were already registered nurses in the Philippines. But because of the testing system in the United States, they had to pass the National Council Licensure Examination (NCLEX) exam. After the first sixteen nurses arrived, they petitioned their family members to join them. "At Swan," Tita Lovelynn told me, "the sixteen nurses started to ask [the owner], can I bring my family? Can I petition them? Can I get my relatives? [The community] grew from there." According to Tita Lovelynn's database, by 2015, two hundred Filipina/ os (not including children) were living in the Urbana-Champaign area. After Swann Special Care Center successfully recruited Filipinos, Carle Foundation Hospital as well as Provena Hospital followed suit.[41] Such migration patterns have come to reflect the racializing and gendering of Filipinas as part of the global care industry.[42] These historical and contemporary immigrant circuits counter dominant ideas of Asian American community formations, which have for so long ignored the viability of the American imperial heartland that sits "East of California" as a potential home for immigrants.[43]

Angelo, Fredrico, Aldrin, and Jacob are all part of a community of working-class first-generation Filipina/o immigrants, as well as a few second-generation Filipino American men, who have settled in Urbana-Champaign and are living within five to ten miles of the state's flagship campus, the University of Illinois, Urbana-Champaign (UIUC). They are only the latest immigrants in a longer history of Filipino immigration patterns of those who came voluntarily or otherwise.[44] Within this region, which is still imagined as white, these Filipina/o communities live in proximity to working-class African American communities and to smaller pockets of Latinx/a/o communities.[45] The Filipina/o community members I discuss in this chapter do not have access to the same educational opportunities, citizenship, capital, or labor as some of the other Filipina/o community members. For example, within the community, there are class differences that are inflected by gender. The Filipina women who came as nurses in the 1990s have much greater income potential and occupy professions with higher social capital than many of the working-class immigrant men with whom I interacted on the basketball courts. A number of these recent immigrant men work in manufacturing industries located in the Urbana-Champaign area. These include an educational company that manufactures and sells educational regalia, a company that makes automated manufacturing products, and a factory producing food and beverage, as well as a company making disposable plastic cups. Other men work for fast-food restaurants or are cooks, and some work at a special care facility for people with disabilities, providing a "labor of care" for the broader Urbana-Champaign community.[46]

Many of the men I interviewed or with whom I had informal conversations, whose ages ranged from eighteen to forty years old, told me how they came to be in the Midwest. Their decisions to migrate were largely the result of the family-sponsored or employment-based category of the Immigration Act of 1965 and, later, the Immigration Act of 1990. For example, family members who had arrived from the 1990s to the 2000s petitioned basketball players like Aldrin, Fredrico, and Jacob. Although I highlight the men's stories in this chapter given the focus on the men's basketball league, women were always present and were crucial to the story of these men. For example, it was Aldrin's aunt, who was already working in Chicago, who petitioned him to come to the United States in 2002. After arriving in Chicago, he moved to Champaign with his girlfriend in 2007, after which she became pregnant. He found work at an educational garment factory as a machine operator with some other Filipino immigrant men. Unfortunately, Aldrin and the other Filipino immigrant men are in many ways an exploitable labor force for the company.

In addition to the players who have settled in Urbana-Champaign within the past ten to twenty years, I also met immigrants who had just arrived, some of whom were undocumented and in the process of looking for jobs. Their status as laborers and undocumented immigrants meant that they held a precarious position in US society. For example, during one of our pickup basketball games, Victor, an immigrant from the Luzon area of the Philippines, shared that he was afraid his status would change to "TNT," short for the Tagalog phrase *tago ng tago*, a reference to being undocumented which translates to "always hiding."[47] Victor had a permanent resident card but needed help finding work because he had a tenuous grasp of the labor market and had a difficult time finding a stable job. Moreover, he was unfamiliar with how to become a citizen. At the time, I was volunteering for the University YMCA's New American Initiative to help legal permanent residents become US citizens. I connected him—as well as other community members who subsequently reached out to me after speaking with Victor—with one of my supervisors to help answer questions about the citizenship process.

The demands of performing manual labor had physical implications for some of the Filipino men. Late one afternoon in March 2015, I met up with a few of the men around the outdoor courts on the UIUC campus. I was shooting around waiting for other people to arrive, when I noticed that Elias, who typically plays, was sitting down. Surprised, I asked him if he was OK. He told me that his back was sore because of his work at the educational garment company. He complained that he had had to move about 1,200 pounds' worth of gowns and consequently needed to rest his back. Similarly, during my interview with Aldrin, we discussed his job as a machine operator for the educational garment company. "You see those big ass presses to iron the gowns? I'm the one that's doing that. That's why I've got burns all over here," he said, pointing to burn marks on his arms. Because of their manual labor in the factories, the men assume the risk of serious bodily harm—injuries that not only affect their ability to play basketball but also limit all sorts of other activities. When in the early twentieth century some working-class Filipino men performed dangerous labor working in agricultural fields and canneries, their work was understood as "tough masculinity." Though the men in Urbana-Champaign are also performing toughness in their jobs, their labor is not seen as commensurate in toughness. In this context, the basketball courts became a site at which to demonstrate a tough sporting masculinity, but one that was desirable to them.

Pickup Basketball and the Formations of the Basketball League

The pickup basketball court was often the men's first introduction to each other and to the broader Filipina/o/ American community. It became an important site for the formation of their community, a site of intimacy, a place for their desires and pleasures to take shape, and a site for male bonding. Aldrin shared that his brother-in-law who was already living in the Urbana-Champaign area was the one who invited him to play basketball on UIUC's outdoor basketball courts or at local parks. "I started working over there at [the educational garment company] and my brother-in-law was already here and playing ball. Playing ball is really like 'Hey, how you guys doing?'" Although the basketball courts were the venue to cultivate these relationships, their social intimacies seeped into other spaces of the men's everyday lives, including hanging out at each other's houses, apartments, and at nearby parks.

The players' social networks grew as they were introduced to other men through the basketball court. As Stanley Thangaraj noticed in his work on the South Asian American basketball cultures, I too saw how the players' social network on the court expands to other aspects of social life.[48] At the UIUC outdoor courts, "players would play and then later on, say 'Let's go drink, BBQ,' and stuff. All that fun. And then we started doing that." Aldrin's coworker Romeo, for example, first invited him to his house to hang out and then introduced Aldrin to other men. "Back then, we started chillin' at Romeo's house. We started chillin' and playing cards while we're drinking. I didn't know any other Filipinos other than my brother-in-law." Such gendered (masculine) intimate spaces of drinking alcohol and playing cards in a private setting enabled the Filipino men to share in the pleasures of homosocial bonding that seeped into and out of the basketball court.

Eventually, some of the men connected with the broader Filipina/o community on Facebook and realized that they had a large enough network to organize the basketball league I described earlier in the chapter. At the time, a weekly co-ed volleyball league was being offered for the community. To satisfy their desire for competition and share their love of basketball, Aldrin, Fredrico, and one of their other friends posted a Facebook message to gauge the community's interest in playing in the basketball league. "We started posting on Facebook and posted a sign-up sheet at [Soriano's]." They generated enough interest and, in 2014, their inaugural season started with four teams. The following year, the league grew to six teams.

Although a volleyball league that had been launched earlier was a cherished sport for both Filipino men and women in the community, the male basketball players established the league to express their own versions of masculinity, a masculinity that was in opposition to their feminized interpretations of volleyball. They viewed volleyball as too passive and lacking the toughness, aggression, and bodily movement that they perceived basketball to have. When I asked Fredrico if women were allowed to play in the basketball league too, he told me, "I wish they would play, but they don't." It could very well be the case that women have not expressed interest in basketball. It could also be the case that basketball, particularly within this community, is generally understood as a sport for men and for performances of masculinity. Tita Lovelynn reasoned that the two most popular sports were volleyball and basketball, but in ways that were delimited by gendered notions of play: "Volleyball [is popular] because the women can get involved. Basketball is mostly male, a male game. There are few Filipinas involved in basketball. There are mostly males who are playing basketball. I don't know if females expressed interest in basketball." An additional reason for this imbalance, potentially, is that there is a larger social landscape that the community in general, and the players in particular, traverses and mediates: The UIUC has a National Collegiate Athletic Association (NCAA) women's volleyball team but only a club men's volleyball team. And, in the broader United States, the number of NCAA men's volleyball teams are few compared to NCAA women's volleyball. Thus, volleyball is typically gendered feminine in the context of the United States and in the Midwest.

Making a Filipino American Place in Basketball

The intentional construction of a Filipino American place and the space it afforded for the performance of masculinity involved social networks as well as a mix of sensory experiences conveyed through food, language, and self-representational strategies. For example, it is worth noting that the sign-up sheet I came across at Soriano's was not posted at corporate-owned grocery stores such as Kroger, County Market, or Meijer. Nor was it posted at other Asian ethnic stores in the area. In addition to being a space of economic exchange, Soriano's served to locate "the basis of a common ethnicity" that then served to recruit Filipino Americans to play in the league.[49]

The Filipino community in Urbana-Champaign did not have enough resources to secure a public space. Tita Lovelynn told me that renting a public recreation space was too expensive for the group. Renting a gym for private use costs approximately $250 per day. However, one of the community members asked Samson, an elder Filipino in the community who was a coach for the local Christian school, which served students from preschool to high school, to reserve space at the school for free. Samson used his social capital to reserve the private Christian school gym to *further privatize* it for the Filipina/o American community every

Sunday. Although the organizers never explicitly excluded the larger African American and Latinx communities, during my tenure playing in the league, they were never present.

The gym looked like an average high school gym with purple banners outlining students' athletic feats in track and field and basketball. One could also see an American flag, an Illinois state flag, and a Christian flag (a white flag with a red cross in the left corner) hanging in the rafters. Although it was devoid of symbolic markers connoting Filipino Americanness, this did not mean that the community did not fill it with their own Filipino American sensibility and place-making practices. Filipino American basketball players, through a number of strategies, creatively appropriated the space to reflect their sense of selves and the larger community through, among other examples, food and language. The public basketball space remains critical for negotiating and expressing their masculine selves, with their athletic feats in the high school gym being one way to express their identity.

Foodways and Space

When the basketball league started, the organizers asked me to bring snacks. I brought artichoke dip, assuming that the food was for the players who needed a quick bite to eat before or after their games. However, I soon realized that the food was not only meant for the basketball players, but for the larger community, including spouses, partners, children, and other friends. When I entered the gym, I spotted Samson and asked him where to drop off my dish. He pointed me to the cafeteria. Upon reaching it, I could smell an amalgamation of foods that was initially difficult to parse. There were various Filipino dishes spread out on the cafeteria's counters, including chicken adobo, pancit, and pork lumpia, alongside foods like pizza, Kentucky Fried Chicken, biscuits, brownies, sodas, and Gatorade. The closer I got to the food, the more I could smell the different Filipino dishes, especially the chicken adobo's pungent soy sauce and vinegar aroma.

Some players, their wives, and children had already filled their plates with the foods. Scents—of food, in this case—are particularly important because they evoke a sense of familiarity in an unfamiliar landscape, triggering for some community members a way to imagine, if not exactly being "back home" in the Philippines, at least a feeling of proximity, as feminist scholar Sara Ahmed would put it, of making a new home.[50] In this case, Filipino food provided comfort amid the community's dislocation and isolation, a vehicle through which they carved out a sense of community and belonging to their new Midwest home. As a symbol of identity, community members in this instance brought food they had grown up eating in the Philippines or that they cooked at home,[51] with the food and its accompanying sights and smells crossing over time, place, and memory. At the same time, pizza and other non-Filipino foods reflected their adaptation to life in America and their expanded set of eating pleasures. Asian American food studies scholar and historian Mark Padoongpatt notes that "taste, smell, and touch are not merely physical acts but also cultural acts infused with meanings."[52] Moreover, this ensemble of food did not simply comprise distinctly American or Filipino dishes but a much more expansive and dynamic rendition of Filipino Americanness and Filipino American culture that is not discrete or anchored to a particular nation or locale.[53]

While food and its accompanying olfactory senses create for some a way to collapse time and space, linguistic strategies also transpired to reflect Filipino American masculine intimacy. As I prepared myself for the upcoming game, I waited on the sidelines with Claudio and Fredrico to warm up. In between breaks in the action—for example, when the teams called a timeout or when the first half expired—we hurriedly jogged to one of the basketball hoops to shoot practice shots. During one of our misses, the ball bounced off the side of the rim and dribbled away from us, landing near one of the other teams. Rather than chase after it, Fredrico, yelled: "Yo, *pogi kunin ang ball!*" ("Yo handsome, get the ball!"). The player nearest to it obliged and threw the ball back at us. Although not everyone spoke Taglish, which is a mixture of Tagalog and English (or a kind of code-switching between English and Tagalog), this was one example among many that illuminated how players interacted with each other. Taglish, as the ethnic studies scholar Rick Bonus reminds us, is a strategy for Filipina/o Americans to circumvent national languages and imperial pasts, as it indexes their linguistic flexibility.[54] It is a kind of code-switching; it involves crossing linguistic borders that enables the community to resist the colonial languages of Spain and the

United States. Rather than reify dominant regimes of Filipino Americanness that roots identity formation in local settings, the community in Urbana-Champaign used elements of mobility, rootedness, and boundary crossing.[55] At the same time, using words like "pogi" confers a sense of masculine intimacy that stays within the boundaries of heterosexuality. In other words, while one might interpret this terminology as evoking queer desire by gesturing toward another man's handsome features, "pogi" is actually a term of endearment. Moreover, Taglish creates a space of intimacy for Filipino immigrant men to carve out a sense of self in an athletic arena. But food and linguistic strategies are not the only ways in which Filipino American men mediate their identities. Another involves asserting a singular version of Filipino Americanness through their team jersey, despite their differences in region and dialect.

Pilipinas Jerseys

Although members of the Filipino community expressed their identities in part through food and language, players also intentionally invoked symbols of their ethnic identity through their team jerseys. A few weeks prior to the start of the league, I went to Fredrico's apartment to pick up my team jersey. When I arrived, Fredrico handed me my jersey and I noticed that they all depicted the same logo. Rather than creatively naming their own teams in line with the NBA style, this community of basketball players assigned teams according to color. I was drafted on the green team while other players were assigned red, blue, purple, or black. Importantly, however, all the jerseys had a uniformly ironed-on logo of the word *Pilipinas* (meaning Philippines) scrawled across the front with the accompanying Philippine national colors of blue, white, yellow, and red. Above the word *Pilipinas* was the Philippine sun's rays, in white and extending outward; underneath sat three stars and half of a basketball in yellow. The half basketball echoed the larger star on the Philippine flag. Appropriating elements of the Philippine flag and placing them on the jerseys, on the one hand, juxtaposed the spatialized version of the white Christian Americanness of the high school gym, and, on the other, contrasted with the figure of white male (on NBA logos) who has become the quintessential masculine symbol of the mythical American heartland of the Midwest.

The choice to use "Pilipinas" rather than "Philippines" or "Filipino American" was intentional. The term Pilipinas is used primarily by first-generation immigrants or those who live in the Philippines and is a rejection of the phonetic use of "Filipino." In the Philippine language, there is no phonetic "ph" or "f" sound; these were introduced by Spain's colonial education system. Interestingly, the sign-up sheet at Soriano's was written as "Filipino-American basketball league," not "Pilipino-American," suggesting that depending on context, there is flexibility in language use within the community. The basketball court was transformed into a "meaningful space and offer[ed] a means by which identities and counter identities can be articulated publicly, and not only vocally."[56] For brief moments, players in the league articulated a sameness as Filipino American even if they came from different regions of the Philippines and spoke different dialects, as these were subsumed under the broader practice of speaking Taglish.

Beyond the sounds of Taglish, shoes squeaking, and the ball bouncing off the hardwood floor with each dribble, one could also hear the sound of a voice booming from a microphone. The high school gym doubled as an auditorium, with an elevated stage and curtains flanking each side. On top of the stage sat a scorer's table with a few seated community members keeping track of time. Players who were not playing in the game voluntarily provided game statistics in the form of points, rebounds, assists, and steals, which were then posted on Facebook. Rather than conventional ways of audience interaction, in which spectators sit in the stands and cheer, the league games involved a community member emcee narrating the game. This immersive engagement of audience and player experience evokes African American leisure spaces' infused call-and-response.[57] This kind of narration commented on both mundane and spectacular plays, while at times providing comedic commentary at the expense of some of the players. There was a symbolic dialogue between players and spectators that forged communal interaction.

For example, during one free throw attempt, Elias, a young Filipino immigrant in his early twenties who works for an educational garment company, badly missed a free throw and hit the side of the backboard. Marlon, the game commentator, had already started laughing and then bellowed, "Shaquille O'Neal!" The players and spectators shared in a laugh. The joke aimed to make fun of Elias's free throw form by equating it and his badly missed free throw attempt to retired African American center Shaquille O'Neal. Although O'Neal was one of the best players to play in the NBA and was widely known for his dominance playing the center position and for wining four NBA championships, he was also known for having a poor shooting form and a poor free throw percentage. Incorporating audience reception and interaction was one way in which the community could participate in the spectacle, blurring the boundaries of athlete and spectator and producing a much more intimate (and playful) environment. Moreover, Marlon's "Shaquille O'Neil" quip further demonstrates the community's knowledge and consumption of broader popular cultural patterns and icons, which the emcee then verbally introduced into the basketball space. As anthropologist Thomas Carter notes, "Sport can also act as a means for reaffirming social ties and unity within a community."[58]

For Filipino immigrant and Filipino American men, their public performances of masculinity on the basketball court engendered communal praise of their bodily abilities. It was a strategy through which they could claim the public space by creating an intimate community to celebrate their basketball skills and the corresponding practices of masculinity. Yet, in addition to their engagement with popular culture practices, Filipino and Filipino American men also organized spaces outside of public view, revealing moments of intimacy and care that are not always attributed to working-class Filipino men in particular and working-class masculinities in general.

The Politics of Ethical Manhood and Care

During my research, I attended several weekly get-togethers, postgame get-togethers, and weekend barbeques that were largely organized by and for Filipino and Filipino American men. Early one Wednesday evening, I met up with some of the men at Angelo's rental house. Angelo was living in a predominantly African American neighborhood located in a working-class neighborhood in Champaign.[59] Some of the other men and I were sitting on the carpet and on folding chairs drinking alcohol and eating snacks, while Anthony, who was in his early twenties, was resting his head on the lap of Elias, a nineteen-year-old. We were conversing about a range of topics, including the competition between teams, the skill levels of the players, and which teams would make the playoffs. Some of the younger Filipino immigrant men spoke highly of Angelo and Renzo's basketball skills.

I was conversing with EJ, a recent immigrant in his twenties, whose mom had successfully petitioned him to join her a few years ago. He was relieved that he had left his food court job at the local mall and had instead been hired at Soriano's. Marlon, the owner, had hired him. "It's more chill," he told me, and he was happy that he didn't have to deal with the hustle and bustle of working at the food court. Amid their disloca-tion from the Philippines and in the context of working in industries that do not always value their labor, the practices of care work that Fili-pino immigrant men forge are central to how they sustain community. These gatherings, whether on basketball courts, in homes, or in apart-ments, are also places of connectivity and exchange, facilitating a kind of strategy that enables Filipinos to navigate the Urbana-Champaign social landscape. Indeed, EJ's relief at now working at Soriano's rather than at the mall food court reflects larger patterns of mutual support, a kind of metaphorical map of solidarity that exists within the community. Thus, for EJ, his relief at working in a space that feels affirming illustrates how Soriano's is a place of belonging. At Soriano's he can speak common languages (in this case, Cebuano, Tagalog, and English), and interact with fellow Filipina/os and other multiracial clientele. Moreover, resting their heads on each other's lap was a common practice among the men whenever I spent time with them in other apartments and houses. Such intimacies through touch reveal the tactile and close nature of some of their relationships. This kind of intimacy challenges the stoicism as-sociated with working-class masculinities and is illustrative of a kind of connectivity and tenderness and a different kind of manhood that does not always subscribe to hegemonic masculine practices.[60] Instead, such men practice what film scholar Celine Parreñas Shimizu describes as ethical manhood, a manhood that works in the service of care for the community by "forg[ing] manhoods that care for others beyond the self."[61] Additional moments of hanging out and spending time together occurred in other intimate and private settings. These were moments in which a seemingly "Filipino" tradition was made meaningful, intimate, corporeal, and connected to notions of self, community, masculinity, and nation. One such tradition is the boodle fight.

Negotiating the Contours of Militarized Masculinity in a Boodle Fight

"Hey, what are you doing on Friday?," asked Aldrin. I told him I didn't have plans and that I was free. He invited me to come over to his house for what he termed a "boodle fight" with some of the guys. I asked him what a boodle fight was, and he said that it was an aspect of life in the Philippine military, that there would be a bunch of food on the table, and that we would eat with our hands.[62] I was thrown off by the word "boodle fight"; I initially thought that Aldrin meant "noodle fight" and imagined that we would literally have a kind of food fight throwing noodles at each other.

After parking on the gravel side road, I walked up to Aldrin's house and immediately smelled a combination of smokey grilled meat and fried fish and heard the sounds of voices coming from the backyard. I walked into the yard with my bowl of grapes and pineapple and greeted the Filipino and Filipino American men. Some of them had brought their kids and were scattered around Aldrin's backyard near the grill and folding table. Aldrin was at his barbeque grilling chicken wings. There were only two women—Celiany and Alexis, Cambodian sisters—who are the wives of Aldrin and DJ. After greeting everyone, I walked over to the plastic folding table, which was covered in banana leaves piled with white rice; the arrangement of the food was neat and tidy. On top of the rice sat a variety of food including tuyo (fried salted fish), chicken wings, boiled eggs with tomatoes, pork adobo with green beans, a vinegar pepper sauce in which to dip meat, and leche flan for dessert. I also noticed apples at the far end of the table.

After Aldrin finished grilling the meat, we stood next to each other, shoulder to shoulder, around the table and commenced eating with our hands at a quick and deliberate pace. It was a sensuous feeling, as some of us first grabbed the rice, squeezing it with the tips of our fingers, pinkies, and thumbs before dropping it on a piece of meat or fish and eating it. As we ate, I heard sounds of lip smacking and slurping with each bite. I indulged in some of the tuyo with rice and picked out some of the adobo-flavored green beans. The feast literally lasted only about fifteen minutes because Aldrin told us that part of the ritual involved eating as quickly as possible. It was meant to reflect how soldiers ate during war time because of the uncertain nature of when they would eat again and whether they'd be called away from the food to fight. We started to slow down before one of the guys blurted out, "Dude, I'm so full!" We shared in a hearty postmeal chuckle. I noticed that the grapes, pineapples, and apples were untouched, and yet most of the meat had been eaten. I jokingly said that my fruit didn't even make it the main table, to which Celiany said, "That's what you get when you boys set it up!" After eating, we drank beers and hung out in the backyard for the rest of our visit, which lasted well into the evening.

For those that partake, the culinary ritual of the boodle fight forges solidarity and cultivates a sense of community. Although Aldrin shared that the boodle fight is a Philippine military tradition, its origins are a product of the US military's conquest of the Philippines. According to historians Daniel E. Bender and Adrian De Leon, the boodle fight was established at West Point military academy in New York. And although its precise origins are unclear, they surmise that it was introduced by the invading American army during the early years of the US colonial period.[63] Boodle fights mainly take place in restaurant establishments in the Philippines and in the diaspora. They are, as Bender and De Leon argue, a form of "militourism," a practice by which military institutions benefit from the tourist industry in places like the Philippines; the tourist industry then assists in obscuring the military's force and influence. However, in Aldrin's backyard we saw a different version of this practice enacted away from restaurants and thus away from public view. Instead, the boodle fight took place in a mundane and private everyday space. Thus, even in a discrete neighborhood backyard in the American heartland of Urbana-Champaign, Illinois, we find residues of US empire that become entangled as a result of the various crossings and crossing overs of various cultural practices (e.g., boodle fights and sports) and their inextricable link to US (military) colonial practices and masculinity-making.

Similarly, as a response to their perceived "feminized" labor as care workers, cooks, or on factory food lines, Filipino ballplayers used the stage of the basketball courts not only to challenge their emasculation but also to disrupt the pain they felt working in such positions. As a performative arena, the boodle fight also enabled them to embody a particular kind of militarized masculinity, revealing how this practice was also about how "the tensions and contradictions about space, nationhood, gender, sex, class, and citizenship unfold and play out through tastes, smells, digestion, and commensality."[64] By standing shoulder to shoulder and waiting for Aldrin to "order" us to commence eating, we carried out what we thought Philippine soldiers do; though with a quickened eating pace, we were nonetheless disciplined and orchestrated in our commensality. This disciplined unity of action and time was incredibly intimate and connective. I felt in place, a Filipino place. The sensory and sensual cues of the boodle fight enabled us to "return" to the Philippines by imagining ourselves as soldiers partaking in a military culinary ritual.[65] This practice of eating with our hands while standing close together produced a tactile and pleasurable form of masculine intimacy among us that fostered a collective a sense of "oneness" throughout our meal.[66]

While one might assume that the boodle fight is simply a fun way of sharing a meal between a group of friends, I read this scene in a much more complicated way. By recreating this culinary ritual in the diaspora, the other men and I forged a sense of diasporic community and (Philippine) national belonging through the sharing of food, albeit in ways that are enmeshed with a "militarized Philippine nationalism." In other words, the boodle fight cannot be separated from the "sedimented" and haunted nature of US colonial history on the archipelago.[67] Although the event was an act of brotherly solidarity and community, we aligned ourselves with a politics of belonging to the Philippine nation that reified dominant tropes of a heteropatriarchal masculine nationalism.[68] This alignment masks the very material ways that US colonialism seeped into our act of eating. Interestingly, given some of the men's relationship to labor and food—as factory workers for a food manufacturing company or as fast-food employees—the boodle fight reoriented this relationship. Instead, we found pleasure through the act of eating, enjoying each other's company, and reveling in the abundance of food before it landed in our stomachs. However, like the boodle fight, other spaces like pickup basketball or the Sunday night basketball league games were a "male preserve."[69] On the basketball court, women were a part of the spectacle in the bleachers to cheer on their partners or husbands, but they did not play. Although the sisters were present in the backyard boodle fight, they did not participate in the eating ritual. When I asked why wives or other girlfriends were not invited, a few of the men demurred without giving me a clear answer. A few seconds later, one of the men said emphatically and simply, "Just the boys." The outdoor space of the backyard became primarily a masculine domain, and grilling and eating food laid out on banana leaves became the ways through which we could participate in a version of Philippine-based, military masculinities.

The boodle fight reveals social relations that are imbricated through hierarchies as well as "inclusion and exclusion, boundaries and transactions across the boundaries."[70] As a form of male bonding and homosociality, Filipino and Filipino American men were welcomed into the space, but, with the exception of Celiany and Alexis, women were not. Moreover, the backyard space functioned as a meaningful social space to carry out gendered roles of manhood. Throughout the gathering, we did not venture into the kitchen, instead staying in the backyard. Aldrin's role as in charge of the grill reflects larger patterns of masculinity-making related to objects and space. Whereas the indoor space of the kitchen is gendered feminine, the backyard evokes masculine roles of commanding the grill, cooking meat, and drinking beer. It aligns in many ways with how white normative masculinity is imagined in backyards with grilling, playing football, and engaging in sport and banter. Objects like the grill and meat are coded as masculine objects; along with the physical space of the backyard, they became the domain for the social practice of masculinity-making. Space and masculinity worked in tandem to produce a "place in gender relations, the practices through which men and women engage that place in gender, and the effects of those practices in bodily experience, personality, and culture."[71]

The various homosocial sites of intimacy and bonding among the group of Filipino immigrant working-class men attest to the critical ways they create community. Their love and joy of playing basketball was something they shared, yet we also see how they negotiated their place in the Midwest, with playing basketball together, eating together, and creating rituals together acting as forms of community-making. One aspect of the crossover is the attempt to destabilize by making sudden moves to fool or trick the defender. As we have seen, Filipinos in the Midwest, and particularly their intimate and proximate relationship to empire through sports, migration, labor, masculinity, and now eating together, disrupt or destabilize the very conventions and stability of our ways of knowing the Midwest.

At the same time, the crossover in basketball (as elsewhere) is also a move of self-expression. It has undergone transformations, appropriations, and manipulations and has evolved through the brilliance of Black players like Dwayne Washington, Tim Hardaway, and Allen Iverson in ways that showcase their creative excellence.[72] The next chapter captures the crossover as a form of self-expression to explore the various ways in which second-generation Filipino American men—in a basketball league called Asian Ballers Syndicate—use the stage of basketball to crossover assimilative logics and assumed identity processes as only or always rooted in the local. Those ways of crossing over point to glocalizing processes that complicate masculinity and identity formations.

3

"They Were Made in the Philippines"

Filipino American Middle-Class Cool and Transnationalizing Identity Formations

I arrived an hour early to the basketball gym on a Sunday night and sat in the bleachers to watch a few other games before my 8 p.m. game. Jackson, a second-generation Filipino American, entered the east side of the gym with a large duffle bag. When he reached the bleachers, he sat next to a group of six other Filipino American men. Following the customary fist bumps, greetings, and salutations, Jackson reached into his bag and pulled out a set of customized basketball uniforms, saying "Here you go boys!" and handing them out to the group. I scanned the jerseys and was impressed by their aesthetic appeal. They looked cool, stylish, and flashy. But this wasn't the first time I had noticed the prevalence of impressive looking uniforms. Many of the young men wore similar uniforms, ones that resembled NBA or collegiate teams. After a few minutes, I approached Jackson and asked, "Where did you get those uniforms?" With a nod, he proudly told me that "they were made in the Philippines," and he shared that he was handing them out to his teammates, who had paid for them.

Throughout my playing tenure in the Asian Ballers Syndicate (AB Syndicate), I noticed a common theme among the Filipino American basketball players. Many of them wore what appeared to be professionally made, customized uniforms during our league games. I was curious about this trend and asked some of my teammates as well as other league players about the uniforms. All of them replied that their uniforms had been made in the Philippines. This was a popular practice not only in AB Syndicate, not only in other Asian American and Filipino American basketball leagues in which I played, and not even only specific in Southern California—I have seen these customized uniforms in the San Francisco Bay Area, California; in Urbana-Champaign, Illinois; and in

Las Vegas, Nevada. It is possible that they are commonplace throughout the United States wherever diasporic Filipina/os play, whether in
pickup basketball spaces, tournaments, or in leagues. This is not unusual
at this point in history. Production of clothes has largely shifted from the
United States to other parts of the world and specifically to Asia. In this
sense, AB Syndicate was only one among many important sites where
such jerseys were most visibly showcased, admired, and celebrated by
the basketball community.

   This chapter charts the transnational movement of material culture—
artifacts like basketball jerseys—the presentation of bodily selves
through tattoos, and the other strategies Filipino American male basketball players use to create a viable ethnic masculine identity in ways that
speak to their simultaneous engagement with the Philippines and the
United States. Such examples of this movement challenge assumptions
not only that popular culture stays within the borders of the United
States but also that there is an overreliance on Black aesthetics. Instead,
those examples show the mobility of goods and ideas at a glocal level,
goods and ideas that shape a distinct Filipino American masculinity. The
glocal level, or "glocalization," is a synergistic process of invention and
creation involving negotiations, connections, and adaptations between
local communities and their consumption patterns as well as their engagement with global phenomena and goods.[1] In this sense, we might
even say the process is one of many kinds of crossing over. Such movement prompts us to rethink linear processes of assimilation whereby
immigrants, and children of immigrants, "let go" of their ethnic ties and
"become" fully American by embracing dominant "American" cultural
regimes. Thus, it is a refusal to see oneself and one's identity as collapsing into dominant ideas of whiteness. In this way, Filipino identity
formations involve making, remaking, and sustaining long histories of
the Philippines and the United States that become spatialized on the
basketball court. Their movements on the basketball court, symbolic
formations, and self-styling are tied to transhistorical and transnational
processes.

Looking Professional and Looking Cool through Kinship, Intimacy, and Exchange

For Filipino American basketball players in the AB Syndicate, uniforms are more than just articles of clothing—they are global cultural products that take on localized meanings and social lives of their own. In the AB Syndicate, a number of the basketball players reported that they found out about ordering customized uniforms from the Philippines through friends, while some saw players from other teams wearing them, asked them about it, and followed suit. Paulo, a second-generation Filipino American who works as an independent consultant for a large technology firm, recalled, "The last three years I'd see other people doing it. We took the lead from other Filipino teams [in other Asian American basketball leagues]. They'd come around and have these full-on jerseys, almost professional looking. I thought, 'If we have a team, we might as well look professional.'"

The uniform designs are digitally created on a computer in the United States. They are then printed (or emailed) and given to the person facilitating the transaction. Depending on the stay of the *balikbayan* (a Filipina/o returning to the Philippines as a visitor or tourist), the turnaround time for the order varies from one to three weeks, and possibly longer. More often than not, obtaining these uniforms in the Philippines involves a teammate, family member, or family friend as a balikbayan traveling to the Philippines and visiting a local store, what Thomas (a second-generation Filipino American who works in the real estate industry) describes as a "swap meet style somewhere in Manila." In terms of labor, a few of the men told me that they saw mainly Filipinas working in the sewing shops, with only a handful of Filipino men. Although the making of these uniforms was a cogendered project, the performance of selves and privileged (national, masculine, and middle-class) visibility was reserved for, and performed by, Filipino American men.

One cannot simply order these uniforms on the web from the Philippines. The movement of these goods and the set of transactions that enables it relies on a system of kinship and intimacy that binds the exchange—one between family members, extended family, or friends. Without these intimate ties, the ability to retrieve these uniforms thousands of miles away is much more difficult and costly because it relies on someone physically traveling to the Philippines. To offset shipping costs, the relative or friend who travels to the Philippines carries the order with them upon their return to the United States. It is considerably less expensive to order from the Philippines than from within the United States.[2] For example, a set of customized uniforms (shorts and a jersey) in the United States costs upwards of one hundred US dollars, while one can order a similar set in the Philippines for approximately ten to twenty US dollars. Rodney recalled that when he went to the Philippines, a teammate asked about the possibility of ordering uniforms, and when he subsequently asked the rest of his teammates if they were interested, "the whole team jumped on the idea."

These uniforms signal an important process through which Filipino *and* American identities are expressed by appropriating elements of popular culture via the NBA and Philippine national symbols, which become mobile sources for crafting identities. By including the Philippine flag and sun on their uniforms, the team demonstrates an identity rooted in the transnational flow of goods, commodities, currency, and exchange.

Players reveled in the fact that their jerseys were unique and stood out in comparison to commercially made NBA jerseys. Their creative self-presentation and style were validated not only by each other, but also by people outside of their communities. Other than saving money on shipping costs and paying less for the labor, Thomas reflected, "there's also the wow factor that comes when you design it. We got compliments of course. 'They look professional. Where did you get it, how did you get it?'" For Thomas and others, wearing professional-looking jerseys that were distinctly made in the Philippines enables them to be publicly acknowledged as cool, generating a kind of social currency, a discursive formation that seeps into their everyday lives. Thomas and a few of the other men are seen as gatekeepers to the uniforms; they have special access to coolness and swagger that few men in the league have.

Rodney recalled that when he wore his customized jersey in a college class, one of his classmates asked him about it. He told me that the experiences "makes me feel good. Knowing that when someone asks where the jersey was made, I tell them, 'The Philippines.' They ask the price and I tell them the converted US dollars. They'll say, 'Next time you go, let me know.'" Here, everyday performances of Filipino American masculinity, through a Philippine-made jersey, allows him a measure of masculine belonging in the most mundane spaces, like college classrooms, where the Philippines is reimagined and geographically consolidated as cool. The sentiment of "looking professional" carries notions of a Filipino American middle-class masculine self informed by Filipina/o labor, transnational consumption patterns, and cosmopolitan sensibilities. Beyond the "wow" factor, players like Rodney and Thomas also garnered a certain level of power as they became the conduits to facilitate ordering the uniform ("Next time you go, let me know"). They have connections, can arrange business deals, and are associated with coolness.

As a form of symbolic capital, some of the Filipino American players wore their uniforms to embody a "basketball cool,"[3] and on the court, they performed a kind of swagger that took the form of a "cool pose," one largely associated with African Americans. The cool pose is a Black masculine act of creative self-expression that Black men employ in sports. As a response to institutional racism, through which Black men are denied various types of access to education, jobs, and institutional power, the cool pose offers them a strategy of cultural resistance through unique and stylish personal presentations manifested in spectacular athletic feats, hairstyle, speech acts, gait, and handshakes; in basketball, the cool pose is meant to elicit affirmations and an overall positive response from others.[4] The cool pose is also linked to cultural Blackness, which is then marketed via sporting conglomerates like Adidas, Nike, and Under Armour, which are some of the preeminent sporting apparel companies in the world. These corporations understand that Blackness sells and is consumed in the larger marketplace. Blackness and Black stylistics permeate basketball spaces like parks, gyms, and recreation leagues. Indeed, some of the Filipino American men in the AB Syndicate adapted the cool pose and elements of cultural Blackness by adorning their bodies with tattoos (which I will detail) and various items of basketball garb, including the latest Nike "signature" shoes promoted by players like the late Kobe Bryant and Derrick Rose and in-vogue shorts, headbands, and wristbands.[5] KC, a digital marketing manager and 1.5-generation Filipino American, acknowledged the popularity of this practice in the AB Syndicate: "I think everybody wants to be a professional athlete. The more you look, by the shoes you wear, by having the nice uniforms. You want [that] look. You want your team uniform to look nice. That look of being the part of a professional. [It's] signified by having these nice uniforms and the Kobe IX's or the D Roses. Just the glamour and the cool feeling. You're an athlete."

In light of the NBA's domination by African American, white, and increasingly international players from Europe, some Filipino American players in the AB Syndicate created a sense of basketball style that reflected their consumption patterns. These consumption patterns both aligned with and yet differed from the ways in which NBA players portrayed their style. Although fashion is always part of the game, Filipino Americans' style in the AB Syndicate is read as masculine and has middle-class connotations that become mapped onto their bodies. Thus, KC folds ideas of basketball cool into desires for the Filipino American sporting body that are facilitated by popular representations of Black aesthetics and are thus cool.[6] The "Kobe IX's" and "D Roses" that KC referenced are Nike- and Adidas-branded basketball shoes cobranded by well-known basketball players Kobe Bryant and Derrick Rose, respectively. At the time of this research, both players were some of the most popular basketball players in the NBA.[7] Such racial identifications are part of a Black popular aesthetic that is tied to dominant modes of representation, identifications that are integral to the production of legible, intelligible forms of basketball cool and, in this case, a Filipino American masculinity. At the same time, for some of the Filipino American men in the AB Syndicate, they appropriated elements of the cool pose and transformed it into a "Filipino cool," one that is informed by and negotiated through their expressions of a Filipino ethnic identity, transnational transactions, and local consumptions of cultural Blackness.

Being "Made" in the AB Syndicate

The AB Syndicate was a relatively new basketball league. It was formed in 2011, about a year and a half before I started playing on the team. Whereas other Asian American basketball players actively sought out competition in other Asian American basketball leagues, the AB Syndicate was established for different reasons. Erik, a second-generation Filipino American who works in the health care industry and is the founder of the AB Syndicate, started the league to match the skill level of players and to build a sense of community. With a look of both disappointment and resentment, Erik shared that many of the players who had played in the Asian Basketball Association (ABA) league became disenchanted with it. "They [ABA] had some semipros [semiprofessionals] playing and it's just too hard when every other team, every other week, you get blown out by thirty to forty points. And ringers [another term for semiprofessionals] would come during playoffs, play once, and not even play during the regular season, come in the playoffs and win the championship." Moreover, some of the other players complained that although there were other Asian American basketball leagues, those leagues restricted the number of players based on ethnicity. For example, one of the Filipino American players shared how he played in a Japanese American basketball league; this league allowed only one or two non-Japanese Americans per team. Although the AB Syndicate did not restrict players based on ethnicity, the majority of the league's players were in fact Filipino American, creating an informal league of Filipino American ballers. While there are a few Filipino American basketball leagues, the majority of them are located in the Los Angeles County area. Most of the players in the AB Syndicate live in proximity to the league, which was in and around Orange County.[8]

With feelings that other Asian American basketball leagues felt incredibly exclusionary and that competition was too steep, the AB Syndicate opened up space to expand renditions of Asian Americanness beyond the dominance of East Asian Americans. Additionally, in popular media, Black and white players are most visibly associated with the sport of basketball and the creativity with which they perform impressive athletic feats like dunking, dribbling, and shooting. Although Filipino American masculinities are informed by the Black-white racial logic, they cross over its binary logics. As basketball is largely coded through the Black-white racial paradigm, it is important to situate these leagues in the longer history of the anti-Asian economic, social, and political exclusion experienced by both Asians and Asian Americans. In the face of this discrimination, various Asian ethnic communities created their own leagues to carve out a sense of place and belonging in a hostile, white supremacist society.

In her book, *Outside the Paint*, historian Kathleen Yep documents how early twentieth-century working-class Chinese Americans in San Francisco created their own basketball leagues in the segregated Chinatown neighborhood. She tells how de facto white privilege affected opportunities for immigration, marriage, housing, and employment there.[9] Sociologists Christina Chin and Nicole Willms likewise report on the creation and sustenance of Japanese American basketball leagues and Japanese American female basketball excellence, established over a century ago. For Japanese Americans, basketball served as a form of civic engagement and a chance for their community to perform their Americanness, especially in the face of Japanese American incarceration and internment during World War II. These performances of Americanness resisted stereotypes of them as "un-American" and "forever foreigners." As a result, we see a particular institutionalization of the sport that created a set of Asian American heroes and became a site of boundary making and claims to citizenship.[10] According to some of the players, in the AB Syndicate, the ABA did not offer the kind of intimacy and camaraderie that the AB Syndicate provides. Many of the league's basketball players in the AB Syndicate already knew each other through their social networks and through playing in college and in other Asian American and Filipino leagues throughout Southern California. Some of the players told Erik that they were dissatisfied with ABA and asked him if might be interested in establishing a league. To gauge interest, he asked other players if they would join his league. Eventually, there was enough interest and he subsequently formed the AB Syndicate.

The players in the ABA did not belong to Erik's version of a basketball community. This was another reason why he founded the AB Syndicate. For example, KC chose to play in the AB Syndicate for recreational purposes and to stay in shape. However, he also sought coethnic bonding and intimacy with his network of friends. "AB Syndicate is where my friends play, and I would rather play with my friends than with people I don't know." He emphasized that his league was much more than simply "showing up and playing and going home with a trophy."

That a number of Asian American basketball leagues span the Southern California landscape, among them Asian Hoops, Asian Ballers Network, Asian Basketball Association, and PacRim Sports, indicates that deep sporting joy and pleasure permeates the Asian American basketball community in the region. While these all cater to Asian American basketball players, their names do not carry the same connotation of toughness and power that the name the Asian Ballers Syndicate suggests. To set the league apart from other Asian American basketball leagues, the AB Syndicate is defined in relation to other Asian American basketball leagues whose names do not inscribe the same masculine markers. "Asian" connotes a unifying pan-Asian identity for Asian and Asian American men to belong to a basketball community, and "ballers" is a common vernacular term for basketball players and contains elements of basketball cool prevalent in African American and South Asian American basketball leagues and communities.[11]

But there is more. Erik shared that he is "a fan of mafia movies and *syndicate* sounds like a mafia. "There's so many Asian leagues out there that most [of them] took names already. So syndicate, nobody really has syndicate." Erik's consumption of popular culture informed how he crafted the league's name, taking inspiration from acclaimed mafia films like *The Godfather* trilogy and *Goodfellas*. These films prominently feature Italian American patriarchs as husbands and fathers who enact their hypermasculinity by intimidating other mobs, asserting their toughness, and perpetrating (or ordering others to perpetrate) violent acts.[12] Because Erik is the founder and organizer of the AB Syndicate, he also carried out the duties as the head of the league. He was responsible for coordinating league matters, including finding a basketball space, collecting registration fees, contacting referees, writing postgame analysis, and having final say on league issues. He is, by all accounts, the head of the basketball syndicate—the don. Yet to call it the AB *Syndicate* is not common basketball parlance. As the "Godfather" of the league, Erik embodies, knowingly or not, the leader, a self-representation based on the patriarch of mafia-based films who signifies control, power, and respect.[13] *Syndicate* also evokes in-group membership, or an exclusivity to an organization in which the members share a common interest. The men in this league became a part of the basketball syndicate through their social networks and shared interests, desires, and pleasures playing basketball that emerged out of processes of inclusion and exclusion. Although the name of the league is Asian Ballers Syndicate, which connotes a pan-ethnic Asian American basketball league, in my estimation, as well as in those of the participants I interviewed, the majority of the players were Filipino American. While not intentionally creating exclusive borders to other Asian Americans, the league was primarily a Filipino American masculine space. For many of the Filipino American men in this league, playing in other Filipino and Asian American leagues and tournaments informally created an exclusive social network that was forged over time.

The league is, in other words, "syndicated" for a predominantly Filipino American basketball community. Bodily performance and the presentation of self through uniforms, tattoos, and self-referencing team names are ways to communicate that this is a Filipino American place. In addition, those who wear uniforms made in the Philippines further assert their "difference" and distinguish themselves as more cool and chic than other men in the AB Syndicate and in other Asian American basketball leagues.[14]

Erik's consumption of mob movies also evokes popular culture references to mafia parlance. In these films, neophytes become "made men" only by being sponsored by other made mafia men in order to be recognized as part of the crime syndicate. Similarly, Filipino Americans reinterpret, adapt, and reassemble mafia-inflected notions of what it means to be "made." They become "made" men through Erik and other men who have privileged information *and* access to the league and the uniforms. The league is ultimately consolidated through this network. Finally, their bodies become legible as they are acknowledged as "made" men from the Philippines, a dynamic that concurrently works with Filipino American sporting masculinity. These distinguishing features further indexed their middle-class networks and resources.

Middle-Class Resources and Digitizing Intimacy

Whereas the majority of the Midwestern men discussed in chapter 2, who were recruited for basketball play out of Soriano's grocery store, were recent, working-class immigrants, the men in this chapter were the children of immigrant parents who arrived in the post-1965 era. These immigrant parents came as nurses, doctors, and engineers and their children (the players in the AB Syndicate) subsequently grew up with middle-class affluence and either graduated from college or were about to graduate. They worked in various white-collar industries including real estate, financial services, and the health care industry. They had the class resources to order uniforms, pay the registration for the league, and accentuate their basketball style by consuming basketball accessories.

Because their uniforms were made in the Philippines, the labor and fabric were considered "cheaper." I was curious about how Filipino American men thought about the unequal global process of consuming products and labor in the Global South. Thomas paused for a few seconds when I asked him whether or not he thought about the people making the uniforms and the relatively "cheaper" option to purchase the fabric in the Philippines. "I think everybody has thought about [sweat shops] one way or another when you buy jerseys in the Philippines. Whoever is making it, I'm sure we thought the labor is cheaper over there. That's probably why they can sell it for cheaper because the cost of living is different." Thomas struggled to find his words and stuttered a few times before replying, "With my background being Filipino, it's almost like you're spending your money where your parents were raised. It feels good that you're kind of spending your money in the homeland." Thomas's reaction to my question demonstrates what literary scholar Denise Cruz calls "affective friction," or "emotional perplexities"—uneasy feelings that are connected to asymmetrical systems of power as a result of global interactions, exchanges, and engagements.[15] Interestingly, Thomas attempts to reconcile these affective frictions by inserting his middle-class privilege and reorienting it through a kind of diasporic philanthropy grounded in ideas of "doing good" for the people. It is akin to what the American studies scholar Joyce Mariano identifies as a diasporic form of "giving back" to the country.[16] In Thomas's view, spending his money in his ancestral homeland will only help the country.

As we saw earlier, the Filipino American basketball league in Urbana-Champaign was formed as a result of the community's grassroots efforts. In this league and in other social spaces, their intimacy involved much more face-to-face interaction that increased their socialization. This was in part because of the community's limited resources and limited leisure time. Players did not have the financial means or technology to sustain a level of institutional infrastructure. Conversely, and in addition to the uniforms, the professionalization of the AB Syndicate was facilitated because of the kind of infrastructure that Erik provided. The league was not accessible to everybody, especially those who did not have the leisure time and capital to play, drive to the venue, purchase uniforms, and register for the league. Even privatizing a public space once a week as a business venture required resources. In Erik's case, he applied for and received a business license, paid for insurance, and hired referees. Then, he found gyms that were willing and able to rent a court to him. Erik's leisure time, technology, and financial resources enabled him to produce a level of digital intimacy for a greater viewing audience beyond the court. This was one of the features that set the AB Syndicate apart from the other leagues in which the men played. Erik personalized the experience by providing pregame and postgame commentary, publishing "news" updates on the AB Syndicate Facebook page, and tracking game statistics. With a look of pride, he told me, "On my website, I write about the games and people really like that. They like to see their name on the Internet. I try to keep the stats up to date as fast as possible." After each Sunday night game, one could log in to Facebook and read Erik's postgame analysis, learn how the team had fared, and track individuals' game statistics. Players reveled in seeing their names featured in postgame summaries and game statistics and in making the "top 10" list of players to watch. During one of my pregame warm-ups, I overheard players from the other team talking about the possibility of being featured on Erik's postgame summary. For KC, this was one of the aspects of the AB Syndicate that he appreciated. "It kinda makes you feel involved in that aspect because it's your name, it's your number. I think it's cool. Typically, when I'm on the report is when I do well. So if I played in a really good game and I contributed x amount of rebounds or x amount of points, that's the stuff that gets displayed in the league reports." For KC, seeing his name on the page solidified his standing in the basketball hierarchy and further set him apart from his peers. Game statistics and summaries created a sense of community and recognized them as skilled basketball players. They celebrated each other's feats by looking up their own or their peers' statistics regarding points, rebounds, assists, and steals.[17]

Statistics provide information about a player's contribution to the game and show proof of one's athletic skill and basketball ability while also generating lively discussions that affect players' homosocial bonding. They reveled in seeing themselves as skillful basketball players and found validation within their basketball community. The AB Syndicate was deemed a safe space for many of these young men, a place in which to feel affirmed. By posting game statistics and summaries as the NBA does, Erik celebrated Filipino and Asian American masculinity by elevating their basketball skills. When players like KC reference prolific scoring, grabbing many rebounds, or making skillful assists, they allude to their peers who perform at an even higher level than the rest of the Asian American ballers. This positions them higher up in the masculine hierarchy of basketball performance.

These digital spaces enabled the players to celebrate each other's athletic prowess, to cultivate male bonding and intimacy, and to affirm each other's presence as athletes. Rodney particularly cherished the leisure time spent playing in the league. When I asked him why he had joined, he shared, "It's [the league] great. It's something to do on the weekends, something to look forward to. After a long week of work, [there is] something to look forward to and cut loose."

The boundaries of community-making and intimacy stretched beyond the basketball court. Erik is not the only one who was actively involved in producing content for the league. Some of the members took to Facebook to post updates and "news" items to solidify their racial and coethnic bonds even more. One of the players, acting as a league "reporter," posted about another player from the team named "The Outsiders": "ESPN BREAKING NEWS: Newly acquired Outsider [Richard Le], goes down in the 3rd qtr. Outsider GM [Erik] was unavailable for comment. Richard was taken by teammates to a nearby UCI Medical." The post was accompanied with an image of Richard on the floor holding his right ankle, while two of his teammates looked on. Some of the league players were tagged in the post while others commented and asked about Richard's ankle and whether he would be able to play in the coming weeks.

The post and image are appropriations of how Disney-owned ESPN. com covers sporting news. The Entertainment and Sports Programming Network (ESPN) is a mainstream public sporting conglomerate that has millions of consumers all over the world. By imitating ESPN's "Breaking News" section, the post showcases not only how these young men are active consumers of American popular culture but also how they maintain an intimate community that incorporates and exists *outside of the basketball space*. The virtual arena, such as Facebook, digitally archives players' experiences, further enabling them to document their sporting history, stay connected, and sustain their love of basketball without actually playing. They can be central to, or at least part of, these basketball stories rather than peripheral to them.

The Outsiders: Negotiating the Outsiderness and Insiderness of Race, Masculinity, and Sexuality

Analyzing how the teams formed illuminates Filipino Americans' creative self-representation. Team names suggest notions of self and consumption of popular culture, and they respond to the Black-white racial binary that Filipino Americans navigate in the sport of basketball. At the same time, team names reveal a paradoxical negotiation of masculinity and sexuality that reinforces patriarchal practices. The style of the uniforms varies from team to team and often reflects mainstream templates of NBA or collegiate jerseys. Most, if not all, include some Philippine national symbol, such as the Philippine flag or sun stitched onto various parts of the uniform. For example, one team named "The Outsiders" used the template and style of the NBA's Atlanta Hawks for their uniforms, and another team used the former Seattle Supersonics template. "The Outsiders" as a team name is rooted and rerouted through complex formations that imply transnational movement, American popular consumption, and basketball playing style.[18] When I asked Erik why his team was named "The Outsiders," he boasted, "Outsiders came from the fact that we don't like to shoot inside. We like to shoot outside and shoot a lot of threes, so we were called 'The Outsiders'—and it's [also the title of] one of our favorite movies." One finds in Erik's comment a bit of joy and pleasure at the prowess of making three-point shots. The Outsiders's style of play, as Erik noted, references the players' specific skill set as shooters who prefer not to shoot layups or two-point shots for easier scores. The 1983 film *The Outsiders* is a coming-of-age film featuring a group of white working-class male youth. It centers working-class masculinity through toughness and violence, acts of intimacy, and homosociality as well as how these young men are treated as outsiders to white, middle-class, mainstream society.

Although the film centers on white aesthetic depictions and cross-racial dynamics, Erik and his teammates did not and of course could not claim whiteness and white masculinity. In fact, Filipino Americans' racialized, sexualized, and gendered (masculine) history has positioned them outside the realm of white, normative masculinity, and therefore, outside the politics of racial belonging.[19] Instead, Erik and his teammates related to the film's premise of outsiderness and feelings of racial belonging, signaling not only their love of the film and consumption of popular culture but also a shared feeling of outsiderness to the Black-white racial paradigm of basketball and performances of masculinity.

Although I did not witness any of the players in the AB Syndicate dunk, this does not mean that the league's players saw their own or their peers' bodies as unmasculine. Shooting and making three-point shots requires practice through repetitive shot-making. It is not easy to consistently make such shots. The rise of NBA three-point shooting specialists like Stephen Curry and Damian Lillard expands versions of basketball masculinity beyond the act of dunking. Indeed, Curry and Lillard have transformed the three-point shot into a performance of basketball cool, not only because of the high degree of difficulty but also because it evokes a sense of supreme confidence, bravado, and swagger. This playing style of these two men also challenges assumptions that African Americans lack the work ethic to develop their skills and that they instead rely on their alleged "natural" ability to jump and simply dunk; that "Black men can't shoot." As the sociologist Scott Brooks reminds us, "Black athletes do work at becoming elite players. They learn and work hard to develop the skills necessary for playing collegiate and professional basketball."[20]

The three-point shot has become part of the repertoire of basketball masculinity.[21] For The Outsiders, shooting and making threes was one way to claim an insiderness to the sport and their place as legitimate basketball players who can also perform a sporting masculinity that departs from the physical act of dunking. Dunking is considered a highly masculine act because it is not only an incredible athletic feat, it is also an act of "dominance over someone."[22] During one late afternoon game, The Outsiders showcased their deft three-point shooting in action. As I observed the game, I noticed a sequence of plays that clearly encapsulated their team name and, thus, their shooting skills. During one sequence, The Outsiders moved the ball inside and outside the key (a rectangular area that extends from the free throw line to the baseline) and around the three-point line to force their opponents to scramble. Their opponents struggled to keep up with their precise and timely passing. As a result, Erik and his teammates were, at times, left wide-open for three-point shots, earning praise from the audience and each other. Although Erik did not have the speed and jumping ability of some of his peers, he was one of the main contributors who shot and made three-pointers. However, Erik and The Outsiders were not the only ones who showcased an impressive set of shooting skills.

Francis, an undergraduate student and 1.5-generation Filipino American, was another such player. He was not particularly known for his speed or ball handling ability, and he did not necessarily rank high on other game statistics like steals, rebounds, or assists. However, he was an excellent three-point shooter and could prolifically score points in a matter of minutes. This was something that some of the young men noticed, including KC, who told me

> These are the guys [referencing players like Francis] you have to contain [watch out for]. These are the guys that have to be stopped. I'm in amazement. On a running clock, to be able to put up *fifty points* [his emphasis]. That's freaking ridiculous [laughs]. Guys who can shoot score fifty a game. Guys who can typically grab seventeen rebounds a game. Those guys can be compared to some of the NBA greats. We say [referring to people like Thomas], "That's the Kobe [Bryant] of the league, that's the LeBron [James] of the league. [He's] the man, the shooter of the league."

Here, KC appraises Francis's masculinity very highly because of the difficulty of making such three-point shots—and of making so many of them per game. Francis has particular masculine value because he deftly shoots three-point shots without relying on other basketball skills to shape the outcome of the game. Writing about South Asian American basketball circuits in Chicago and Atlanta, the anthropologist Stanley Thangaraj notes, "These ostentatious acts are performances of difficult skills validated through flawless execution and legitimated by the other people in this arena."[23]

Impressively shooting and making three-point shots was not the only way some of the young men displayed their basketball skill. Game statistics and their accompanying hierarchical placements work concurrently with bodily performance. Players manipulated their bodies in ways that required basketball skill as well as the ability to perform innovative acts, creativity, and spontaneity. During one of my league games in the AB Syndicate, I was guarding Ricky, a second-generation Filipino American who was a few strides in front of me. His teammate Payton, also a second-generation Filipino American and one of the best players in the league, dribbled down the court during a fast break possession. I ran back to catch up to Ricky; when I finally caught up to him, I did not think he was a threat to score because he did not have possession of the ball. But in quick succession, Ricky looked back, raised his arm to signal to Payton that he was open, then Payton passed the ball through my legs and into Ricky's hands, and Ricky took a couple of strides toward the basket to finish with an easy layup. I heard a handful of spectators react with "Oooh!" after Ricky scored. Payton, sporting a grin, nonchalantly jogged to the other side of the court and, with a kind of bravado, nodded his head to acknowledge the spectators' reactions. Witnessing Payton's impressive feat was not new to me, nor was it surprising to other players in the league. In fact, I observed Payton's basketball skill on display a number of times over the course of my playing tenure in the league. Far from ordinary, his feat required skill, anticipation, improvisation, and creativity. After the game, Payton gathered his belongings, including a large Nike duffel bag, and removed his Nike shoes. With a self-assured gait, he then walked toward other Filipino American men who were his teammates and opponents as they greeted each other with half handshakes and chest bumps.

The US imagination does not tend to associate Filipina/os with basketball—other than by the scant media coverage of Manny Pacquiao and his ownership of one of the teams in the Philippine Basketball Association (PBA). Despite the PBA being the second oldest professional basketball league in the world, Filipina/o Americans do not often come to mind when thinking about basketball cultures, skills, and excellence. However, the play sequence suggests pleasures and counterhistories. Despite the increasing numbers of Filipino American collegiate and professional basketball players, the various Filipino American basketball leagues and tournaments throughout the United States, and the long history of US colonialism's role in institutionalizing sports in the Philippines,[24] we know very little about what these spaces mean for Filipino American men in the diaspora.[25]

Payton's impressive basketball feat demonstrated his temporary dominance, an act of masculinity bound up with athletic ability and swagger not commonly associated with Asian American men. Although swagger has its origins in the embodiment of white masculinity, as the sociologist Oliver Wang notes, it is much more clearly associated with working-class African American men and found in cultural forms like hip-hop and basketball.[26] It is part of a performance of "racial posturing" that other men of color have since borrowed and appropriated.[27] Filipino Americans' alignment with Blackness works against the assimilative promise of white normative masculinity and instead becomes a pathway for them to appropriate its elements through stereotypical performances of Black hyper- and heterosexuality. This strategy has been one way to free themselves of enduring Oriental stereotypes mapped onto Asian American men, stereotypes which presuppose a racially castrated masculinity.[28] Although Black men did not make up the majority of the AB Syndicate's players, cultural Blackness was still prominently featured through basketball style and desired by some of the Filipino American men. It permeated the league through racialized and sexualized registers refracted through a Filipino American masculinity. I recall one such incident when I was warming up with my teammate Rodney, a 1.5-generation Filipino American college student. He was wearing a customized black basketball jersey with the head of a snake as the mascot. Above the snake was the team name "Mambas."

When Filipino Americans enter the AB Syndicate basketball space, they perform manifestations of self with particular inflections of gender, race, and sex. Their own consumption patterns, ethnic identity, gendered performance, and heterosexual desires and pleasures inform these contours. In Rodney's case, he uses artifacts of popular culture to craft a presentation of self that responds to, and resists, mainstream stereotypes of effeminate Asian American men.[29] Rodney shared that the Mambas jersey was an ode to the late Kobe Bryant, an African American basketball player who played twenty years for the Los Angeles Lakers and was nicknamed "the Black Mamba." The black mamba is a venomous snake found in parts of Africa, and Bryant used this animalistic nickname as part of his basketball performance and corporate image brand, which is "meant to sell blackness" locally and in the global marketplace.[30] Moreover, Bryant was known to perform what he called a "mamba mentality," which connotes aggression, stoicism, and toughness. Through his persona, he created a hypermasculine performance on the court, where he dominated opponents en route to winning five NBA championships. In this light, when Rodney shared that "everyone on the team loved Kobe," this was no surprise given these Filipina/o Americans' proximity to Los Angeles and the regional fandom that enables fans to belong to an imagined community and to recognize the Black Mamba snake symbol and name.[31] Many of my interlocutors in the basketball league were Los Angeles Lakers fans and admitted that Kobe Bryant was their favorite player.

For some Filipino Americans like Rodney, embracing the team name "*Mambas*" was not only an ode to Bryant and Black masculinity but also an embrace of the phallic signifier of heterosexual masculinity. Linking Bryant's self-referencing Black Mamba persona to the Black phallus enables Filipino Americans to appropriate Black stylistics and hyperheterosexual masculinity that then creates distance from dominant representations of Asian American lack of masculinity.[32] However, this embrace also worked sociohistorically when, in the early twentieth century, perceived fears of working-class Filipino men as sexual predators over white women drove anxieties about Filipino masculinity and sexual improprieties.[33]

Beyond the "Mambas" moniker, other team names also alluded to ideas of sexual dominance and conquest. One team was called "Bang Bus." I was curious about this, so I asked Erik what it meant to the team. I sensed his hesitation about discussing the name and, after a short pause, admitted that Bang Bus is a "pretty bad name." After sensing his discomfort and reaction to my question, I immediately understood what he meant. Bang Bus has gendered and sexualized implications, referring to a symbolic and imagined space to perform an act of heterosexual conquest of forcefully penetrating women. Through the name "Bang Bus," the team reaffirms patriarchal practices of symbolically exercising power and control over women's bodies.[34]

For Filipino American ballers, however, performing swagger in the AB Syndicate is not confined to metaphors of sexual prowess and processes of extraction and appropriation of Black cultural forms.[35] Although the performance of basketball can contain forms of cultural Blackness and Black aesthetics,[36] Filipino Americans consume, reappropriate, and reassemble their meanings in ways that exceed appropriation. Payton and other Filipino American men's swagger in the AB Syndicate, for example, while tied to working-class Blackness, is also situated within a movement of goods and ideas ushered in from the Philippines. Thus, Filipino American swagger in the AB Syndicate is fully realized only when placed in transnational linkages to the Philippines materially and symbolically. In this way, consuming or alluding to Black style does not operate in a vacuum. What we witness are movements and trickery (e.g., the crossover) that take on transnational forms of consumption and production. Filipino American basketball players also adopt bodily tactics which set them apart from other Asian American men, and it is to these that we now turn.

Inking Pride, Ethnicity, and Nation

Being "made in the Philippines" does not refer only to uniforms that were literally created in the Philippines. In saying that the jerseys were made in the Philippines, Filipino Americans are also asserting that in order to be legible as American *men*, they must claim their ethnic bodies as made in the Philippines, even if some of them were not born there. *Made* thus takes on polyvalent meanings that travel across time, space, generations, and (trans)national borders. In addition to uniforms, some of the Filipino American men tattooed their brown bodies with ethnonationalist symbols to further differentiate their bodies and themselves. Although one might assume that skin operates as a blank canvas, skin is also a visual marker of difference. Filipino American bodies are still social (raced) bodies onto which social meanings are imposed.[37]

Tattoos are clear visual markers of difference that allow the players to deliberately brand their bodies with their ethnic background without entirely appropriating Black, working-class aesthetics.[38] Thus, the creation of ethnic bodies also occurs at the nexus of ethnicity, sporting masculinity, and class. Although uniforms have an ephemeral quality to them, "made" bodies, through tattooing, preserve a kind of permanency, a statement. Unless the wearer chooses to have them removed, their markings remain on their bodies for the rest of their lives. In the AB

Syndicate as well as in other multiracial basketball teams, some of the Filipino American ballers prominently showcased their tattooed arms, shoulders, and calves; they literally showed off their ethnicity every time they played, with the overt purpose of identifying their bodies as ethnic and desirable. These tattooing practices signal transnational connections and transnational intimacies by weaving in Philippine national symbols. These tattooing practices signal transnational connections and transnational intimacies by weaving in Philippine national symbols, showcasing creativity, production, and consumption that involve the multiple crossing of imagined borders historically and contemporaneously.[39]

Tattooing is a form of bodywork, a way for Filipino Americans to mark their identities permanently as *ethnic men* in a public situation like the basketball league. Tattooing creates a multivalent process of self-representation of their masculine identities through transnational contours. Basketball uniforms enable players to accentuate their bodies, physiques, and muscularity, especially in showcasing their arms and legs. These tattoos are typically placed on shoulders, biceps, forearms, and calves—in short, on the most visible parts of the uniformed body, to ensure the overt display of their Filipinoness. Thomas, for example has an outline of the Philippine sun and the three stars inked on his right shoulder, as well as his children's astrological signs. Rather than tattooing the entire flag with its blue, yellow, and white colors, he chose to have inked on him only the sun and the three stars. The sun represents liberty while its eight rays extending outward note the eight provinces who resisted Spanish colonial rule. The three stars represent the three major islands (Luzon, Visayas, and Mindanao) of the Philippines.[40] By appropriating elements of the Philippine flag on his Filipino American body, he embodies a masculinized version of an ethnic-nationalist identity he can express and claim on the basketball court. His tattoos also create a sense of community through communicative competence; only those who know the flag recognize and affirm the symbols' meanings.

When I asked Thomas why he chose to ink his tattoo on his shoulder (rather than somewhere more visible), he shared that he was aware that many people still regard tattooed bodies to cross a line of social acceptability: "You don't do *that* [his emphasis] to your body." In the social consciousness, tattooed bodies are linked to deviance, criminality, and a working-class masculinity.[41] Although these ideas are not necessarily rooted in reality, Thomas was conscious of people's perceptions when they "read" him. This dynamic combined with his racial presentation influenced how he wanted to be and was perceived. Thomas is noticeably dark-skinned, stands close to five feet, nine inches tall, and has a shaved head. These features in white public spaces can hypermark his body as deviant while unmarking white middle-class respectability. However, outside of his leisure time, Thomas, who works in the real estate industry, can cover his body with middle-class attire. He wears a collared button-down shirt, a tie, and slacks to work, which mark his middle-class identity and his privilege navigating middle-class spaces. "People looked at tattoos a different way. I wanted to make sure I was conscious about all of that like if I was going to work." On the basketball court, however, he strategically chose ways to showcase the tattoos, wearing basketball jerseys cut in such a way as to leave the shoulders and arms visible. Thomas's observations are important in helping us to understand how he perceived his brown body in basketball spaces as well as in everyday (work) spaces, reflecting concerns about the exhibition of working-class and middle-class aesthetics.

On the basketball court, displaying tattoos is commonplace among the Asian American and Filipino American ballers. For Thomas, on the basketball court, his body is made legible through a cool, working-class aesthetic while he simultaneously negotiates his middle-class professional life off the court. I observed a number of players who had tattoos on their arms and legs. Some showed different designs, but quite a number of them had tattoos with Philippine-based national symbols. Like Thomas, many inked the Philippine flag or the cartographic outlines of the Philippine islands on their shoulders as one way to showcase their ethnicity and pride. Thomas asserted, "I know one thing. You choose a location on your body. You want people to see that. You want people to know that you're proud to be a Filipino American." Tattoos carry positive value associated with toughness and basketball cool. This practice is not unique to Filipino Americans. It is also prevalent within and outside broader Asian and Asian American communities.[42]

On the basketball courts, tattoos do not carry the same kind of social stigmas that they tend to carry in everyday life. Rather, they are one way for these young men to display their bodies publicly, feel proud of their ethnic identity, and perform their ethnic-masculinity overtly and *in motion*. During one game, one of the players was dribbling toward the baseline of the basketball hoop to make a layup. Sensing that his defender was about to challenge him, he quickly jumped from the baseline, "scooped" the ball underneath the basket, and laid it in. It was a spectacular shot inflected with flair and creativity. One of his teammates put his arm around him as if to acknowledge his play. Afterward, as he was running down the court, he pointed to his shoulder, which was tattooed with an outline of the Philippine sun.

Tattoos signifying contemporary iterations of the Philippines and its national symbols are not the only tattoos Filipino Americans sport. Other Filipino American players ink Baybayin[43] tattoos with their last names. Baybayin is a precolonial writing script that existed prior to Spanish colonialism in the Philippines. Indigenous people of the Philippines used this script to communicate on palm leaves or bamboo shoots. It was never meant to be tattooed on one's body.[44] However, tattooing Baybayin is a phenomenon practiced by some 1.5- and second-generation Filipino Americans. There is a sense among some Filipino Americans that by inking a precolonial and pre-Western writing script, they can embody a "pure" Indigenous Filipino identity that rewrites and therefore subverts Spanish and US colonial histories.[45] Understood like this, Baybayin tattoos are an "indigenous narrative,"[46] one adopted primarily by college-educated Filipina/o Americans with middle-class aesthetics. In the basketball league, the young men have a precolonial writing script inked onto their bodies to accentuate a "politics of difference" within Asian America.[47]

Moreover, this ethnic-specific cultural practice not only marks *difference* within the pan-ethnic Asian American basketball community, it also indexes a kind of opposition to cultural and social forces that have historically and contemporaneously marked Filipino male bodies as being outside of normative masculinity.[48] While the tattoos are *one* way to assert their Filipino American masculinity, they are also part of a larger ethnic-nationalist repertoire that connects to how these young men claim a sense of community. With conviction in his voice, Thomas told me that "[getting tattoos] has to do with why we wanted matching uniforms. It was an unconscious sense of belonging to something." The uniforms and tattoos further served to differentiate Filipino American ballers from other Asian American ballers in ways that expanded the rubric of "Asian America" while also troubling the presence and dominance of East Asian Americans as the quintessential faces of Asian America.

"Jeremy Lin Is Just another Asian": Asserting Difference in the AB Syndicate

While I was doing my research, Jeremy Lin was a Taiwanese American point guard for the New York Knicks and was capturing the imagination of the NBA in the United States and globally. As an Asian American, Lin burst onto the popular cultural scene because of his performance on the basketball court. He was the first player in NBA history to score at least twenty points and have five assists in his first five starts.[49] He was dunking, crossing over players, and hitting game-winning shots. With time, Lin became an Asian American icon and challenged the many stereotypes of Asian American masculinity as lacking athletic ability and being "all brain" and no brawn.[50] He was performing these spectacular feats against some of the most accomplished and well-known players in the NBA including Kobe Bryant, John Wall, and DeMar DeRozan. His basketball skills and "underdog" story created what mainstream media pundits termed "Linsanity," and his success led to his embrace by Asian Americans seeking to claim someone in the mainstream imagination.[51]

At the same time, much of the discourse featuring Asian American fan reception focused on East Asian Americans (Chinese and Japanese in particular), with the category of Asian American (and to a lesser degree, "Asian American athlete") phenotypically represented through Jeremy Lin's East Asian American body. The dominance of this representation did not reflect the heterogeneous Asian American community.[52] Some of my Filipino American interlocutors did not see Jeremy Lin as representative of their lived experiences and did not claim him as one of their own. When he was making spectacular plays in the NBA, I barely heard a whisper about his athletic performances from some of the players in the AB Syndicate. Indeed, some of them did not have the same kinds of strong reactions to Lin as their East Asian American counterparts.

For example, when I asked Erik if he was following Jeremy Lin's rise to prominence, he responded matter of factly, "Not too much, 'cause I'm not a big New York fan. Jeremy Lin is just another Asian. I know Asians are talented, but it's not a big wow factor to me." Erik's response to Jeremy Lin's success is grounded in local fandom (Erik is a Lakers fan), and while he affirms Asian American basketball skill he does not necessarily celebrate Lin's Asian Americanness, despite his impressive basketball feats and performances of masculinity against his Black and white peers. At the same time, Erik, along with the other Filipino American men, has been playing basketball against other Asian American men throughout his life. Erik's response, and that of other Filipino American men, to Jeremy Lin is also a way of making Asian American basketball excellence routine and not exceptional. Rather than celebrate Jeremy Lin, Filipino Americans celebrate each other in more mundane spaces like the AB Syndicate, and through symbolic constructions or markers of ethnicity, such as clothing and tattoos. Whereas some Filipino Americans do not look to the Philippines as a site of diasporic identity,[53] my interlocutors intentionally incorporated Philippine symbols on their clothes and skin to stake claims to a diasporic Filipino American identity.

As a site of social relations and a stage for identity formation, the AB Syndicate was transformed into a space for Filipino American men to carve out and contest dominant constructions of Asian American bodies devoid of athletic ability and to challenge the US colonial institution's goal of sporting assimilation. Consumption of popular culture, and in particular NBA commodity culture and NBA style, shaped the contours of a middle-class Filipino American heterosexual masculinity that rejected white normative masculinity while also embracing Black aesthetics. Filipino Americans craft their identities through a technology of self in the form of Philippine-made uniforms and body modification.[54] The uniforms involved a transnational web of social actors from the United States and the Philippines, raw material from the Philippines, and Filipina/o labor and culminated in public performances of Filipino American sporting masculinity on the basketball court and beyond. The processes complicate how we understand Filipino American ethnic and racial identity in the twenty-first century. The uniforms and tattoos cross over singular understandings of Filipino American identity formation that are solely situated within the United States and completely destabilize stories of migration and diaspora that imagine movement, enculturation, and cultural production as linear.[55] In this way, we see how Filipino Americans manage diasporic contours in the AB Syndicate and perform masculinity through a repertoire of bodily movements and symbols, quantifiable proof of sporting skill, and sporting artifacts.

Although Filipina and Asian American women did not play in the Asian Ballers Syndicate, this does not mean that they were passive spectators at the basketball games. Beyond dominant constructions of female spectatorship as "objects" on the sidelines or as "irrational" fans who only watch sports out of a heterosexual desire for men's bodies,[56] the women attending the league games displayed a degree of agency as spectators and were part of the construction of Filipino American heterosexual masculinity. In fact, throughout my playing tenure, a number of Filipina Americans brought their children to the games and were often the most vocal supporters of their boyfriends, husbands, and partners. In the next chapter, I center Filipina American athletic performance by discussing how athletic Filipina and Asian American women assert their agency through flag football acumen, skill, and technique by playing against white women and against the institution of whiteness in flag football tournaments.

4

"We're Just as Good and Even Better Than You!"

Filipina American and Asian American Flag Footballers and the Racial Politics of Competition

You know, women's flag football, they've been getting some attention on ESPN. A couple of months ago, they were highlighting [a white female flag football player] that made some kind of crazy play. It was on the "Top 10" on SportsCenter. And I'm like, "Ok we've done that many times." It wasn't even that serious but it was on "Top 10" on SportsCenter. I was like, "Really? I'm sure we've done that at least six times when I was playing."

Keena, a second-generation Filipina American, spoke to me about a popular video featuring Michelle Roque, a white female college-age flag football player from Florida State University (FSU), performing spectacular football plays including spin moves and jukes, which are meant to fake out or deceive defenders.[1] Although these moves are difficult to execute, they are common in flag football and tackle football across the country.[2] However, women are not often highlighted for their sporting abilities in the realm of (flag) football. Thus, when SportsCenter's "Top 10," a popular segment on the Entertainment and Sports Programming Network (ESPN), featured Roque's plays, it was celebrated by athletes and fans. "Top 10" plays recognize athletes performing spectacular athleticism. Among other performances, these can include a game-winning touchdown, a home run, or a basketball crossover.

However, Keena offers a reading of this ESPN feature of Roque that challenges notions of equivalence within the category of woman. She is aware of the larger cultural politics around gender, race, and (sporting) representation. Racialized and gendered difference operates not only within the category of woman, but also across Asian American communities.[3] Keena, in other words, is embedding a broader commentary about flag football visibility and its association with race, gender, ability, and claims to national belonging. While she offers a cursory acknowledgment of Roque's flag football feats, which are spectacular in their own right, she also draws upon her own sporting success and skills to make claims to athletic mastery. In the process, she provides her own archive that extends beyond dominant media frames that center white femininity.

By asserting that she and her fellow Asian American teammates performed incredible athletic feats on many occasions, Keena interjects Filipina American athletic femininity into the realm of sporting identity, sporting pleasures, sporting excellence, and (Asian) Americanness. In my observations playing alongside and training with Asian American female flag football players, I often witnessed the kinds of athleticism that ESPN's "Top 10" segment celebrates. Like Roque, Asian American women faked out their defenders, threw touchdown passes, and made one-handed catches. They not only used their bodies to fake out their defenders but also "crossed over" stereotypical imaginings of Asian exoticism and Orientalism as well as white racist readings of their racialized and gendered bodies.[4] However, as we see in the excerpt, and in the mainstream imagination, Asian American women and their sporting feats are largely rendered invisible. Asian American athletic femininity in general and Filipina American athletic femininity in particular are deemed impossible within larger US sporting discourses. Whiteness operates to solidify its feminine Western ideal in which Asian American bodies are imagined as the nonathletic, racialized other.

In this chapter, I highlight how Asian and Filipina American women narrate their participation in flag football and how, through the sport, they formulate their sense of self, especially through their experiences interacting with and playing flag football against predominantly white college-age women. Their stories demonstrate how their marginalization in the mainstream sporting imagination was not because they were women. *Women* is not an equivalent category. Rather, these Filipina and Asian American women articulate an experience of marginalization based on the intersections of race and gender. Asian American women embodied and performed "heterogeneity, hybridity, and multiplicity" as a refusal and a challenge to dominant ways of knowing and imagining

Asian American women.[5] In this process, they also expanded notions of Asian Americanness and Asian American culture.

Although their racial difference was perceived through essentialist representations of Asian American women that dislocated them from the terms of belonging in flag football, it is this exclusion and invisibility in the larger media and narrative landscape that informs how cultural productions operate through difference while stereotypes operate through equivalence.[6] Although she shares Asian American experiences of marginalization within the larger national sporting landscape, Keena and her teammates offer their own sets of pleasures and desires through sporting feats, acts of aggression, overt physicality, pain, and desire for bodily contact. Their performance of flag football athleticism is also an inversion of the relationship between race, gender, and ability.[7]

Asian Americans' pleasure at playing flag football opens the boundaries of belonging, inverts racializations, and affirms athletic identities. Football is a treasured American pastime with a large consumer fanbase. Football is considered a hypermasculinized American national pastime played primarily by men.[8] Yet within the confines of the flag football field, Filipina and Asian American women expand what constitutes acceptable sporting bodies, exceed the racializations of Asian American femininities, and spatialize the meanings, values, and pleasures of flag football. As we will see, the flag football tournament is a site of exclusion because the contours of normative femininity stayed within communal boundaries of white, heterosexual, and middle-class constructions. In this sense, Asian American women are racialized as petite, small, and nonaggressive, and their bodies are never seen beyond their exoticism and Orientalism to reflect the aggression required for sport. Instead, they are expected to conform to stereotypes that often cast them as submissive, demure, and fragile within their families and in larger US society. Part of these stereotypes stem from dominant understandings of the "model minority" moniker that frames them as submissive in the political arena and in all other arenas of life, with the exception of the academy and their profession. Even in the academy, there is minimal engagement with Asian American women athletes. Moreover, such stereotypes imagine them through yellow peril tropes through which they are hypersexualized and, therefore, only legible as hyper-heterosexual objects in places like spas and in spaces of prostitution and pornography.[9] These opposing poles produce static renditions of Asian American women that position them as caricatures incapable of athletic excellence, obscuring their athletic ability in favor of more stringent ideas about what constitutes normative sporting bodies.[10] As Sucheta Mazumdar argues, "their identity has been formed by the lore of the majority community, not by their own history, their own stories."[11] Asian American women have simultaneously experienced exclusion in subtle and overt ways. They were treated like outsiders and their cultural practices were perceived as "un-American"; once they proved their athletic prowess, stereotypes about them as "foreign" to the game faded, and they were perceived as too good of a team and therefore, too dominant, which justified their exclusion from participating in an annual flag football tournament called the Lambda Tournament. Rather than dismissing flag football tournaments as trivial interactions or subscribing to the fallacy of classifying sports as "post-racial"[12] arenas, we should be clear that social relations between white and Asian American women and their bodies constitute racial projects.[13] The "honorary white" status, which is often seen as evident in Asian American communities, has not garnered the Asian American women's team full inclusion and instead has exposed racial hierarchies on the playing field.[14] Yet, Asian Americans have asserted their bodies in ways that undermine prevailing discourses of Asian American female fragility, reconfigure the relationships between femininity and athletic ability, and foreground aspects of female masculinity while also showcasing their opposition to white femininity.[15] Flag football tournaments are simultaneously political and pleasure-laden sites where people struggle over, negotiate, and contest racial, gendered, and sexualized meanings. Because of this, Asian American women mobilized around ideas of Asianness as empowerment rather than as powerlessness as flag football athletes. They wanted to "ball out" (a sporting vernacular term for playing well) and dominate on the field.

In addition to employing critical theory approaches to race and Asian American feminism,[16] approaches that center the voices of Filipina American and Asian American women, this chapter employs critical race theorist Cheryl Harris's whiteness as property. For these women, flag football tournaments become spaces of social critique that reveal how they use their bodies, football skills, and techniques as improvisational tools of athletic excellence and identity formation that cross into realms of pleasure and desire not often afforded to Asian American women. These cultural productions become arenas for them to simultaneously claim Asian Americanness and to disclaim the model minority status and its relevant racializations.

Complicating Sport, Gender, and Race Beyond Black, White, and Male

Scholarship on gender and sport has critically examined the gendered aspects of women's sporting experiences, taking into account how gender and power ideologies circulate in sporting spaces at the crossroads of class, race, and sexuality.[17] Such scholarship has also critiqued how sport has historically been constructed as a male preserve,[18] a site for reproducing hegemonic masculinity where patriarchal codes of authority are reaffirmed, and where sport ideologies and practices structure dominance, subordination, and agency along gendered and racial lines.[19] Similarly, the literature has also addressed how the increased presence of women has entrenched patriarchy and its pattern of social relations.[20] At times, this scholarship has ignored the racial and ethnic differences among women, referencing middle-class white women—such as Michelle Roque and her FSU team—as symbolic of all women.[21] When the scholarship has discussed women of color in sport, its focus on race is generally uncritically equated to African American women.[22] Black women's bodies, their narratives, and experiences become representative of the "raced" body, a move which fails to account for differences within the categories of race, Blackness, and woman, as often pointed out by Black feminist theory.[23] By creating an equivalence and essentializing "race" and "woman," the focus on Black women does not adequately address the multiple racialized and gendered experiences of women of color in general and Asian American women in particular.[24] In many ways, sporting agency is reduced to that of a white female figure; the person of color is portrayed perpetually as the victim, always passive, and always in need of white support. Some Asian and Asian American women, for example, confront discourses about the powerful constraints of patriarchy, labeling men in these communities as always and already perpetrators of misogyny and sexism. These patriarchal practices render

Asian and Asian American women as helpless, powerless, and without avenues of resistance or agency. Such gendered interactions are seen as naturalized and commonsense. As a result, some white women become the universal subject of care and the *only* advocate for Asian and Asian American women.[25]

Negotiating Racialized, Gendered, and Sexualized Meanings in Flag Football

The origins of flag football (also called touch football), like those of the more popular variation, tackle football, date back to the US military in the 1930s. However, tackle football carried higher bodily risks. To minimize injuries and preserve US servicemen's bodies for combat, flag football became the preferred game. It has remained a relatively popular leisure activity for college-age students.[26] Although some of the women played flag football in middle and high school, their long-term commitment to playing the sport began when they were college students and, later, alumni playing intramurals. Many also participated in coethnic sports tournaments organized by Filipina/o American student groups throughout Northern and Southern California. These coethnic tournaments have existed for over thirty years. Filipina and Asian American women involved in the sport have found it a site of great joy and social intimacy, as well as of coethnic, and coracial bonding. Moreover, we can think of flag football spaces as "counterspaces"[27]—spaces outside the traditionally imagined spaces of cultural festivals—where Asian American women undermine racial and gendered stereotypes of Asian American female bodies. Flag football remains a popular sport played by both men and women, sometimes starting with kids as young as ten years old and extending to college-age, and by amateur athletes and beyond.

Flag football offers a way to reconfigure the meanings of sexualized femininity imposed upon Asian American female athletes. It does so by displacing Oriental framings of Asian exoticisms, fragility, physical lack, and docility. When participants revel in the pleasures and pain of playing flag football, they do so knowing that the game is coded through hypermasculinity; through their play, they critique the hegemonic and taken-for-granted ideology of flag football as the domain of men alone while also collapsing the dichotomous realms of male-female and masculinity-femininity in sport.

As a counterpoint to tackle football, flag football also allows discourses of heterosexual femininity and heterosexual desires to emerge that simultaneously showcase athletic abilities. Both Asian American and white women challenge normative gender expectations while simultaneously performing a "hetero-sexy"[28] sense of self. That is, they perform acceptable acts of toughness and athleticism that, at times, stay within the confines of heterosexual femininity. Their acts are read as feminine because of the strong connection between women's flag football and heterosexual desire. Flag football offers a compelling way to understand how Filipina Americans, as well as white women, navigate a cultural terrain that incorporates hypermasculinity and female hyperheterosexuality. Because flag football (and even more so tackle football) is so intimately tied to the American nation,[29] Asian American and white women players can temporarily stand in as national representatives while also destabilizing normative belonging.[30]

Sports Memories, Interviews, and the Politics of Racial Remembering

As a member of an Asian American men's flag football team, my teammates and I trained and practiced with Asian American women. As a man, I benefited from the "patriarchal dividend":[31] my access to sporting spaces like the football field was never called into question. My football skills were seen as an asset to the Asian American women's flag football team. As an informal coach, I helped teach them flag football's fundamentals like how to maneuver through tight spaces and how to catch and throw. I also taught them offensive plays and concepts to further their knowledge of the game. Thus, I used my cultural capital from years of playing and I took great pleasure in sharing my football knowledge with some of the players. Although patriarchal masculinity governs sporting spaces like flag football and socializes women and children along these lines, Asian American women performed their sporting brilliance and flag football prowess. I draw from nine interviews and observations to understand how Filipina American and Asian American women make sense of their lived experiences, sporting memories, and perspectives competing in a predominantly white flag football tournament. Although the majority of the team members are Filipina American, I also include interviews from a Japanese American and a Vietnamese American. I discuss their experiences playing in the Lambda Tournament from 2000 to 2006. Currently, these Asian American women variously work in real estate, health care, sales, law, and in nonprofit sectors and their ages range from thirty to thirty-eight years old.

At first, I was interested in interviewing Asian American female athletes about their experiences playing in Filipina/o American and Asian American sporting tournaments. But these experiences became secondary when a number of the women discussed their college playing experiences in what they called the Lambda Tournament—a weekend-long tournament that the Lambda Delta fraternity organized at Cal State South Bay. The fraternity was part of the white mainstream Interfraternity Council (IFC), a national fraternal organization that serves as an umbrella group for hundreds of fraternities throughout the United States. The IFC fraternity members and the sororities against whom these Asian American women played were predominantly white. At the conclusion of the tournament, Lambda Delta awarded trophies and engraved the name of the tournament's champion on them. Throughout the weekend, sororities and other Greek-identified organizations played against each other in a number of nine-on-nine flag football games.[32] These sororities were also members of a national umbrella organization called the Panhellenic Council and were deeply embedded in the white mainstream of Cal State South Bay's Greek life.[33] While some of my research participants were members of an Asian American interest sorority, the organization they represented was not part of the Panhellenic Council. This meant that they did not have institutional power within the council and were not part of the dominant Greek community on campus.

Camaraderie, Competition, Passion, and Joy: Why Women Play Flag Football

Whereas some Asian American girls and women participate in sport to be part of a larger and long-standing ethnic community,[34] Asian American women flag football players had a wide assortment of desires for, motives for, and pleasures in playing. One of the reasons they played was because they had been fans of football from an early age. Some recall watching games with their brothers or fathers. Nora had never played flag or tackle football, but she had a deep admiration for and interest in the sport. It was not until college that she had an opportunity to play. Her sorority sister from Beta Zeta Delta was a player and invited her to join the team. Nora recalled, "I love football. I knew a lot about it growing up. I remember watching it but I never played, so I thought it'd be fun."

Nora's desire to play flag football is also about larger claims to local, diasporic, and national belonging, particularly because football historically excluded women.[35] In this sense, flag football is one space of leisure where women perform and embody the nation, albeit in ways that contain differential outcomes based on race, gender, sexuality, and nation. Asian American women experienced deep pleasure and competitive joy in playing with each other. As did the men profiled in Stanley Thangaraj's *Desi Hoop Dreams*, they cultivated their own sporting public among whom they could gauge and appreciate their athletic abilities free of mainstream racializations.[36] This subsequently cultivated a sense of coracial camaraderie woven through their sporting pleasures. When I asked Keena why she continued to play, she replied:

> I enjoyed playing. I really did. I enjoyed the camaraderie between all of us on the team. I'm passionate about the game. I love the game so that was big for me. I liked the competitiveness of it. It was just fun. Win or lose, it was always a good time. And I still miss it to this day. I haven't played in over ten years but I still miss it. When I watch videos of our teams play, I still miss it and I always think in the back of my head, "Should I go play one more time?"

Keena's teammate Allyson shared, "It was the camaraderie, the sportsmanship, [and] the teamwork. I was used to that playing sports in high school" and to "being part of something that was also Asian and Asian American."

For Allyson, the pleasures arising from camaraderie, sportsmanship, and teamwork were also about aspiring to be a college athlete. As a first-generation college student, she was not familiar with how to become a student athlete. This partially explains why she was interested in playing flag football and desiring to *feel* like a college athlete: "I played be-cause I always wanted to play collegiate sports. I felt like if I trained hard enough, I could have been a walk-on on the track team. Maybe not a D1 but D2 or D3, I think I would have been good enough for a track team. But I didn't know. That's why [flag] football was an outlet for that to hap-pen without being a collegiate athlete."[37] As Allyson shares, because of the lack of a flag football infrastructure in her community, she came to the sport in a nontraditional way.

Some of the white women were also part of a community that cel-ebrated athletic achievement and the female body and reveled in the pleasures and joys of their competitive desires. Playing flag football was a way for them to participate in a subculture and relish in performing a flag football identity, defying expected feminine gender conventions and being able to "choose and execute a fuller range of endeavors" beyond simply challenging flag football's lack of feminine performance.[38]

Although one might assume that flag football does not carry the same kinds of physical demands as tackle football, Asian American women were acutely aware of the sport's risks and potential for bodily injury. This did not discourage them from playing. Cynthia, a second-generation Filipina American, remembered, "[Flag] football was really hard because of the physical contact." Indeed, Allyson proudly recol-lected that she and her teammates had experienced "broken bones, broken ankles, dislocated fingers," and readily acknowledged that play-ing flag football is just as physical as playing tackle football. Some of the Filipina and Asian American women viewed the traumas to their bodies as something to show off and of which to be proud. Kaya, a 1.5-generation Filipina and white American told me that the injuries she sustained playing football were "like badges of honor," symbols of ag-gression and toughness. She also shared that one of her teammates has since "retired" from playing after suffering multiple concussions from playing flag football. These matter-of-fact responses to bodily injury are one way for her to claim a measure of belonging to the sport and claim such aggressive and physically demanding play. Because flag football requires significant physicality, such demands enabled Asian American women (and white women) to see themselves as an integral part of the sport's normative practices and to resist norms of "respectable hetero-sexual femininity."[39]

Expelled to the Sidelines: The Margins of Flag Football

In flag football tournaments, Asian American women were cultural producers who simultaneously embodied and performed dominant and subordinate positions as successful athletes, but others imagined them as outside of whiteness and athletic ability.[40] While participants shared that they enjoyed playing in several of the annual Asian American club-sponsored tournaments, they were especially proud of their success playing against white women. In Asian American tournaments, the women socialized with other teams, admired other Asian American female athletes, and, despite the highly competitive games, found joy in competing against them. They were part of a "community [of] athletic women" and celebrated their peers' impressive feats on the flag football field.[41] These tournaments also provided a venue in which to normalize athletic excellence and Filipina and Asian American femininity without engendering feelings of exclusion. These were spaces of affirmation and admiration where such women could expand their versions of Americanness without feeling as if they did not belong; they could be players instead of racial stereotypes and racial caricatures.[42]

However, in my talks with the women, a point of contention emerged time and time again once the conversation steered toward their memories playing against white women in white-dominated tournaments. In these flag football tournaments, competition became a contest of racial and gendered meanings on the playing field. There were hierarchical values of athletic ability that left Filipina Americans and Asian American women out of this white space. Nora recalled, "We played [in tournaments] on campus with the other sororities, which was nice because it was between ten teams who were Caucasian, tall women, and we were the minority team out there." Keena remembered, "We always went into games with people underrating us and not thinking we would perform well." For Filipina and Asian American women, these tournament spaces symbolized feelings of marginalization and exclusion both figuratively and materially. When they first started playing in the tournament, Asian American women noticed some of their white counterparts' condescending attitude toward them. With an irritated tone, Minh, a second-generation Vietnamese American shared, "They would say, 'Look at these ninjas, look at these little Asian girls; what are they? They probably don't go to school here. I can't believe they even know how to play this sport." Nora had felt slighted for their perceived athletic inferiority: "Some of the [white] girls were really kinda big and tall and they assumed because we're all short, that we're not good. They would just [make] snide [remarks]. I know when we first started the tournament, we would get laughs from the [white] girls like, 'Oh yeah, this is gonna be easy.'"

Height and size, amplified by race and gender ideologies about Asian American women,[43] became a way for white women to racialize Asian American women as small, frail, and certainly not athletic.[44] We see here how race is a spatializing practice that mapped particular racial meanings onto the bodies of the Filipina and Asian American women while spatially dislocating them from the field of American sport. Whereas Nora saw white female bodies as physically imposing, some of the white women used the common racialization of Asian American women as petite dolls and combined this with the actual diminutive stature of a few of the Asian American athletes. Such ideas essentialized all the players as lacking physical skills and cultural knowhow of flag football. Recalling her interactions with white sororities, Allyson described, "They [white teams] really didn't interact with us. We were kind of isolated in the corner." The "corner" signified not only a figurative recollection of exclusion but also how the spatial arrangement of the tournament was racially demarcated; Asian American women were typically the only women of color playing in the flag football tournament. Participants, for example, shared how a Latina team played in only one tournament and African American teams were never present.[45] Asian American women literally inhabited their marginalization. They were provisionally accepted as competitors because their perceived unathleticism did not threaten the racial and gendered status quo of white female athleticism. Because Asian Americans are positioned outside of the dominant Black-white racial logic, they embodied a "racial ambiguity" that afforded them greater mobility in various sporting realms like flag football spaces.[46] They were also gendered and racialized in ways that made them sexually exotic and set them with within frames of domesticity and sexuality such that they were not perceived as a threat to the sporting field.

The racial and gendered meanings mapped onto their bodies denoting demureness and fragility allowed them access to the flag football tournament that African American sportswomen could not access. Given dominant stereotypes of African American female bodies as too "mannish" and hypermasculine,[47] one wonders whether and how these dominant ideas shaped their limited opportunities to participate in the tournament since, at times, Black sportswomen are deemed threats to sporting spaces.[48]

Furthermore, some white women drew upon dominant popular cultural representations of Asians as martial artists in ways that consequently categorized their bodies outside of cultural Americanness (i.e., flag football) and, therefore, beyond the boundaries of the American national fabric. Although the martial arts are athletic forms that demand toughness and aggression, they are not as highly valued as other sports because they are imagined outside of the geographic boundaries of the United States and outside the cultural practices of an American sport like flag football. Asian American *difference* contributes to how the women were racialized. Yet imposing generic caricatures of Asian American women as martial artists fails to account for the differences within this sporting community.[49] In this way, some white women symbolically inscribed *Asian* popular cultural forms to *Asian American* identities that then dislocated their claims to American belonging. Even though they were born in the United States and were socialized along US norms of citizenship, they were not seen within the legible frames of normative white femininity.[50] Yet common to all of them was that they had grown up participating in multiple American mainstream sports like basketball, baseball, softball, volleyball, and track and field. These practices were one way in which these women performed their sporting pleasures that also bolstered their claims to Americanness, which countered how some white women perceived them.

Racial insults associated with body size, Asian martial artistry, and objectification (e.g., "What are they?"), as well as their racially undetermined status, all reinforced assumptions and even accusations that Asian American women did not belong. By being denied cultural claims to a quintessentially American sport, Asian American women could not claim Americanness. Their experiences are an accumulation of exclusionary experiences that seep into their everyday lives. They bring these personal experiences with them into the racialized and gendered realms of the flag football tournament. Instead of being the "easy" game for the

white teams, though, they dominated the Lambda Tournament to challenge these racial classifications and attain a position at the top of the
flag football pyramid.

Performing Swag, Appropriating Thug, and Embodying Female Masculinity

Although the flag football tournament generated feelings of exclusion,
for some of my Filipina and Asian American interlocuters it offered a
means to subvert dominant stereotypes about Asian American women.
Filipina and Asian American flag football skills, confidence, and swagger were strategies through which they claimed flag football superiority
and an athletic identity. In 2001, during one remarkable play on offense,
Elia, the quarterback, pitched the ball to Minh. As Minh started running to the right side, a defender anticipated the play and converged
on her to grab Minh's flag. It appeared that she would be ruled down
because she had nowhere to run. As the defender reached for her flag,
Minh lowered herself, quickly stopped, and stepped back, before accel-
erating past her defender. She managed to fool her defender and score
a touchdown. As the play was unfolding, a few of the young men on the
sidelines screamed "Oh, oh, oh, did you see that juke!?" while another
yelled "Juke mode!" to acknowledge her spectacular feat. When the
referee signaled a touchdown, instead of celebrating, Minh casually
strutted toward the referee and tossed him the ball. Minh, it seemed, had
performed this athletic feat many times over and was used to juking her
defender. Indeed, given the number of spectacular and noteworthy plays
by Filipina and Asian American athletes, it is worth mentioning that
the players themselves knew they had skills. As Allyson told me, "Our
team ha[d] so much swag[ger]!" Self-assurance and bodily comport-
ments manifested in football skill, talent, and dominance, all of which
constituted their swagger, which refers to a multitude of masculine
behaviors primarily associated with and embodied by men of color and
white men.[51] Notions of swagger rarely acknowledge how women can
perform or attach meanings of masculinity and swagger to their own
bodies.[52] For these women, swagger emanated from self-confidence and
knowing that their skills and talents were superior to that of their white

counterparts. They also garnered symbolic capital from playing flag football and reaped the rewards as legitimate athletes in their respective community.[53]

In addition to swagger, their sense of flag football style was gendered masculine by their appropriation of Black cultural forms, embodiment of the cultural politics of the cool, and identification as "jocks," all of which were bound up in Asian American female masculine performances. For example, Julianna, a fourth-generation Japanese American recalled that her team "[played] with cut off T-shirts [and] bandanas." She proudly remembered, "We just looked like little thugs." Wearing cut off T-shirts and bandanas accentuated an urban cool by which they could display their muscularity and female physicality. Moreover, the self-definition of *thug* is linked to representations of working-class African American men who perform a tough and aggressive masculinity. *Thug*, however, does not carry the negative racial overtones that Filipino American youth confronted in Southern California or in Hmong communities. Importantly, the "thug identity" is something that some of the Asian American women called themselves, not something that others called them.

Because some sports like football and basketball are embodied physical cultures, Asian American women are not expected to use their bodies in a "combination of force and skill."[54] Julianna used racial grammar and a class-inflected signifier that temporarily enabled Asian American women to inhabit working-class Black aesthetics that are distinct from racially normative Asian American middle-class, model minority references.[55] Although "thug" enabled Asian American women to invert dominant stereotypical images of Asian American women as passive or weak model minorities to accentuate instead an aggressive and tough female masculinity in a football setting, this does not mean that they aligned themselves with political Blackness.[56] Embracing the thug moniker was spatiotemporally bounded, a fleeting gender nonconforming performance of female masculinity that was acceptable because it happened precisely (and only) during sporting time. They crafted their identities in opposition to respectable Asian American femininities by portraying their bodies as athletically empowered, aggressive, and tough. These characteristics stand in stark contrast to those in typically feminine sports like tennis and golf, where, at times, Asian American female athletes are represented through Orientalist frameworks.[57] Whereas pejorative terms like "butch" and "dyke" are mapped onto the bodies of Asian American women who play in sports that are considered masculine,[58] these women collapsed "female masculinity" and heterosexual desires and pleasures on the sporting field. They did not consistently face simplistic representations of Asian American femininity from their Asian American male counterparts. Although participants' Asian American male friends celebrated their athleticism and treated them equally and respectfully, patriarchy still regulated the flag football space. Both Asian American and white women's bodies were sexualized; the bodies of those known to be in heterosexual relationships were policed according to norms of what is acceptable as hetero-sexy and fit bodies.

While Asian American flag football players could scramble essentialist meanings of Asian American femininity, especially within their community of friends, some of them did not feel entirely supported by their families. For example, Vanessa, a second-generation Filipina American, shared that her mother did not support her flag football pursuits. "She thinks sports [are] for boys. And she still feels strongly about that. When I played [flag football], she [told me], 'That's for boys, why do you play that? Are you butch?'" Because Vanessa played an often-masculinized sport like flag football, her mother read her body as nonnormative in relation to normative ideas about Filipina American femininity. This reading also worked alongside the sexualizing of female athletes that played mainstream American sports like basketball, football, and baseball.[59] Conflating sport (seen as masculine) with conservative gendered and sexualized expectations of Filipina Americanness, Vanessa's mother did not see her performing appropriate Filipina American diasporic subjecthood because to the mother, her daughter's body did not represent heterosexuality, demureness, chastity, and femininity.[60] Despite this, some of the players challenged and reassembled meanings of masculinity to then mobilize around a shared sense of coolness. Allyson explained how accruing "cool" status as football players shaped interactions with people who did not play. She was also cognizant of how football privileges men and traditional forms of masculinity: "Maybe just being a woman knowing about football, knowing how to play [and] knowing the game is huge. I think for all of us that play, it gives us an extra kick in our step. We feel like jocks, [we feel] cool. It gives us a cool factor [and] cool points." This was especially heightened in female-to-female peer interactions. "Because we know the game and people hear [that we play flag football]. You tell people, 'Yeah, I play football.' They're like, 'Oh. Really? You *play, play*?' [emphasis added] 'Yeah, I play real flag football.' It gives all of us a boost of confidence that we know a game that's male-dominated. It makes all of us feel good outside [of] when we're playing." Beyond boosting their self-confidence by playing this sport, Allyson and her teammates generated a sense of coolness that was social capital and could be carried to other spaces outside of sport. In doing so, they laid claim to sporting masculinity and defined themselves in relation to other women who did not play. As the term *jock* is generally linked to boys, men, and heterosexual masculinity,[61] Allyson represented herself and her teammates as athletically masculine and allowed Asian American women to accrue symbolic capital not only in gendered terms but also in ways that reflected the politics of cool. Their presentations of self and subsequent athletic performances critiqued dominant ideas of race and normative femininities while opening up the space to imagine sporting femininities as well.[62] Importantly, Allyson's very playing enabled her and her teammates to have privileged access to male spaces that were unavailable to women who did not play.

Asian American "Invaders" and the Politics of Exclusion

Despite feeling like outsiders, Asian American women mobilized their underdog status to prove they belonged, and they consequently spoke confidently of their football success over white women. Nora recounted how her team's underdog status angered—but also provoked, irritated, and inspired—her: "It would make me mad. We're just as good and even better than you!" Nora's "Asian American anger" stems from accumulated resentment toward her white counterparts, who she felt underestimated Asian Americans' athletic abilities.[63] Indeed, she and her Asian American peers mobilized this anger through their bodies and against white women. Anger, as ethnomusicologist Deborah Wong notes, had to do with whiteness encroaching on Asian American moments of intense pleasure and the irritation that they harbored against their white counterparts. In this way, Asian Americans' flag football pleasures became politicized.[64] When I asked Nora how her team fared against the white women's teams in the tournament, she proudly remembered, "We won, we killed them. We played them like four years in a row and we won the tournament every year." By saying "We're just as good and even better than you!," Nora makes claims to Asian American athletic superiority. She affirms dominance over white teams as a result of defeating them four consecutive years, which positioned them as athletes atop the sporting hierarchy. In a way, sport as a racial project leads to a different reading of racial dynamics while still inserting racial difference into the space. It does so by positioning Asian American women as athletically legible and superior to white women. Allyson, Nora's teammate who continued to play a few years after Nora "retired," matter-of-factly remembered, "We're good at it. We kick[ed] ass. We take a lot of pride in that. We were just that good. We were such a well-oiled machine." With each touchdown, interception, and tournament win, the Asian American women derived pleasure from their athletic feats and inverted static assumptions of Asian American race and ability.[65]

Whereas using the phrase "well-oiled machine" might recall Orientalist tropes framing Asian bodies as rote, stoic, and emotionally detached,[66] Allyson instead used it to emphasize how they had cultivated their self-confidence through hours of practice, and how that practice had resulted in their perennial flag football success. In sporting vernacular, "machine" is also a reference to a team working in synchrony while displaying toughness and athletic coordination. I recall the numerous times Allyson used her low center of gravity and speed to accelerate through tight spaces and run past her defenders. In fact, her teammates called her Reggie Bush, alluding to the retired African American running back who won the Heisman Trophy and starred on two national championship teams for the University of Southern California. He had tremendous football skill because of his footwork, speed, and ability to fake out defenders. Like Bush, Allyson had a great football acumen and made difficult bodily maneuvers look easy.

Akin to the crossover, Asian American women excelled through speed, fakery, and misdirection plays to score touchdowns or gain chunks of yardage. Allyson explained, "The 'bread and butter' for me was pitch left [or] pitch right. Minh would block for me. Another would be a pitch left or right to Minh and she would pitch it back to me. Or, if I wasn't open, she would just keep it. If Minh was with me in the backfield, if she was running left or right, depending on who was coming at her, she would pitch it back to me. I'd catch it but I'd run the opposite direction. We scored a lot on that play." With a chuckle, Allyson asserted, "That's because Minh and I were hella [really] fast and they couldn't catch us."

The players were equally skilled on defense. During the 2002 tournament, the opposing team's quarterback dropped back, scrambled left, then right, before spotting her receiver running across the middle of the field. Silvina was playing safety and the defense was in zone coverage. Zone coverage means defensive players were responsible for covering a particular assigned area of the field. If an offensive player runs through their zone, the defensive player must cover them. Silvina was responsible for covering the middle of the field. With her eyes looking at the quarterback and using her peripheral vision, Silvina mirrored the quarterback's movements shuffling her feet left and then right. The quarterback set her feet and threw the ball downfield to her seemingly wide-open receiver. However, standing at around five feet, six inches tall, with a long and lanky frame, Silvina quickly analyzed the play and spotted the receiver running toward her zone. In an instant, Silvina ran toward her opponent and reached around the wide receiver's torso to bat the ball away. Both the receiver and Silvina fell to the ground, but Silvina quickly got up and pumped her fist to signal her satisfaction at thwarting the play. Such plays demonstrated Filipina and Asian American women's knowledge of the game, including tactics, strategies, and techniques, and their incredible athletic speed which they used to execute successful plays on both offense and defense.

Asian Americans' dominance on the field during the tournaments changed the way in which white teams viewed them. Initially seen as a novelty and not taken seriously, racialized ideas about them morphed; white teams now regarded them as athletic intruders. When I asked Silvina, what she recalled about playing in the Lambda Tournament, she said she remembered "feeling very hated. Because we were good. Our team was really, really good. I just remember the sorority teams being frustrated." Although some of the white women did not initially see Asian American women as legitimate athletic competitors, their initial assumptions of race and perceived lack of Asian American athletic ability were quickly inverted.[67] The Asian American team's dominance challenged the racial meanings that structured the playing field, which then destabilized the white women's claims to the space. Instead of owning the space, the white women were now the ones owned on the playing field—by Asian American sporting excellence.

While race shaped the competitive relations between Asian American and white players during the Lambda Tournament, it also extended to unequal power relations between white men and Asian American women. Changing ideas about Asian American athletic threats influenced how white male referees managed the games, as their judgment for impartiality was called into question. This was especially so when their calls disproportionally favored some of the white teams. Minh recalled: "The [fraternity] referees [were] very close to the sororities. They didn't want their girls to lose. And the girls didn't want to lose against us. Talk about hearing it from the other team. We were hearing it from the referees too. They did not hide how they would say, 'You have to understand. We have to come home to these girls.'" In this example, Asian American women confronted incredible odds against white teams. Heterosexual alliance between white men and white women meant that Asian Americans were also playing against the institution of whiteness, prompting them to question universal ideas of fair play and meritocracy. There were times, however, when white men (who were partners of some of the white players) broke from their expected roles as intimate partners and acknowledged the legitimacy of certain plays. Allyson, for example, remembered, "There were times we were so good [that] when they tried to call in favor of the other team, it was so hard for them to go against us, because they're like, 'Dang, that play was totally legit [fair].'"

Legit, along with meaning "legitimate" or "fair," also refers to Asian Americans' football skills as impressive and spectacular. The 1990s hip-hop artist MC Hammer popularized the term "legit" to assert that his skills were "too legit to quit" making music. Like Hammer's self-confidence in his hip-hop artistry, Asian Americans also proclaimed that their football skills were "too legit to quit" playing flag football. Although many of the Asian American women felt that the white teams had disparaging attitudes toward them, there was one instance, prior to the 2002 championship game, in which one of the white women approached the Asian American team to offer her support. This, however, was a rare exception and the overall sense that Asian American women were indeed, just as good and even better than white women resulted in them being prevented from playing the following year. Minh recalled, "They were fine with us until they found out that we were a threat to them because we were winning, and we were winning against white sororities. I strongly felt that they weren't fair with us and it's because we posed as competition to them." After winning the tournament four years in a row, they were never invited back. Allyson remarked, "2004 is when they stopped inviting us for, I don't know, whatever reason. We heard from the grapevine that the white sororities did not want to play us anymore." Julianna added, "All the other [white sorority] girls were able to vote us out. Plus, we were the only Asians there."

These Asian American women were well aware of their racial subjectivity and clearly understood that as "the only Asians," they did not hold the power to influence Lambda Delta's decision to exclude them. Since they were not part of the Panhellenic sorority system, they had insufficient social capital and power to protest their exclusion. Because white women read these Asian American bodies as athletic threats (having been beaten by them four years in a row), their desire to keep the flag football spaces white meant that Asian Americans could no longer participate in the pleasures of sporting competition. In fact, their physical exclusion mirrored their symbolic exclusion. This was captured in the fraternity's refusal to engrave their team name on the tournament trophy. Julianna elaborated, "The first time we won, it was embarrassing for everybody else cause they didn't take us seriously. We killed them. We didn't get our name on the trophy that year because they didn't want to put our name on [it]. And they didn't invite us back because the girls told the fraternity that was sponsoring it, it was no fun. They weren't gonna play if they asked us to play."

These Asian American flag footballers' physical exclusion and subsequent erasure from the tournament archive is an example of white women's desire to erase Asian Americans' presence from the tournament's history. That exclusion and erasure meant that their success was not documented. That the trophy was kept in the fraternity's house—a predominantly white space—is symbolic and material evidence of Asian American erasure. However, the stories re-narrated here and their own personal video collection offers an archive for Asian American women's stories of sporting success. The process of exclusion parallels a form of whiteness as property. Although intangible, whiteness confers institu-

tional, social, and cultural benefits and therefore produces material outcomes. As Black critical race scholar Cheryl Harris reminds us, part of
the power of whiteness as property involves white people's privilege and
subsequent power through four characteristics: rights to disposition,
right to use and enjoyment, reputation and status, and the absolute right
to exclude.[68] Of these four characteristics, the white women's teams in
the tournament used their whiteness both as a right to use and enjoyment and as the absolute right to exclude.

The white women's intentional refusal to invite the Asian American
women back to the annual tournament meant that they could sanitize
or whiten the flag football space for themselves and enjoy the pleasures
of competition *with each other*. Although they could not overtly say
they desired a white-only space, their silence about (dis)inviting Asian
Americans spoke volumes about their institutional power to maintain
their ability to control who can play and who cannot and, thus, who *has
the right enjoy* playing flag football. Because whiteness is an identity and
a powerful resource, it therefore "can move from being a passive charac-
teristic as an aspect of identity to an active entity that—like other types
of property—is used to fulfill the will and to exercise power."[69] Indeed,
prior to the Asian American women's dominance, the white women did
not activate the power of their whiteness in this way. It was only when
perceptions of Asian American athletes as "little Asian girls" were transformed into a flag football community with swagger and football dominance that the white women engaged this particular form of the power
of their whiteness. Their interpretation of racial dynamics showcases
how Filipina and Asian American exclusion in flag football is also one
sign of their broader exclusion from the national fabric.[70]

Moreover, when the white women deployed their whiteness for their
right to use and enjoyment, they did so not by coalescing around a unified
notion of whiteness and white identity but by mobilizing around the fact
that Asian American women were "not white." In other words, as Harris
reminds us, "the concept of whiteness is built on both exclusion and racial
subjugation."[71] The annual flag football tournament was built on informally excluding Asian American women in order "to include only the
cultural practices of Whites."[72]

However, one of the ways that these women responded to their erasure and reinstated themselves was by creating a highlight video docu-

menting their football exploits and talent. During our interview, Allyson shared a six-and-a-half-minute video montage of their 2002 tournament games with hip-hop music featuring artists like Erick Sermon and Fabolous playing in the background. The highlight video is an alternative archive that re-presents Asian American female subjectivity in more complex ways. It starts by showing the trophy that Julianna referenced earlier, followed by clips from the football games.

The video narrates a community in motion—choreographed Asian American bodies using misdirection plays on offense to score touchdowns. It also showcases their speed, agility, and overall football acumen to trick and distract their white counterparts. In doing so, the video offers visual evidence of how hours of practice, coupled with understanding strategies and tactics, honed their flag football skills. The video shows Minh and Nora scoring touchdowns, performing spin moves, and faking out their defenders. Silvina, who also plays wide receiver and is known among her teammates for her ability to catch passes with ease, intercepts a pass intended for a white offensive player. In this way, the video archive is their source of truth, one that centers and makes visible Filipina and Asian American pleasures and desires.[73]

Like the Asian American actresses in film studies scholar Celine Parreñas Shimizu's book *The Hypersexuality of Race*, my informants claimed power over their bodies by appropriating the flag football tournament space as a site of pleasure that was simultaneously about "personal strength and self-authoring."[74] Their athletic bodies and the accompanying video rescripted and challenged dominant norms of Asian American women's racialized sexuality. It depicted their bodies as innovative, improvisational, and tough, and therefore countered the narratives of mainstream media outlets like ESPN and those of their white opponents.

Negotiating the Boundaries of Sporting Belonging

Sports are one way in which the body is central to the production of racial spectacles. Asian American women's athletic feats are embodied critiques and negotiations of power. Playing football allowed these women to experience physicality on their own terms and they enthusiastically reveled in their athletic pleasures. They confronted exclusionary ideologies and racist sentiments by performing feats of athleticism, dominance, and alternative forms of femininity and masculinity that destabilized the racial platform on which they were playing. Flag football tournaments, while offering a critique of white femininity, also became a way for Asian American women to perform gender in ways that transgressed middle-class and respectable Asian American femininities.

Moreover, for Asian American women, these sporting spaces became a racial proving ground against their white counterparts that allowed them to claim a measure of belonging as athletic equals and thus to challenge their subordinated status. This, however, does not mean that power relations were neutralized. Though the Asian American women challenged the racial and gendered order, the white patriarchal order remained more or less intact. Collegiate belonging and sporting belonging are often symptomatic of greater national belonging. Because tournament organizers denied the Asian American women's access to subsequent flag football tournaments, the homogeneity and sanctity of the white sporting space was preserved.

Whiteness is taken for granted and becomes the unmarked category through which racial otherness is amplified and the place where the privilege of the "somatic norm" of the white body is seen to belong.[75] Whiteness then becomes the normative standard of womanhood and sporting femininity, which Keena and her team interrupt and question. The flag football tournament remained a liminal space imbued with possibility and contradiction; Asian Americans' presence was not fully guaranteed. However, the video footage serves as a form of visual protest to their symbolic exclusion from the flag football tournament—and yet that video does nothing to affirm or to validate their claims to athletic mastery beyond their Asian American peer networks. Still, the video is one way for Filipina and Asian American women to challenge and to recognize, in Mitsuye Yamada's words, "[their] own invisibility [and] to finally be on the path toward visibility."[76]

Filipina and Asian Americans used flag football tournaments to attempt to straddle or cross over racial and gendered boundaries, and their play allowed them to reimagine their bodies in relation to white women, their peer networks, and a larger society that too often renders them outside of sporting cultures. Their exclusion in amateur flag football also offers insights into the experiences of exclusion in sporting spaces from high school to college to professional sports.

Conclusion

The poet Hanif Abdurraqib brilliantly captures what the crossover does. "A crossover, more than about getting space, is about who can briefly be humiliated inside of the space you make."[1] In this book's opening story, when Jenilyn executed the crossover and faked out her defender, she created a space for herself within the racialized and gendered parameters of belonging and enjoyed a brief moment of pleasure. It was a moment in which her athletic prowess enabled her to embody something other than what her community of peers thought of her. In other words, the crossover was her version of asserting an Americanness and a challenge to masculinity, albeit a temporary one, that she thoroughly enjoyed.

I began this book with Jenilyn's story of her crossover move as an entry point to talk about the larger issues and concerns I have highlighted in this book. In it, I have sought literally, metaphorically, and analogously to capture both how the crossover operates in Filipina/o and Filipina/o American sporting spaces and the complexity it reveals about the nature of sports and in Filipina/o America. Instead of the celebratory narrative of sporting assimilation that US colonists desired, I have applied the metaphor of the crossover to complicate how we understand someone like Manny "Pac-Man" Pacquiao beyond the fact that he is globally adored and loved by thousands, if not millions, of Filipina/os living in various diasporic hubs. Although his masculine performance in the boxing ring and in his everyday life serves as a kind of antidote to Asian emasculation and reimagines the Philippines as a muscular, Christian nation, it is also worth asking why and how we got to this point in the first place. This discussion has aimed to ground our understandings of the broader colonial context and its contemporary manifestation, especially in understanding masculinity and Christianity at the nexus of class, race (especially anti-Blackness and white supremacy), and homophobia. In doing so, I do not intend to minimize Pacquiao's accomplishments or the various ways in which Filipina/o Americans attach affective meaning to his iconicity and success. Indeed, as my fieldwork observations and interviews have illuminated, Pacquiao is a cultural powerhouse and he conjures intense diasporic fandom through affective behaviors (feelings and emotions) that manifest in physical and digital spaces of fandom. But part of his, and this, narrative is anchored in a much deeper history of colonial gendering and subjugation of the Philippines economically, politically, and socially. The cross he bears for the nation and the diaspora comes at the cost of demarcating barriers of exclusion, especially against queer people, women, and various "others." Far from laying the burden solely on Pacquiao to effect change in the service of transgender or queer rights, I return to Analissa's sentiments about the power of Pacquiao's voice. He does carry symbolic weight and his words do resonate across various realms of the diaspora. But what might it look like if Pacquiao became a champion not only for the poor, but for those with intersecting identities who are targets of transphobia and homophobia in the Philippines and the diaspora?

As a theoretical move, I have also shown how crossovers create entanglements in the Midwest that are informed by the movements of various colonial state agents, colonized peoples, Indigenous peoples, and the institutions and social actors that structured sporting spectacles. Although the Midwest is hegemonically imagined as a space of rural, white farmer life and reproductions of white masculinity, we have seen that for Filipina/os and Indigenous people of the Philippines it is also a site of trauma, violence, and surveillance, with sports, like those in the Special Olympics, also about asserting US colonial state power. At the same time, the Midwest is also about stories of intimacy, contact, and long histories of community formations that challenge not only how we imagine Asian America but also how we understand working-class immigrant lives, intimacy, and homosociality and how these in turn shape formations of Filipino masculinity.

The crossover is also a challenge to assumptions of assimilation logics and identity formations as a smooth, seamless, and linear process. Although cultural Blackness is embedded in the sport of basketball in amateur, collegiate, and professional ranks, we also see how 1.5- and second-generation Filipino American men in the AB Syndicate "make" and remake their identities and selves not only in relation to cultural Blackness but also through transnational networks and connections, as well as through appropriating symbols and clothing that intentionally mark their difference as ethnic Filipino American men.

As Jenilyn's story illustrates, the crossover is an agentive act, especially for a community that has largely been rendered invisible to the mainstream athletic imagination. In the context of gender, it forces us to consider athleticism beyond assumptions that only men and masculinities can be considered "athletic." This book also refuses to settle for static representations of model minority tropes, Asian American masculine lack, or the various iterations of Asian American women's alleged hyperfemininity and hypersexuality. When we apply the crossover, in all of its complexities, we enter into a site of liminality and therefore possibility in thinking about what could be, where we might go, and what sports can reveal about the nature of citizenship, belonging, agency, contradiction, and possibility. For Filipina and Asian American women playing flag football, the tournaments were an opportunity to excel in a sport against white women who underestimated the former's talent and skills. The flag football field was an arena in which Filipina and Asian American women negotiated their racialized and gendered identities and one in which, through their athleticism, toughness, and swagger, they negotiated and undermined how we conceptualize maleness and masculinity.

This book has aimed to contribute to various academic fields including ethnic studies, Filipina/o studies, American studies, and the anthropology of sport. First, my analysis of sports has built on the existing scholarship of the relatively small but growing cohort of scholars who critically center not only Asian American sporting cultures but also the diverse ways that these communities negotiate different relationships to their community and society and how their sporting identities are shaped by issues of race, class, gender, and sexuality.[2] In building a project informed by ethnic studies, I have prioritized the minoritized community voices of my research participants through oral histories, home movies, and participant observations in global sporting spectacles and smaller-scale, community-created sporting spaces, among other ways. Given the rise of anti-Asian violence in the context of the COVID-19 pandemic, murders of Black people at the hands of the police state, and conservative assaults on critical race theory, this book reminds us of the kinds of ethnic studies scholarship needed to highlight how sporting cultures and practices are not value-free sites of meaning. This book has not only centered an understudied ethnic group and its members' engagement with sports, it has also revealed the various ways that racialized, sexualized, and gendered stereotypes can be usurped, and the paradoxical practices of symbolic and literal exclusion from the fleeting moments of play, joy, pleasure, and pain.

Second, past Filipina/o Studies scholarship on leisure has tended to focus on expressive forms of culture including Pilipino Culture Nights, music, DJing, taxi dance halls, and contemporary dance forms like hip-hop.[3] Although the US sporting industry recognizes and caters to Filipina/o Americans as key consumers, we know very little about how sports are critical arenas to understand larger questions of Filipina/o identity formations, racialization, diasporic contours, and postcolonial sporting cultures. This book has, I hope, broadened conversations with the aforementioned scholarship by placing sports front and center. It is the first of its kind to offer in-depth ethnographic examinations of the significance of sports to the lives of Filipina/o Americans and their enduring connection to the afterlife of US empire, immigration, labor, belonging, citizenship, transnationalism, and identity.

In addition, this book grounds scholarship in the larger contexts of American studies scholarship that critiques the American exceptionalism ethos of sports as a meritocratic institution. Scholars including Neil Lanctot, Adrian Burgos, Bryan Niiya, and Samuel Regalado have explored how race and racism challenge baseball as being an "all American" game in the face of racism, segregation, and Japanese American incarceration.[4]

This book has also challenged the sexist structure of sports whereby, as scholars like Merrie Fidler and Amira Rose Davis show, white women and women of color had, and continue to have, disproportionate access to sports and the pleasures that may be derived from them.[5] I have expanded this scholarship by highlighting how Filipina/o American bodies constitute racial projects as their sporting practices contest, negotiate, and manage racial meanings in relation to their Black and white counterparts. Looking at Filipina/o Americans in basketball, boxing, and flag football spaces disrupts the dominant narratives of Black, white, and to a lesser degree, Latinx athletes. By examining the different experiences of the sports players in this book, I have reexamined historical discourses of participation, and have demonstrated how race as ideology and sport as practice help *make race real* beyond Black and white.

I have contributed to the anthropology of sport to highlight ritual-istic processes and sporting spaces as important sites for the making of selves,[6] spectatorship,[7] and racialized masculinities as well as kinship and care and simultaneous engagements with diaspora, nationalism, transnationalism, and the glocal.[8] In this process, I have also compli-cated current scholarship that, with the exception of Thangaraj's *Desi Hoop Dreams*, does not adequately theorize how gender, race, class, and sexuality are coconstituted within the terrain of identity formation in sporting cultures. Filipina/o Americans are an understudied population in the literature on sports despite US colonialism's role in institutional-izing sports in the Philippines, their relationship to US empire through the Special Olympics, and the long histories of their engagement with sporting cultures in the Philippines, the United States, and in various diasporas around the world.

For Filipina/o diasporas in the United States, sports remain one im-portant social arena in which to cultivate a sense of ethnic community, a sense of belonging to the American national fabric, and in which to crossover into various forms of belonging. Such crossovers destabilize normative strains of belonging to the nation(s) and diasporas, while reimagining terrains of identity formations in nationalist and ethno-nationalist spaces.

I hope that by theorizing the term *crossover* I have demonstrated the management of Filipina/o American identities across spaces and times, identity managements that destabilizes normative understand-ings of Filipina/o American identity to refuse nation, territory, or re-gion. The crossover move is a form of skillful athletic fakery through which one can realize broader ways of understanding nation(s) and diasporas—in this case, Filipina/o Americans' ways of understanding themselves in diaspora and of understanding themselves as part of the US nation too. My engagement with racializations of Asian Americans in general and Filipina/o Americans in particular have questioned and, I hope, disrupted our racializations of these communities as "not Ameri-can enough" nor capable of performing American sporting identities.[9] I have mined the use of the crossover as a conceptual, theoretical, and methodological framework not only to capture how Filipina/o Americans performed a kind of dissimulation in sporting contexts (e.g., by undermining dominant racialized stereotypes through their athletic feats) but also to argue that the performative realm of sport analogously enables them to *cross over* into the porous racialized, gendered, classed, sexualized, and national borders and boundaries.

Because diasporic Filipina/os have traversed borders prior to and during Spanish and US colonialisms that continue in the postcolonial moment, Filipina/o, Spanish, and US culture have always been influenced by cross-pollination, interchange, cultural intermixing, and contact. This book has engaged with this transmission, breaking the footing of scholarship that portrays static and monolithic renditions of Filipina/o lives. Playing and participating in sports like basketball or flag football or cheering on Pacquiao are not simply isolated incidents of pleasure, play, and fandom. Rather, Filipina/o American sporting experiences are mediated by the afterlife of US colonialism and the persistence of social hierarchies at the nexus of race, ethnicity, gender, class, and sexuality. These sporting cultures enable understandings of a wide spectrum of Filipina/o communities and individuals with different relations to belonging. Although their play and fandom can offer political critiques of existing social hierarchies, it is imperative to recognize that these same critiques might not always liberate us from the very same categories we wish to transform. A reckoning with US empire and a much more expansive and intersectional political practice of belonging to the nation and diaspora is necessary if we aim to make sporting spaces truly transformative.

ACKNOWLEDGMENTS

This book is a product of a series of starts, stops, twists, turns, and detours that at times felt incredibly difficult and isolating. And while the words in this book are my own, there are many people who collaborated with me to make it a finished product. I would be remiss if did not acknowledge the community of people who have supported, advocated, and believed in me. I have so many people to thank for their unwavering support. First and foremost, I am grateful to the folks who generously shared their time and energy and, more importantly, their stories with me. A special thank you goes out to the Filipina and Asian American female flag football players for sharing their love, joy, and passion for flag football. I am also thankful to the players in the AB Syndicate, especially its founder, Erik, and some of the players including KC, Thomas, Paulo, and Rodney for allowing me to observe and play ball in the league. To the Urbana-Champaign Filipina/o crew, thank you for welcoming me into your community. I will forever remember the time we spent together on basketball courts, in apartments and houses, and at barbeques.

A special thank you goes out to family and friends who supported me by letting me crash in their spare bedrooms or couches for the summers, winter breaks, or while I was conducting fieldwork. Thank you to Chris and Orchid Arnaldo, Ned and Carisa Realiza, Lori and Eric Cruz, Robbie and Jeanette Rogan, and Lani Desembrana. I especially appreciate Aiza Galdo. Our friendship has spanned decades and I am incredibly grateful to her for being in my life. She has been so supportive of me, was my roommate while I conducted fieldwork, and took on the burden of paying more rent.

My friends from the Bay Area to Long Beach have been incredible sources of inspiration and support. Kathleen Andal and Angie Carillo inspired me go to graduate school and to this day, I'm hella in awe of their brilliance. I am fortunate to have met Carolyn Sideco. I admire her commitment to making sports a much more welcoming, diverse, and transformative space.

I am grateful to Amber Ng, who continues to remind me that I have a place in the academy. Jocelyn Sarigumba is one of the few who knows what it feels like to move far away from home and to live in the Midwest. I appreciate our late evening iChats, especially around a shared understanding of the grad school Midwest struggle. Rachelle Samson is a dear friend and has been a constant advocate of me and my work.

I still remember taking my first ethnic studies class as a third-year college student in Linda España-Maram's Filipino American Experiences class. I was an undeclared major and trying to figure what I wanted to do as a career. Linda is the reason why I chose a PhD in the first place. She encouraged me to pursue a PhD, even when I didn't know what it was. I am forever grateful for her mentorship and friendship. I have relied on her so much at various moments of my life as I navigated college, graduate school, the academy, and life! I owe her a debt of gratitude that I don't think I will ever be able to pay back. I carry her mentorship with me to this day. Her book, *Creating Masculinity in Los Angeles's Little Manila*, especially the chapter "From Living Doll," has deeply shaped how I think about US colonialism and sports in the Philippines.

At the University of Hawai'i, Manoa (UH Manoa), in the American studies department, a number of friends, mentors, and professors guided me through my master's program. I am thankful to David Stannard for his practical advice on how to finish in two years, and I am fortunate to have learned from the late Haunani K. Trask, who taught me so much about resistant politics, settler colonialism, and Hawaiian sovereignty. Thank you to Theodore Gonzalves, Patricia Halagao, Jon Okamura, and Mari Yoshihara. A cohort of friends provided the kind of emotional and intellectual support I needed throughout my time at UH Manoa. Johanna Almiron, Daya Mortel, and J. Lorenzo Perillo sustained me. I carry fond memories of us going to Zippy's to celebrate birthdays or Bubbies to get mochi. They became my family and affirmed me in so many ways. Stephanie Noehlani Teves reminded me that my ideas were important and that my voice mattered. Kristy Ringor, Chihiro Komine Sakihara, and Rochelle Fonoti generously shared their experiences of how to survive graduate school. Although Erin Felarca (in memoriam) was with us a short time, I think about her often.

At California State University, Long Beach, in the department of Asian and Asian American studies, I had the pleasure of working with a group of colleagues and friends who supported me fresh out of my master's program. Thank you to Ferdinand Arcinue, Stewart Chang, Larry Hashima, Barbara Kim, Zeus Leonardo, Linda Maram, and John Tsuchida.

A great many thanks to my colleagues at Miami University, Ohio. Although I was only there for one year, I felt supported. I'm grateful for the lunches, dinners, and coffees and for the advice I received as I was starting my career. A heartfelt thank you to Ken Chaplin, Yu-Fang Cho, Rodney Coates, Roland Sintos Coloma, Anita Mannur, Brian Roley, and Liz Wilson.

While writing a book can feel like an isolated process, this research has benefited from a number of people who believed in my ideas and provided critical and generative comments since its inception. I am thankful to Ryan Buyco, Faith Kares, and J. Lorenzo Perillo for their careful reading of my book proposal. Lorenzo and Rosemary Candelario provided analytical insight to an earlier version of chapter 4, "We're Just as Good and Even Better Than You!" My debt of gratitude also goes out to Tracie Canada and Veena Mani. In addition to keeping me accountable, their sharp comments, insights, and suggestions made the book that much better. I always look forward to our monthly meetings and have learned so much from their brilliance. I am so grateful for their friendship. The book's transformative moments unfolded during a writing retreat organized by Stanley I. Thangaraj, James E. Heydon chair at the Center for the Study of Race, Ethnicity, and Social Justice at Stonehill College. During this retreat, the book became more clear and focused, and the discussion helped clarify the book's narrative arc. It was so great to "get down on it" with Stephanie George, Lauren Hindman, Sara Seweid-DeAngelis, Stanley Thangaraj, and Lucia Trimbur. They pushed my ideas in such profound and critical ways, and they did so with a commitment to a politics and ethics of care. My gratitude to my brother Stan is beyond measure. He is a constant reminder of how to unconditionally love, care for, advocate, and support through a social justice practice. I thank him for his brotherhood and friendship. Thank you also to Alena, Jeya, Louis, and Mango Thangaraj for their generosity, hospitality, and love. I will always carry with me such fond memories of walking and playing board games (I look forward to defending my and Stan's Pictionary title soon!), pool, laser tag, and basketball. I hope to read the rest of Jeya's book one day!

I have met a community of scholars and dear friends in the Association for Asian American Studies (AAAS). Connecting with folks at the annual AAAS conference has kept me grounded. AAAS is my academic home and a place where I feel a sense of belonging. Thank you to Christine Balance, Victor Bascara, Rick Bonus, Tracy Buenavista, Lucy Burns, Pawhan Dhingra, Chris Eng, Kale Fajardo, Mae Farrales, Allen Punzalan Isaac, Lili M. Kim, Valerie Menchavez-Francisco, Bernard Remollino, Robyn Rodriguez, Thomas X. Sarimento, and Allyson Tintiangco-Cubales. The 2018 Association for Asian American Studies Junior Faculty Workshop folks provided feedback of an earlier draft of chapter 3, "They Were Made in the Philippines." Thank you to Jennifer Huynh, Nishant Upadhyay, and Jeannette Roan for pushing my analysis. Many thanks to Jeannette Roan and Oliver Wang for organizing the workshop. A number of critical sports studies scholars have supported me throughout. My thanks to Scott Brooks, Daniel Burdsey, Judy Liao, Jeffrey Montez de Oca, Jorge Moraga, Aarti Ratna, and Nicole Willms. Daniel Burdsey has been especially encouraging and supportive. I thank him for his check-ins and feedback on drafts and for being someone I can always count on.

At the University of Nevada, Las Vegas (UNLV), I have had the pleasure to get to know a number of colleagues who have become allies, close friends, and family. I thank colleagues in the small, but mighty, Interdisciplinary, Gender, and Ethnic Studies (IGES) department for fostering a space of collaboration and support. My gratitude goes out to Erika Abad, Sheila Bock, Lynn Comella, Kendra Gage, Tim Gauthier, Javon Johnson, Brandon Manning, Mark Padoongpatt, Tyler Parry, Allyson Remigio, Anita Revilla, Danielle Roth-Johnson, Susana Sepulveda, Anne Stevens, Valerie Taylor, and Chris Willoughby. They have fostered a critical intellectual space that values research, all while ensuring that our students learn from their brilliance and expertise. Sheila Bock took the time to meet with me and to offer practical advice during our conversational walks on campus. She kept reminding to keep writing. I appreciate Javon Johnson for reminding me to forgive myself when writing days did not feel as productive. Anita Revilla is a dear friend and helped ease my transition to the department. She has been a fierce advocate, reminding me, among other things, to engage in self-care and to give myself grace. She has shown me what radical, loving, social justice practice looks like. I am grateful to have Mark Padoongpatt in my corner. I appreciate him for checking in, meeting for coffee, lunch, and dinner, reading drafts of my work, and ensuring that my benchmarks were met. I am grateful to the IGES department's administrative assistants for ensuring that our department runs smoothly. Thanks to Marian Anderson, Jessica Bradley, Caitlin Moscato, Laurence Reese, and Taylor Iida. Anita Revilla, Anne Stevens, Mark Padoongpatt, and Lynn Comella have been terrific IGES department chairs.

I have also been fortunate to form relationships with a number of people in the College of Liberal Arts (COLA), the College of Education, and Lied Library. Thank you to Mike Alarid, Emma Bloomfield, Raquel Casas, Maile Chapman, Su Kim Chung, Christine Clark, Georgiann Davis, Kristine Espinosa, Desiré Galvez, Tammi Kim, Kari Kokka, Danielle Mireles, Jean Munson, Johansen Pico, Ranita Ray, Cassaundra Rodriguez, Marcela Rodriguez-Campo, Noah Romero, Jeff Schauer, Brittani Sterling, Gary Totten, Karen Villa, Doris Watson, Claytee White, A. B. Wilkinson, and Gloria Wong-Padongpatt. I am profoundly indebted to Christine Clark and Anita Revilla. They both took a chance on me by advocating on my behalf and made it possible for Norma and I to start our careers together. Kari Kokka, Ung-Sang Lee, Lisa Lei, Mark Padoongpatt, Gloria Wong-Padoongpatt, Cassaundra Rodriguez, Jose Avila, Bento, Georgiann Davis, Ranita Ray, Tessa Winkelmann, and Zach Poppel have made Las Vegas feel like home.

My brilliant students at UNLV remind me why I decided to pursue a career as a professor. Thank you to Janah Esplana Balane, Ava Carino, Nicole Espinosa, Enzo Imperial, Isabelle Chen Rice, Angela Tampol, and Izzy Tollefson. Special thank you goes out to my Spring 2023 Filipinx American Experiences students who read the opening narrative of chapter 1, "He's Not Your Champ!" They provided such critical commentary and helped smooth out the vignette.

A number of people at the University of Illinois were such important mentors and friends and have been an integral part of my intellectual journey: Paul Michael L. Atienza, J. B. Capino, Christina Chin, Genevieve Clutario, David Coyoca, Mary Ellerbe, Augusto Espiritu, Sarah

Park Dahlen, Anna Gonzalez, Xavier Hernandez, Kenny Importante, Anthony Jerry, Moon-Kie Jung, Susan Koshy, Viveka Kudaligama, Soo Ah Kwon, Yaejoon Kwon, Esther Kim Lee, Alex Lee, Melissa Littlefield, Christine Lyke, Joyce Mariano, Shantel Martinez, Brian Montes, Ellen Moodie, Lisa Nakamura, Fiona Ngo, Mimi Nguyen, Andy Orta, Naomi Paik, Yoon Pak, Viraj Patel, Christine Peralta, Teresa Ramos, Carolyn Randolf, Ariana Ruiz, Mark Sanchez, Merin Thomas, Mirelsie Velázquez, Tessa Winkelmann, Daniel Wong, and Caroline Yang.

I am immensely grateful to Martin Manalansan, Lisa Cacho, Alejandro Lugo, Junaid Rana, and Richard T. Rodríguez. Their sophisticated analysis and insights throughout graduate school profoundly influenced me. A debt of gratitude goes to Martin Manalansan. He embodies the kind of scholar, mentor, and teacher I strive to be. He provided practical advice whenever I was stuck writing and reminded me, in true ethnographic fashion, to start with a story as an entry point to examine larger themes. He made writing less daunting by talking me through ideas, providing feedback on some of my drafts, and was gentle, kind, and encouraging. His presence is felt throughout the book. During the early stages of this research, Lisa Cacho poked and prodded me to think more deeply about sports, nation, race, masculinity, and belonging. I am grateful to her for enriching my analysis and for her astute observations about my own lived experiences playing and watching sports. Alejandro Lugo advocated for me to come to the University of Illinois anthropology department. I thank him for nurturing a sense of community, especially during my first year as I navigated the Midwest. I also thank Junaid Rana for his mentorship and for his feedback on some of my early research proposals. He knew I had more to explore and more to say. Richard T. Rodríguez has been a source of support from the beginning and has become a dear friend. I love our conversations about popular culture and the minutiae of everyday life. I am a better scholar because of Martin, Lisa, Alejandro, Junaid, and Ricky.

This book was supported by funding from the Asian American, Native American, Pacific Islander Serving Institutions (AANAPISI) summer research program, as well as the UNLV COLA summer research fellowship. The AANAPISI program enabled me to visit the Filipino American National Historical Society archives. At the archives, I met

Dorothy Cordova, and she graciously shared her knowledge about Filipina/o Americans and sports and pointed me to a number of archives that provided important context for this research. Many thanks also goes to Dorothy Fujita-Rony who helped workshop some key ideas for the book's themes. UNLV's COLA fellowship allowed me to carve out precious summer writing time to finalize the book proposal and complete two chapters.

The folks at NYU Press have been a pleasure to work with and have made publishing the book feel like a seamless endeavor. Many thanks to Veronica Knutson and Ainee Jeong for fielding my many questions about image and copyright use. My deep appreciation to the anonymous reviewers who provided critical and generative feedback throughout the book's stages. I am so thankful to my editor, Jennifer Hammer for believing in this project. She has such an incredible eye for detail, rigor, and critical engagement. I appreciate her feedback and for ensuring I was clear, concise, and accessible. I owe a special thanks to Jordan Beltran Gonzales, Ulrike Guthrie, and Martha Murray for helping clarify my ideas and helping me write with a clearer authorial voice.

Thank you to the Arnaldo families for supporting me throughout my journey. A special thank you to the Realiza clan for nourishing my love for sports and sharing in the joys and pains of Bay Area team fandom. There are four people in my family who didn't live to see the book published. My late father Constancio Buclatin Arnaldo, my maternal grandmother Lucia Castillo Realiza, my uncle Daniel "Danny" Mendoza, and my uncle Frederick "Freddie" Rodrigo. My father died when I was young and while my memories of him are sparse, I still remember how much he loved watching the Oakland A's and the San Francisco 49ers—and watching my brothers and I play little league baseball. Lucia Realiza, who dedicated her life to teaching children in the Philippines, was my spiritual adviser and greatest teacher. Although my uncle Danny passed away while I was in graduate school, I know that he would have celebrated this book. He was the first to share his knowledge of Filipina/o American history with me and was a living testament to the pursuit of knowledge. My uncle Freddie passed away as I was completing the book. I'm grateful to him for being such a constant presence in my life, especially after my father passed away. He always reminded me of how proud he was of my educational accomplishments.

My love for sports began with my parents. While my late father was the reason my brothers and I played sports, my mother, Beulah Arnaldo-Dionson, was responsible for our continued engagement. I thank my mom for the love she gave to my brothers and I, for a work ethic I try to emulate, and for her unwavering faith and love for me. I thank my stepfather Ruben Dionson for his unconditional support. Nat and Chris have been supremely supportive of me and my book journey. Although they don't quite fully understand what I'm writing about, they still found time to check-in and ask how my book was coming along. I can't thank my sisters-in-law Diane Arnaldo and Orchid Arnaldo enough for their support. I'm grateful to have such wonderful relationships with them. I'm grateful to my extended family, Nena Castañeda, Mama Esperanza Guzman, as well as Mama Josefina and Papa Ricardo Marrun for treating me like family.

My furry family companions and desert tortoise bring me tremendous joy. Smokey, our fiercely loyal maltipoo reminds me that it never hurts to ask (especially for treats). Bruno, our bundle of energy, mixed wheaten terrier poodle reminds me to have fun, play, and go for walks. And of course, Bernie, our desert tortoise, reminds me that it's OK to sleep for extended periods and to be patient because I will eventually get to my destination.

Finally, to my partner, Norma A. Marrun, my best friend and confidante. It is difficult to capture in writing how much she has enriched my life. Norma has sustained me through the arduous process of graduate school, applying for jobs, writing a book, and more. She has been on this journey with me since day one, reading every draft, helping me hash out ideas, asking me critical questions, and forcing me to think about how and why *sports matter* to me and my community. She has witnessed how writing the book has frustrated me and, at times, brought me despair. And yet she has seen my excitement when an idea emerges that captures the poetics, politics, and deep pleasures of sports, play, and fandom. She reminds me to forgive myself when I am being too hard on myself and to celebrate the big wins as well as the small ones. She reminds me that there is another day if yesterday wasn't a good one. And she reminds me that no matter what, she loves and supports me.

NOTES

INTRODUCTION

1 The majority of this fieldwork occurred during a time (from 2009 to 2019) when the term "Filipinx" was not commonly used in community circles or in the academic community. Although the *x* signifies gender neutrality and gender inclusion for transgender, genderqueer, or nonbinary people, it is also a political act of solidarity with the Latinx community. However, to honor how my interlocutors self-identified based on gender, I use the terms *Filipino* American or *Filipina* American as an identity marker. See Coráñez Bolton, "Tale of two Xs"; Nievera-Lozano, introduction to *Pilipinx Radical Imagination Reader*.

2 To maintain confidentiality, I assigned pseudonyms to all interview participants.

3 Thangaraj, *Desi Hoop Dreams*.

4 Bayne, "Schoolyard Game."

5 Connell, *Masculinities*.

6 España-Maram, *Creating Masculinity*, 92.

7 US Census Bureau, "Filipino Alone," 2020.

8 Shankar, *Advertising Diversity*.

9 Anthropologist Rachael Joo and literary scholar Sameer Pandya note that there is a critical mass of Asian American fans in the NBA. Joo and Pandya, "On the Cultural Politics of Asian American Sports."

10 Thangaraj, *Desi Hoop Dreams*.

11 Ferguson, *Aberrations in Black*; Fujiwara and Roshanravan, *Asian American Feminism and Women of Color Politics*; Hong and Ferguson, *Strange Affinities*.

12 Ferguson, *Aberrations in Black*; Reddy, *Freedom with Violence*; see also Manalansan, "Messing Up Sex."

13 Hong and Ferguson, *Strange Affinities*.

14 Gopinath, *Impossible Desires*.

15 Manalansan, *Global Divas*, 144.

16 Halberstam, *Female Masculinity*, 1.

17 Rodriguez, *Migrants for Export*; Francisco-Menchavez, *Labor of Care*; Fajardo, *Filipino Crosscurrents*.

18 Rodriguez, *Migrants for Export*.

19 Francisco-Menchavez, *Labor of Care*.

20 For an excellent analysis of deprivileging land-based approaches to Filipina/o movement and immigration, see Fajardo, *Filipino Crosscurrents*.

21 Thangaraj, "We Share the Same Ancestry."

22 Gonzalves, *Day the Dancers Stayed*; Balance, *Tropical Renditions*; Tiongson, *Filipinos Represent*; Wang, *Legions of Boom*; España-Maram, *Creating Masculinity*; Burns, *Puro Arte*; Perillo, *Choreographing in Color*.

23 Diaz, Largo, and Pino, *Diasporic Intimacies*, 183–98; Farrales, "Colonial, Settler Colonial Tactics."

24 Aquino, "More than a Game."

25 James, *Beyond a Boundary*.

26 Yep, *Outside the Paint*, 2009; Thangaraj, Arnaldo, and Chin, *Asian American Sporting Cultures*; Thangaraj, *Desi Hoop Dreams*; Willms, *When Women Rule the Court*; Chin, "We've Got Team Spirit!"

27 Baldoz, *Third Asiatic Invasion*; Jamero, *Growing Up Brown*; Empeno, "Anti-Miscegenation Laws." Although *brown* is a US-based racial signifier for Filipino Americans, we must not forget how Black Filipino Amerasians in the Philippines are marginalized and continue to face discrimination. See Allen, "Black Filipino Amerasian Identity."

28 Brown, as a fluid concept is not unique to Filipina/o Americans. Critical sports studies scholar Jorge Moraga deploys brown to analyze how Latino/a/x people negotiate the Black-white racial paradigm. He writes, "'Brownness,' therefore, is not simply a substitute to understand or consider Latino/a/x people in relation to socio-political systems." Moraga, "Riverboat Ron," 11.

29 See also Ho, *Racial Ambiguity in Asian American Culture*.

30 Lasco, "Little Brown Brothers."

31 Parreñas, "'White Trash' Meets the 'Little Brown Monkeys.'"

32 España-Maram, "Brown 'Hordes' in McIntosh Suits," 5.

33 Posadas, "Hierarchy of Color."

34 Parreñas, "'White Trash' Meets the 'Little Brown Monkeys.'"

35 Burns, *Puro Arte*; Espiritu, *Home Bound*.

36 España-Maram, *Creating Masculinity*, 81, 102; Remollino, "Scrapping into a Knot."

37 Mabalon, *Little Manila Is in the Heart*.

38 For a discussion on how Filipino Americans made claims to belonging through racial heteronormativity, see Volpp, "American Mestizo." For a discussion on their claims to citizenship, Chuh, *Imagine Otherwise*. For a discussion on diasporic subjectivity, see Vergara, *Pinoy Capital*.

39 Lowe, *Immigrant Acts*.

40 Thangaraj, *Desi Hoop Dreams*.

41 Ngo, "Punk in the Shadow of War"; Ferguson, *Aberrations in Black*; Gopinath, *Impossible Desires*; Gopinath *Unruly Visions*.

42 Thangaraj, Arnaldo, and Chin, *Asian American Sporting Cultures*.

43 Thangaraj, "Playing through Differences"

44 Manalansan, *Global Divas*; Gopinath, *Impossible Desires*; Reddy, *Freedom with Violence*; Ferguson, *Aberrations in Black*.

45 Thangaraj, "I Was Raised Buddhist."

46 Rafael, *White Love and Other Events in Filipino History*; Ocampo, *Latinos of Asia*; Empeno, "Anti-Miscegenation Laws"; Balce, "Filipino Bodies, Lynching, and the Language of Empire," 43–60.

47 Theberge, "Toward a Feminist Alternative to Sport as a Male Preserve."

48 Chin and Andrews, "Mixed Martial Arts."

49 Reft, "From Perpetual Foreigner to Pacific Rim Entrepreneur."

50 Analyzing Black films, Sheppard uses the term *critical muscle memory* as a kinesthetic metaphor "to theorize Black corporeality, individuality, and sociality." Sheppard, *Sporting Blackness*, 14.

51 The anthropologists Nancy Scheper-Hughes and Margaret M. Lock assert, "We will begin from an assumption of the body as simultaneously a physical and symbolic artifact, as both naturally and culturally produced, and as securely anchored in a particular historical moment." Nancy Scheper-Hughes and Lock, "Mindful Body," 7.

52 Francisco, "First Vietnam"

53 Kramer, *Blood of Government*.

54 See España-Maram, *Creating Masculinity*.

55 Lasco, "Little Brown Brothers." See also Kramer, *Blood of Government*, 200; Bernardo, "From 'Little Brown Brothers' to 'Forgotten Asian Americans.'"

56 Balce, "Filipino Bodies, Lynching, and the Language of Empire."

57 Kramer, *Blood of Government*, 200.

58 Remollino, "Scrapping into a Knot."

59 Of course, simian characteristics were also mapped onto Filipinos bodies and manifested in other spaces of leisure like taxi dance halls. See Burns, *Puro Arte*; España-Maram, *Creating Masculinity*; Parreñas, "'White Trash' Meets the 'Little Brown Monkeys.'"

60 *Philippine Souvenir Booklet*.

61 de la Cruz, Baluyut, and Reyes, *Confrontations, Crossings, and Convergence*; Parezo, "Special Olympics."

62 Reyes, "Image into Sequence." See also Vergara, *Displaying Filipinos*; Balce, *Body Parts of Empire*.

63 Unknown artist, *Boston Sunday Globe*, March 5, 1899, reprinted in de la Cruz et al., *Forbidden Book*, 80. See also Winkelmann, *Dangerous Intercourse*. Running "amuck" was also about racializing Filipinos in Mindanao.

64 Mills, *Racial Contract*.

65 Perillo, *Choreographing in Color*, 9.

66 See Perillo, *Choreographing in Color*.

67 Hong and Ferguson, *Strange Affinities*. See also Thangaraj, *Desi Hoop Dreams*.

68 España-Maram, *Creating Masculinity*.

69 Sociologist Oliver Wang refers to Filipina/o immigration as "waves." Wang, *Legions of Boom*.

70 The *Filipino Student Bulletin* was a newsletter that circulated throughout various Filipino student organizations.

71 Note for example, how one *Student Bulletin* emphasized the following: "Remember at all times that you are representing the Filipino people and the thousands of Americans will judge the whole Filipino race by the way you live. You have been sent here primarily to acquire scholarship, but the development of your moral fiber and the maintaining of high moral standards are essential for your future usefulness in life as well As for the instilling of a high conception of Filipino character into the minds of the American people. For patriotic motives alone, for no other reason you are duty bound not only to live an exemplary life yourself, but also encourage other Filipino students to live the same." *Filipino Student Bulletin* II, no. 1 (October 1923), Filipino American National Historical Society Archives. See Anderson, *Colonial Pathologies*.

72 España-Maram, *Creating Masculinity*; Mabalon, *Little Manila Is in the Heart*; Poblete, *Islanders in the Empire*; Posadas and Guyotte, "Unintentional Immigrants."

73 Mabalon, *Little Manila Is in the Heart*. See also, Doolan, "Transpacific Camptowns."

74 DeWitt, "Watsonville Anti-Filipino Riot of 1930."

75 Dewitt, "Watsonville Anti-Filipino Riot of 1930."

76 Volpp, "American Mestizo."

77 Bulosan, *America Is in the Heart*, 101.

78 Litsky, "Victoria Manalo Draves."

79 Mabalon, *Little Manila Is in the Heart*; Yep, *Outside the Paint*.

80 Jamero, *Growing up Brown*.

81 Herbert, "Growing up Brown in America," 51.

82 Herbert, "Growing up Brown in America," 61.

83 For seminal work on Filipina nurses see Ceniza Choy, *Empire of Care*.

84 Nursing and the military are directly connected to US colonialism in the Philippines. See Suarez, "Militarized Filipino Masculinity."

85 Thangaraj, "I Was Raised Buddhist," *Desi Hoop Dreams*.

86 Joo and Pandya, "On the Cultural Politics of Asian American Sports."

87 Appadurai, *Modernity at Large*.

88 Manalansan, introduction to *Cultural Compass*, 5.

89 Twitter has since changed its name to X.

90 Arnaldo, "I'm Thankful for Manny."

91 Marcus, "Ethnography in/of the World System."

92 Specifically, the MGM Grand Garden Arena and the Las Vegas Strip.

93 1.5-generation connotes a person who was born in the Philippines but migrated to the United States at a young age. However, more than simply migrating to the United States as children, the 1.5-generation experience simultaneous feelings of belonging and exclusion in both the country of origin and the receiving country. At the same time, they have the ability to navigate the cultural terrain in both countries. See Rumbaut, "Ages, Life Stages, and Generational Cohorts."

94 Sands, *Sport Ethnography*. See also De Garis, "Experiments in Pro Wrestling"; Thangaraj, *Desi Hoop Dreams*.

95 Diaz, *Postcolonial Configurations*; San Juan, "Overseas Filipino Workers."
96 It is worth noting that despite the US institutionalizing Western-style medicine in the Philippines, her father *was still* expected to pass an additional exam in the United States.
97 Shah, *Contagious Divides*; Eng, *Racial Castration*.
98 Lipsitz, *Possessive Investment in Whiteness*; Harris, "Whiteness as Property."

1. "HE'S NOT YOUR CHAMP!"
1 Arnaldo, "Undisputed Racialised Masculinities."
2 Mossière, "Sharing in Ritual Effervescence."
3 Andrews and Jackson, *Sports Stars*; Jacobs, "Get Used to Me."
4 Joshi, *White Christian Privilege*. See also Kim, *Race for Revival*. In the introduction to *Race for Revival*, Helen Jin Kim describes how in Korea, Billy Graham's white Christian masculinity works in relation to Korean pastor Billy Kim in what is one of Graham's largest groups of Christian converts ever.
5 Moore, *I Fight for a Living*.
6 Putney, *Muscular Christianity*, 6.
7 Ladd and Mathisen, *Muscular Christianity*.
8 Arnaldo, "Manny 'Pac-Man' Pacquiao."
9 Tadiar, *Fantasy Production*.
10 Woodward, "Material Culture and Narrative," 61
11 Comella, *Vibrator Nation*; Maginn and Steinmetz, *(Sub)Urban Sexscapes*.
12 *Pan de sal* is a type of bread roll.
13 Manalansan and Espiritu, *Filipino Studies*.
14 Velasco, *Queering the Global Filipina Body*.
15 Antolihao, *Playing with the Big Boys*, 29
16 España-Maram, *Creating Masculinity*; See also Antolihao, *Playing with the Big Boys*.
17 Gems, *Athletic Crusade*, 10.
18 Montez de Oca, *Discipline and Indulgence*.
19 Hoganson, *Fighting for American Manhood*.
20 España-Maram, *Creating Masculinity*, 84.
21 España-Maram, *Creating Masculinity*; Svinth, "Origins of Philippines Boxing, 1899–1929"; Sheehan, "Little Giants of the Ring."
22 España-Maram, *Creating Masculinity*.
23 España-Maram, *Creating Masculinity*.
24 Murashako, "Manny Pacquiao is a 'Bible-Quoting Maniac.'"
25 Mitchell, "Manny Pacquiao."
26 Murashko, "Manny Pacquiao Is a 'Bible-Quoting Maniac."
27 Arnaldo, "I'm Thankful for Manny."
28 Putney, *Muscular Christianity*.
29 Thangaraj, *Desi Hoop Dreams*; Eng, *Racial Castration*; Kim, *Writing Manhood in Black and Yellow*.

30 España-Maram, *Creating Masculinity*, 81.
31 See Hall, *Representation*.
32 Hall, *Representation*, xxv–xxvi.
33 Hall, "Encoding and Decoding in Televisual Discourse."
34 Hall, "Cultural Identity and Diaspora."
35 Interestingly, Filipina American boxer, Ana Julaton, a highly successful boxer in her own right, was not mentioned as a successful athlete.
36 See Okamura, *Imagining the Filipino American Diaspora*.
37 Goffman, *Presentation of Self in Everyday Life*.
38 Appadurai, *Modernity at Large*.
39 In 2010, Pacquiao and comedian Will Farrell appeared on *Jimmy Kimmel Live!* and sang John Lennon's "Imagine." Walter Fraizer, "Will Ferrell, Manny Pacquiao Cover John Lennon's 'Imagine,'" *Billboard*, November 2, 2010, www.billboard.com.
40 See Vergara, *Pinoy Capital*.
41 See Basch, Schiller, and Blanc, *Nations Unbound*.
42 Osborne, "Boxer, Godfather, Politician."
43 Osborne, "Boxer, Godfather, Politician."
44 INCITE! Women of Color against Violence, *The Revolution Will Not Be Funded*.
45 Aguilar-San Juan, "Filipinx American Activism."
46 Putney, *Muscular Christianity*.
47 Johnson, "Sincerely, These Hands."
48 Thangaraj, *Desi Hoop Dreams*.
49 Southpaw means that the boxer stands with their right foot forward and jabs with their right. Orthodox means the boxer stands with their left foot forward and jabs with their left.
50 Arnaldo, "Undisputed."
51 Novio, "Why My God Won't Show Up."
52 Carrington, *Race, Sport and Politics*, 2.
53 Jun, *Race for Citizenship*.
54 Carrington, "Race."
55 Feagin, *White Racial Frame*.
56 Carrington, *Race, Sport and Politics*.
57 See Omi and Winant, *Racial Formation in the United States*.
58 Manny Pacquiao (@mannypacquiao), "I rather obey the Lord's command than obeying the desires of the flesh," February 15, 2016, https://www.instagram.com/p/BB1Nk83OdzT/.
59 See Sullivan-Blum, "It's Adam and Eve, Not Adam and Steve."
60 Dudley Rutherford, for example, was part of a group of two hundred church leaders who condemned *Christianity Today*'s op-ed criticizing former US president Donald Trump and calling for his removal. Rutherford, "Nearly 200 Evangelical Leaders Slam Christianity Today." See also Thangaraj et al., "Leisure and the Racing of National Populism."
61 Gopinath, *Impossible Desire*.

62 Kang, "Idols of Development."

63 Velasco, *Queering the Global Filipina Body.*

64 I honor how Annalisa identifies as Pilipinx American that reflects both their ethnic identity and gender pronoun (i.e., *x* as more gender inclusive and gender neutral). Whereas all my interlocuters self-identified according to their gender identities (e.g., Filipina or Filipino American), Annalisa self identifies as "Pilipinx" instead of Filipinx because there is no phonetic *ph* or *f* sound indigenous to the Philippine language. See note 1 in the introduction of this book.

65 de la Cruz et al., *Forbidden Book*, 83–84.

66 Muñoz, *Disidentifications.* See also, Siu, "Queen of the Chinese Colony."

2. "YO, POGI!"

1 Soriano's is a pseudonym.

2 Lumpia is a type of Filipino spring roll.

3 US Census Bureau, "Quick Facts," 2020.

4 Bonus, *Locating Filipino Americans.*

5 Vega, *Latino Heartland.*

6 See Thangaraj, *Desi Hoop Dreams.*

7 Halvorson and Reno, *Imagining the Heartland*, 5.

8 Halvorson and Reno, *Imagining the Heartland*, 16.

9 Sugrue, *Origins of the Urban Crisis.*

10 Lowenstein, "Health Industry."

11 Baseball as the American national pastime is a metaphor for the US nation itself. As Jacques Barzun famously quipped, "Whoever wants to know the heart and mind of America had better learn baseball." Cited in Guthrie-Shimizu, *Transpacific Field of Dreams*, 10.

12 The "Black Sox Scandal" involved eight white male baseball players who were accused and later acquitted of intentionally losing the 1919 World Series against the Cincinnati Reds.

13 Sobchack, "Baseball in the Post-American Cinema," 14.

14 Thangaraj, "Masculinities"; Vega, *Latino Heartland.*

15 Manalansan et al., "Queering the Middle."

16 Manalansan et al., "Queering the Middle." See also Fajardo, "Queering and Transing the Great Lakes."

17 I follow literary scholar Stephen Sumida's lead in decentering the West Coast. Sumida, "East of California." See also Manalansan et al., "Queering the Middle."

18 Hoganson, *Heartland*, xxv.

19 Bulosan, *America Is in the Heart*; Castillo, *America Is Not the Heart.*

20 de la Cruz et al., *Confrontations, Crossings, and Convergence*; Reyes, "Image into Sequence." This did not mean that Indigenous people did not assert their agency. Antero, who was part of the Bontoc Igorot tribe on the Philippine reservation, came to the United States for a sense of adventure. He also sought to earn money to make a living and improve his life once he returned to the Philippines. He

eventually married and has a daughter who was born in the United States. See Public Broadcasting Service, *Asian Americans.*

21 Foucault, *Discipline and Punish.* This Special Olympics in 1904 is distinct from our contemporary understanding. The Special Olympics today is an annual sporting event organized for people with intellectual and physical disabilities.

22 Pilapil, "Dogtown U.S.A."

23 See Guiliano, *Indian Spectacle.*

24 Approximately 1.5 hours northeast of Urbana-Champaign is Pekin, Illinois. In 1820, surveyors believed that the town was geographically linked to Peking, China, and named the local town Pekin. In the 1930s, Pekin High school named their school mascots after a "Chink," a Chinese racial slur. After several attempts by the Organization of Chinese Americans to remove the school mascot it was not until 1975 when it was officially "retired." See Billings and Edward Black, *Mascot Nation.*

25 I intentionally use Igorot or Indigenous people of the Philippines to complicate hegemonic and taken-for-granted readings of "Filipinx/a/o" ethnoracial categories. See Ruanto-Ramirez, "Why I Don't (Really) Consider Myself a Filipinx."

26 Pilapil, "Dogtown U.S.A."

27 Thaman, "Wydown Middle School's Mascot."

28 Mendoza, *Metroimperial Intimacies*; Sarmiento, "To Return to Saint Louis."

29 Sarmiento, "To Return to Saint Louis."

30 Parezo, "Special Olympics."

31 Sarmiento, "To Return to Saint Louis."

32 For a cogent analysis of conceptualizing the Midwest as the heartland of American empire, see Sarmiento's "To Return to Saint Louis"; see also Posadas and Guyotte, "Unintentional Immigrants," 2.

33 Posadas and Guyotte, "Unintentional Immigrants," 27.

34 We must not forget that Chicago also has a large Latinx (specifically Mexican American) community. See Vega, *Latino Heartland*

35 Posadas and Guyotte, "Unintentional Immigrants."

36 Posadas and Guyotte, "Unintentional Immigrants"; Parreñas, "'White Trash' Meets the 'Little Brown Monkeys'"; España-Maram, *Creating Masculinity*; Burns, *Puro Arte.*

37 Burns, *Puro Arte*; España-Maram, *Creating Masculinity*; Parreñas, "'White Trash' Meets the 'Little Brown Monkeys'"; Posadas and Guyotte, "Unintentional Immigrants."

38 See Puar and Rai, "Monster, Terrorist, Fag." Puar and Rai showcase the discursive constructions of South Asians after 9/11 as emasculated, nerdy, and queer and thus hypomasculine while also framing them as terrorists and monsters. Such discursive productions allow us to see the queering of South Asian American racialization and the unmarking of whiteness through the patriot. See also Thangaraj, *Desi Hoop Dreams.*

39 Ho, *Racial Ambiguity in Asian American Culture*; Thangaraj, *Desi Hoop Dreams*; Bow, *Partly Colored*.

40 Lowenstein, "Health Industry."

41 Lowenstein, "Health Industry."

42 Francisco-Menchavez, *Labor of Care*; Parreñas, *Servants of Globalization*; Velasco, "Performing the Filipina 'Mail-Order Bride.'"

43 Dhingra, "Being American Between Black and White"; Lee, "Asian American Studies in the Midwest"; Sumida, "East of California"; Thangaraj, *Desi Hoop Dreams*.

44 Posadas and Guyotte, "Unintentional Immigrants." As the literary scholar, Thomas X. Sarmiento notes, the United States is a "critical node in the circuits of Asian migration to the United States—whether forced or voluntarily—disrupting the conventional narrative that positions the Pacific and, to a lesser extent, the Atlantic coasts as always central to Asian America." Sarmiento, "To Return to St. Louis."

45 Vega, *Latino Heartland*.

46 Francisco-Menchavez, *Labor of Care*.

47 See Manalansan, "'Stuff' of Archives."

48 Thangaraj, *Desi Hoop Dreams*.

49 Bonus, *Locating Filipino Americans*, 60.

50 Ahmed, *Queer Phenomenology*.

51 Mabalon, "As American as Jackrabbit Adobo."

52 Padoongpatt, *Flavors of Empire*, 4.

53 Gupta and Ferguson, "Beyond 'Culture.'"

54 See Bonus, *Locating Filipino Americans*.

55 Bonus, *Locating Filipino Americans*; and Manalansan, *Global Divas*.

56 Bonus, *Locating Filipino Americans*, 71.

57 Stuckey, *Slave Culture*.

58 Carter, "On the Need for an Anthropological Approach to Sport," 412.

59 African Americans have experienced long histories of police brutality, including the 2009 murder of fifteen-year-old African American Kiwane Carrington, while also demanding justice. See, for example, Cha-Jua, "We Believe It Was Murder."

60 See Burton, "Captivity, Kinship, and Black Masculine Care Work under Domestic Warfare." See also Arnaldo, "'Undisputed' Racialised Masculinities"; Inhorn, *New Arab Man*; Thangaraj, "Masculinities."

61 Shimizu, *Straitjacket Sexualities*. See also Thangaraj, "I Was Raised Buddhist."

62 Boodle means candy or treat, and fight also means a party. Thus, a boodle fight is a party where candy or treats are enjoyed by its consumers.

63 Bender and De Leon, "Everybody was Boodle Fighting."

64 Manalansan, "Beyond Authenticity," 291.

65 Manalansan, "Beyond Authenticity."

66 Bender and De Leon, "Everybody was Boodle Fighting."

67 Bender and De Leon, "Everybody was Boodle Fighting." For further exploration of the relationship between food, immigration, authenticity, and US colonialism, see Orquiza *Taste of Control*; Mabalon, *Little Manila Is in the Heart*; and Manalansan "Beyond Authenticity."
68 See Velasco, *Queering the Filipina Body*.
69 Theberge, "Toward a Feminist Alternative to Sport as a Male Preserve."
70 Douglas, "Deciphering a Meal," 61.
71 Connell, *Masculinities*, 71.
72 Abdurraqib, "It Rained in Ohio."

3. "THEY WERE MADE IN THE PHILIPPINES"

1 Tsing, *Friction*.
2 Literary scholar Denise Cruz writes about the complexity and politics of ethical fashion through Filipina Canadian Caroline Mangosing's couture fashion line. She discusses the transnational, gender, and labor politics embedded in its production. See Cruz, "Splitting the Seams."
3 Thangaraj, *Desi Hoop Dreams*.
4 Majors and Billson, *Cool Pose*.
5 A key aspect of South Asian American masculinity-making involves consumption and appropriation of cultural Blackness and Black stylistics as an acceptable basketball style. However, as Thangaraj reminds us, consumption of Black stylistics is "devoid of its political embers" as some of the South Asian American men discriminate against African American men. See Thangaraj, *Desi Hoop Dreams*, 64.
6 Boyd, *Young, Black, Rich, and Famous*.
7 Kobe Bryant has since died as a result of a helicopter crash in Calabasas, California, in 2020.
8 Although there are significant pockets of Asian Americans (Vietnamese especially), Orange County has a history of racism and white supremacist violence against people of color. See Lewinnek, Arellano, and Vo Dang, *A People's Guide to Orange County*.
9 Yep, *Outside the Paint*.
10 Chin, "We've Got Team Spirit!"; Willms, *When Women Rule the Court*.
11 Majors and Billson, *Cool Pose*; Thangaraj, *Desi Hoop Dreams*.
12 Larke-Walsh, *Screening the Mafia*. See also Stanley I. Thangaraj's excellent ethnography of South Asian American basketball players taking cues from popular culture films like *Untouchables*. Thangaraj, Desi Hoop Dreams.
13 Larke-Walsh, *Screening the Mafia*.
14 Hong, *Ruptures of American Capital*.
15 Cruz, "Splitting the Seams."
16 "Doing good," Mariano writes, involves "philanthropic initiatives, related discourses and collective practices of generosity, obligation, and the context of their institutionalization—as an interpretive framework for understanding the

processes of Filipino diaspora formation animated by linked moral figurations of migration and returns." Mariano, *Giving Back*, 34–35.

17 The website keeps track of basketball statistics including scoring, rebounds, steals, assists, and blocks.

18 Clifford, *Routes*.

19 See España-Maram, *Creating Masculinity*.

20 Brooks, *Black Men Can't Shoot*, ix.

21 Thangaraj, *Desi Hoop Dreams*.

22 Brooks, *Black Men Can't Shoot*, 31.

23 Thangaraj, *Desi Hoop Dreams*, 94.

24 I have found over twenty-five Filipino American basketball leagues and annual tournaments throughout the United States.

25 For scholarship on diasporic Filipino men playing basketball, see Aquino, "More than a Game"; Farrales, "Colonial, Settler Colonial Tactics"; Diaz, Largo, and Pino, *Diasporic Intimacies*.

26 Wang, "Living with Linsanity."

27 Thangaraj, *Desi Hoop Dreams*. See also Gilroy, *Black Atlantic*.

28 See Eng, *Racial Castration*.

29 Kim, *Writing Manhood in Black and Yellow*; Thangaraj, *Desi Hoop Dreams*.

30 Carey, Millington, and Prouse, "Branding Boundaries," 226.

31 Anderson, *Imagined Communities*.

32 Shimizu, *Straitjacket Sexualities*.

33 España-Maram, *Creating Masculinity*; Parreñas, "'White Trash' Meets the 'Little Brown Monkeys.'"

34 Fujiwara and Roshanravan, *Asian American Feminism and Women of Color Politics*.

35 For an astute analysis of how Filipina/o and Filipina/o Americans navigate hip-hop in the context of race and US empire, see Perillo, *Choreographing in Color*.

36 Kelley, *Yo Mama's Disfunktional!*.

37 Lock and Farquhar, *Beyond the Body Proper*.

38 Aquino, "More than a Game."

39 Lowe, *Intimacies of Four Continents*.

40 Arevalo, "Philippine Flag."

41 DeMello, *Bodies of Inscription*; Fisher, "Tattooing the Body, Marking Culture."

42 Thangaraj, *Desi Hoop Dreams*; Aquino, *Racism and Resistance in the Filipino Diaspora*.

43 This is more commonly known by Filipino American ballers as *alibata*.

44 Arugelles, "Alibata Tattoos and the Search for Indigenous Filipino Culture."; Arguelles, "More than Skin Deep."

45 Arugelles, "Alibata Tattoos and the Search for Indigenous Filipino Culture."

46 Strobel, "Born Again Filipino."

47 Thangaraj, "Ballin' Indo-Pak Style."

48 Fisher, "Tattooing the Body, Marking Culture"; Chuh, *Imagine Otherwise*.

49 "Jeremy Lin," NBA, accessed January 9, 2021. http://www.nba.com/players/jeremy/lin/202391.
50 Thangaraj, "Ballin' Indo-Pak Style"; Prashad, *Karma of Brown Folk.*
51 Joo and Pandya, "On the Cultural Politics of Asian American Sports"; Wang, "Everybody Loves an Underdog"; Yep, "Linsanity and Centering Sport."
52 Chin, "Aren't You a Little Short to Play Ball?"; Thangaraj, *Desi Hoop Dreams*; Willms, *When Women Rule the Court.*
53 Tiongson, *Filipinos Represent.*
54 Fouché, *Game Changer.*
55 Tiongson, *Filipinos Represent.*
56 Toffoletti and Mewett, *Sport and Its Female Fans.*

4. "WE'RE JUST AS GOOD AND EVEN BETTER THAN YOU!"

I thank the *Journal of Asian American Studies* for allowing me to publish chapter 4. I have added a few ethnographic moments and applied Cheryl Harris's whiteness as property theoretical framework. Constancio R. Arnaldo, Jr., "'We're Just as Good and Even Better than You': Asian American Female Flag Footballers and the Racial Politics of Competition," *Journal of Asian American Studies* 24, no. 1 (February 2021): 115–44.

1 Eisenberg, "FSU Sorority Sister Is Back."
2 Flag football is played differently than tackle football for one glaring reason: it does not require tackling. Whereas in football, a player is ruled down after the opponent either knocks or tackles them to the ground or pushes them outside of the playing boundary, in flag football, the players pull flags to down an opponent. In flag football, offensive and defensive players wear cloth belts with Velcro flags hanging from their waists. When an offensive player possesses the football, the defender pulls the flag from the belt in order for the play to be ruled down. Tackling is prohibited.
3 Hong, *Ruptures of American Capital.* See also Fujiwara and Roshanravan, *Asian American Feminism and Women of Color Politics.*
4 Chin and Andrews, "Mixed Martial Arts."
5 Chin and Andrews, "Mixed Martial Arts."
6 Hong, *Ruptures of American Capital.*
7 See also España-Maram, *Creating Masculinity.*
8 I am aware that flag football is played differently than tackle football. However, the former is still considered a masculine sport and contains some of the same kinds of cultural processes in tackle football.
9 The March 16, 2021, Atlanta Spa shootings were yet another reminder of how Asian and Asian American women are imagined as sex-workers, prostitutes, and whose bodies are racialized, gendered, and sexualized and stereotyped as bringing immorality, sexual contamination, and disease.
10 Willms, *When Women Rule the Court.*
11 Mazumdar, "General Introduction."

12 Yep, "Peddling Sport."

13 Carrington, *Race, Sport and Politics*; Omi and Winant, *Racial Formation in the United States*.

14 Tuan, *Forever Foreigners or Honorary Whites?*.

15 Halberstam, *Female Masculinity*.

16 See Carrington, *Race, Sport and Politics*; Hartmann, *Race, Culture and the Revolt of the Black Athlete*; Omi and Winant, *Racial Formation in the United States*; Yep, "Peddling Sport." I follow Karín Aguilar-San Juan's lead when she writes that Asian American feminism has its own "feminist paradigm with its own cultural and political reference points." Aguilar-San Juan, "Foreword: Breathing Fire," x; Asian Women United of California, *Making Waves*; Bow, *Asian American Feminisms*; Fujiwara and Roshanravan, *Asian American Feminism and Women of Color Politics*; Hune, "Introduction: Through 'Our' Eyes"; Shah, *Dragon Ladies*; Yamada, "Asian Pacific American Women and Feminism."

17 Birrell and Cole, *Women, Sport, and Culture*; Caudwell, *Sport, Sexualities and Queer/Theory*.

18 Theberge, "Gender and Sport."

19 Birrell, "Feminist Theories for Sport," "Racial Relations Theories and Sports."

20 Brown, "Pierre Bourdieu's 'Masculine Domination.'"

21 Bolin and Granskog, *Athletic Intruders*.

22 Lee, "Beyond Black and White"; Ratna, "Not Just Merely Different."

23 hooks, *Ain't I a Woman?*; Lorde, *Sister Outsider*.

24 Lee, "Beyond Black and White"; Smith, "Women of Color in Society and Sport."

25 Nguyen, "Biopower of Beauty."

26 Bird, "History of Flag Football."

27 Chin, "We've Got Team Spirit!"; Willms, *When Women Rule the Court*.

28 Samie, "Hetero-Sexy Self/Body Work and Basketball."

29 Crepeau, *NFL Football*.

30 Brownell, *Training the Body for China*. Sporting cultures are one avenue for women to display their bodies as strong and physical while also attaching their sense of selves to the nation.

31 See Connell, *Masculinities*.

32 For example, Asian American women played under the team name "Sigma Sisters," a program sponsored by a fraternity named Sigma Alpha Psi whose membership comprised predominantly Asian American men. The program recruited women to be a part of the fraternity.

33 Asian American women shared these views of the Panhellenic sorority system as the white mainstream.

34 Chin, "We've Got Team Spirit!"; Willms, *When Women Rule the Court*.

35 Oriard, *Reading Football*.

36 Thangaraj, *Desi Hoop Dreams*.

37 By D1, D2, and D3, Allyson is referring to Division I, II, and III colleges.

38 Green and Chalip, "Sport Tourism as the Celebration of Subculture," 281.

39 Adjepong, "They Are like Badges of Honour," 1494. Although not equivalent, I find similar sentiments in scholarship about women playing rugby.

40 Reddy notes that South Asian American women embody contrary poles simultaneously; they are fetishized over their white female counterparts along Western-centric realms of beauty or as tragic figures who ultimately cannot escape its fetishizing processes.

41 Yep, *Outside the Paint*, 33.

42 Flag football has gained popularity in other Asian ethnic communities. For example, Hmong Americans in the Midwest play flag football much more than other sports like soccer and volleyball. See Vang, "Hmong Youth."

43 Yep, *Outside the Paint*, 33.

44 Willms, *When Women Rule the Court*.

45 The regulation of flag football spaces concurrently worked with historically white university spaces. This meant that Black women were already not prominent on the campus or on its sporting fields. See for example, Walker, *Their Highest Potential*.

46 Thangaraj, *Desi Hoop Dreams*.

47 Schultz, "Reading the Catsuit."

48 Fleetwood, *On Racial Icons*.

49 Lowe, *Immigrant Acts*.

50 Tuan, "On Asian American Ice Queens and Multigeneration Asian Ethnics."

51 Leonard, *Playing While White*; Thangaraj, *Desi Hoop Dreams*.

52 Halberstam, *Female Masculinity*.

53 Bourdieu, "Forms of Capital."

54 Connell, *Which Way is Up?*, 18.

55 Thangaraj, "Playing through Differences."

56 Thangaraj, *Desi Hoop Dreams*.

57 Brake, *Getting in the Game*; Joo, *Transnational Sport*.

58 Halberstam, *Female Masculinity*.

59 Thangaraj, *Desi Hoop Dreams*.

60 Espiritu, "We Don't Sleep Around like White Girls Do."

61 Pronger, *Arena of Masculinity*.

62 Collins, *Black Sexual Politics*.

63 Chin, "Aren't You a Little Short?" For a poignant analysis of how Japanese American taiko drummers express their anger, see Wong, *Louder and Faster*.

64 Wong, *Louder and Faster*, 119.

65 España-Maram, *Creating Masculinity*.

66 Joo, *Transnational Sport*.

67 España-Maram, *Creating Masculinity*.

68 Harris, "Whiteness as Property"; see also Lipsitz, *Possessive Investment in Whiteness*.

69 Lipsitz, *Possessive Investment in Whiteness*, 281.

70 Carrington, *Race, Sport and Politics*.

71 Harris, "Whiteness as Property," 1737.
72 Harris, "Whiteness as Property," 1721.
73 Hune, "Introduction: Through 'Our' Eyes"; Yamada, "Asian Pacific American Women and Feminism."
74 Shimizu, *Hypersexuality of Race*, 51.
75 Puwar, *Space Invaders.*
76 Yamada, "Invisibility Is an Unnatural Disaster."

CONCLUSION

1 Abdurraqib, "It Rained in Ohio." I thank Tracie Canada for introducing me to Hanif Abdurraqib's poetry.
2 Yep, *Outside the Paint*; Joo, *Transnational Sport*; Regalado, *Nikkei Baseball*; Thangaraj, *Desi Hoop Dreams*; Thangaraj, Arnaldo, and Chin, *Asian American Sporting Cultures*; Willms, *When Women Rule the Court*; Szto, *Changing on the Fly.*
3 Gonzalves, *Day the Dancers Stayed*; Balance, *Tropical Renditions*; Tiongson, *Filipinos Represent*; Wang, *Legions of Boom*; España-Maram, *Creating Masculinity*; Burns, *Puro Arte*; Villegas, *Manifest Technique*; Perillo, *Choreographing in Color.*
4 Lanctot, *Negro League Baseball*; Burgos, *Playing America's Game*; Niiya, *More than a Game*; Regalado, *Nikkei Baseball.*
5 Fidler, *Origins and History*; Davis, "No League of Their Own."
6 Sands, *Sport Ethnography.*
7 Carter, *Quality of Home Runs*
8 Canada, *Tackling the Everyday*; Brownell, *Training the Body for China*; Joo, *Transnational Sport*; Rios, *Transnational Sport in the American West*; Uperesa, *Gridiron Capital.*
9 Thangaraj, *Desi Hoop Dreams*, 18.

BIBLIOGRAPHY

Abdurraqib, Hanif. "It Rained in Ohio the Night Allen Iverson Hit Michael Jordan with a Crossover." In *They Can't Kills Us until They Kill Us*. Columbus, OH: Two Dollar Radio, 2017.

Adjepong, Anima. "'They Are like Badges of Honour': Embodied Respectability and Women Rugby Players' Experiences of their Bruises." *Sport in Society: Cultures, Commerce, Media, Politics* 19 (2016): 1489–1502. https://doi.org/10.1080/17430437.20 15.1133602.

Aguilar-San Juan, Karín. "Filipinx American Activism—and Why I once Loved Manny Pacquiao." In *Filipinx American Studies: Reckoning, Reclamation, Transformation*, edited by Rick Bonus and Antonio T. Tiongson, Jr., 256–66. New York: Fordham University Press, 2022. https://doi.org/10.2307/j.ctv2gmhh8s.

Aguilar-San Juan, Karín. "Foreword: Breathing Fire, Confronting Power, and Other Necessary Acts of Resistance." In *Dragon Ladies: Asian American Feminists Breathe Fire*, edited by Sonia Shah, ix–xi. Boston: South End Press, 1997.

Ahmed, Sara. *Queer Phenomenology: Orientations, Objects, Others*. Durham, NC: Duke University Press, 2006.

Allen, Angelica. "Black Filipino Amerasian Identity." In *Filipinx American Studies: A Critical Registry of Terms*, edited by Rick Bonus and Antonio T. Tiongson, Jr. New York: Fordham University Press, forthcoming.

Anderson, Benedict. *Imagined Communities: Reflections on the Origin and Spread of Nationalism*. New York: Verso, 1991.

Anderson, Warwick. *Colonial Pathologies: American Tropical Medicine, Race, and Hygiene*. Durham, NC: Duke University Press, 2006.

Andrews, David, and Steven J. Jackson. *Sports Stars: The Cultural Politics of Sporting Celebrity*. New York: Routledge, 2001.

Antolihao, Lou. *Playing with the Big Boys: Basketball, American Imperialism, and Subaltern Discourse in the Philippines*. Lincoln: University of Nebraska Press, 2015.

Appadurai, Arjun. *Modernity at Large: Cultural Dimensions of Globalization*. Minneapolis: University of Minnesota Press, 1996.

Aquino, Kristine. "More than a Game: Embodied Everyday Anti-Racism among Young Filipino-Australian Street Ballers." *Journal of Intercultural Studies* 36, no. 2 (2015): 166–83. https://doi.org/10.1080/07256868.2015.1008430.

Aquino, Kristine. *Racism and Resistance in the Filipino Diaspora: Everyday Anti-racism in Australia*. New York: Routledge, 2017.

Arevalo, Carminda R. "The Philippine Flag: Symbol of our Sovereignty and Solidarity." Accessed April 2, 2024. https://nhcp.gov.ph.

Arnaldo, Constancio R., Jr. "'I'm Thankful for Manny': Manny 'Pac-Man' Pacquiao, Pugilistic Nationalism, and the Filipina/o Body." In *Global Asian American Popular Cultures*, edited by Shilpa Davé, LeiLani Nishime, and Tasha Oren, 27–45. New York: New York University Press, 2016.

Arnaldo, Constancio R., Jr. "Manny 'Pac-Man' Pacquiao, the Transnational Fist, and the Southern California Ringside Community." In *Asian American Sporting Cultures*, edited by Stanley I. Thangaraj, Constancio R. Arnaldo, Jr., and Christina B. Chin, 102–25. New York: New York University Press, 2016.

Arnaldo, Constancio R., Jr. "'Undisputed' Racialised Masculinities: Boxing Fandom, Identity, and the Cultural Politics of Masculinity." *Identities: Global Studies in Culture and Power* 27, no. 6 (2020): 655–74. https://doi.org/10.1080/1070289X.2019.1624068.

Arugelles, Randolf. "Alibata Tattoos and the Search for Indigenous Filipino Culture." Paper presented at the Association for Asian American Studies conference, Philadelphia, PA, March 31–April 3, 1999.

Arugelles, Randolf. "More than Skin Deep." *A. Magazine: Inside Asian America* (April/May 1999): 18–20.

Asian Women United of California. *Making Waves: An Anthology of Writings by and about Asian American Women*. Boston: Beacon Press, 1989.

Balance, Christine Bacareza. *Tropical Renditions: Making Musical Scenes in Filipino America*. Durham, NC: Duke University Press, 2016.

Balce, Nerissa S. *Body Parts of Empire: Visual Abjection, Filipino Images, and the American Archive*. Ann Arbor: University of Michigan Press, 2016.

Balce, Nerissa S. "Filipino Bodies, Lynching, and the Language of Empire." In *Positively No Filipinos Allowed: Building Communities and Discourse*, edited by Antonio T. Tiongson, Jr., Edgardo V. Gutierrez, and Ricardo V. Gutierrez, 43–60. Philadelphia: Temple University Press, 2006.

Baldoz, Rick. *The Third Asiatic Invasion: Empire and Migration in Filipino America, 1898–1946*. New York: New York University Press, 2011.

Basch, Linda, Nina Glick Schiller, and Cristina Szanton Blanc. *Nations Unbound: Transnational Projects, Postcolonial Predicaments, and Deterritorialized Nation-States*. Philadelphia: Gordon and Breach 1994.

Bayne, Bijan C. "The Schoolyard Game: Blacktop Legends and Broken Dreams." In *Basketball in America: From the Playgrounds to Jordan's Game and Beyond*, edited by Frank Hoffman, Robert P. Batchelor, and Martin J. Manning, 67–81. New York: Routledge, 2013.

Bender, Daniel E., and Adrian De Leon. "Everybody Was Boodle Fighting: Military Histories, Culinary Tourism, and Diasporic Dining." *Food, Culture & Society: An International Journal of Multidisciplinary Research* 21, no. 1 (2018): 25–41. https://doi.org/10.1080/15528014.2017.1398469.

Bernardo, Joseph A. "From 'Little Brown Brothers' to 'Forgotten Asian Americans':
Race, Space, and Empire in Filipino Los Angeles." PhD diss., University of Washington, 2014.

Billings, Andrew C., and Jason Edward Black. *Mascot Nation: The Controversy over
Native American Representations in Sports*. Urbana: University of Illinois Press,
2018.

Bird, Beverly. "History of Flag Football." *SportsRec*, July 8, 2011. www.sportsrec.com.

Birrell, Susan. "Feminist Theories for Sport." In *Handbook of Sports Studies*, edited by
Jay Coakley and Eric Dunning, 61–76. Thousand Oaks: SAGE, 2000.

Birrell, Susan. "Racial Relations Theories and Sports: Suggestions for a More Critical Analysis." *Sociology of Sport Journal* 6 (1989): 212–27. https://doi.org/10.1123/
ssj.6.3.212.

Birrell, Susan, and Cheryl L. Cole, eds. *Women, Sport, and Culture*. Champaign, IL:
Human Kinetics, 1994.

Bolin, Anne, and Jane Granskog. *Athletic Intruders: Ethnographic Research on Women,
Culture, and Exercise*. Albany: SUNY Press, 2012.

Bonus, Rick. *Locating Filipino Americans: Ethnicity and the Cultural Politics of Space*.
Philadelphia: Temple University Press, 2000.

Bourdieu, Pierre. "Forms of Capital." In *Cultural Theory: An Anthology*, edited by Imre
Szeman and Timothy Kaposy, 81–97. Chichester, UK: Wiley-Blackwell, 1986.

Bow, Leslie. *Partly Colored: Asian Americans and Racial Anomaly in the Segregated
South*. New York: New York University Press, 2010.

Boyd, Todd. *Young, Black, Rich, and Famous: The Rise of the NBA, the Hip Hop Invasion, and the Transformation of American Culture*. New York: Doubleday, 2008.

Brake, Deborah. *Getting in the Game: Title IX and the Women's Sports Revolution*. New
York: New York University Press, 2010.

Brooks, Scott N. *Black Men Can't Shoot*. Chicago: University of Chicago Press, 2009.

Brown, David. "Pierre Bourdieu's 'Masculine Domination' Thesis and the Gendered
Body in Sport and Physical Culture." *Sociology of Sport Journal* 23, no. 2 (2006):
162–88. https://doi.org/10.1123/ssj.23.2.162.

Brownell, Susan. *Training the Body for China: Sports in the Moral Order of the People's
Republic*. Chicago: University of Chicago Press, 1995.

Bulosan, Carlos. *America Is in the Heart*. Seattle: University of Washington Press,
1946.

Burgos, Adrian. *Playing America's Game: Baseball, Latinos, and the Color Line*. Berkeley: University of California Press, 2007.

Burns, Lucy Mae San Pablo. *Puro Arte: Filipinos on the Stages of Empire*. New York:
New York University Press, 2013.

Burton, Orisanmi. "Captivity, Kinship, and Black Masculine Care Work under
Domestic Warfare." *American Anthropologist* 123, no. 3 (2021): 621–32. https://doi.
org/10.1111/aman.13619.

Canada, Tracie. *Tackling the Everyday: Race, Family, and Nation in Big Time College
Football*. Berkeley: University of California Press, forthcoming.

Carey, R. Scott, Rob Millington, and Carolyn Prouse. "Branding Boundaries: Colonial Sporting Identities and the Racialized Body." In *Sport, Animals, and Society*, edited by James Gillett and Michelle Gilbert, 209–32. New York: Routledge, 2014.

Carrington, Ben. "'Race,' Representation and the Sporting Body." CUCR Occasional Paper Series. London: Goldsmiths College, 2002.

Carrington, Ben. *Race, Sport and Politics: The Sporting Diaspora*. Los Angeles: SAGE, 2010.

Carter, Thomas. "On the Need for an Anthropological Approach to Sport." *Identities: Global Studies in Culture and Power* 9, no. 3 (2002): 405–22.

Carter, Thomas. *The Quality of Home Runs: The Passion, Politics, and Language of Cuban Baseball*. Durham, NC: Duke University Press, 2013.

Castillo, Elaine. *America Is Not the Heart: A Novel*. New York: Penguin, 2018.

Caudwell, Jayne. *Sport, Sexualities and Queer/Theory*. New York: Routledge, 2006.

Ceniza Choy, Catherine. *Empire of Care: Nursing and Migration in Filipino American History*. Durham, NC: Duke University Press, 2003.

Cha-Jua, Sundiata Keita. "'We Believe It Was Murder': Mobilizing Black Resistance to Police Brutality in Champaign, Illinois." *Black Scholar* 44, no. 1 (2014): 58–85.

Chappelle, Dave. *The Age of Spin: Dave Chappelle Live at the Hollywood Palladium*. Performed Los Angeles, CA. Video, 01:07:00, Netflix, 2017.

Chin, Christina B. "'Aren't You a Little Short to Play Ball?': Japanese American Youth and Racial Microaggressions in Basketball Leagues." *Amerasia Journal* 41, no. 2 (2015): 47–65. https://doi.org/10.17953/aj.41.2.47.

Chin, Christina B. "'We've Got Team Spirit!': Ethnic Community Building and Japanese American Youth Basketball Leagues." *Ethnic and Racial Studies* 39, no. 6 (2015): 1070–88. https://dx.doi.org/10.1080/01419870.2015.1103878.

Chin, Jessica W., and David L. Andrews. "Mixed Martial Arts, Caged Orientalism, and Female Asian American Bodies." In *Asian American Sporting Cultures*, edited by Stanley I. Thangaraj, Constancio R. Arnaldo, Jr., and Christina B. Chin, 152–79. New York: New York University Press, 2016.

Chuh, Kandice. *Imagine Otherwise: On Asian Americanist Critique*. Durham, NC: Duke University Press, 2003.

Clifford, James. *Routes: Travel and Translation in the Late Twentieth Century*. Cambridge, MA: Harvard University Press, 1997.

Collins, Patricia Hill. *Black Sexual Politics: African Americans, Gender, and the New Racism*. New York: Routledge, 2005.

Comella, Lynn. *Vibrator Nation: How Feminist Sex-Toy Stores Changed the Business of Pleasure*. Durham, NC: Duke University Press, 2017.

Connell, R. W. *Masculinities*. Cambridge, MA: Polity Press, 1995.

Connell, R. W. *Which Way is Up?: Essays on Sex, Class, and Culture*. Boston: George Allen & Unwin, 1983.

Coráñez Bolton, Sony. "A Tale of Two 'X's: Queer Filipinx and Latinx Linguistic Intimacies." In *Filipinx American Studies: Reckoning, Reclamation, Transformation*, edited by Rick Bonus and Antonio T. Tiongson, Jr., 284–90. New York: Fordham University Press, 2022.

Crepeau, Richard C. *NFL Football: A History of America's New National Pastime.* Urbana: University of Illinois Press, 2014.

Cruz, Denise. "Splitting the Seams: Transnational Feminism and the Manila-Toronto Production of Filipino Couture." In *Fashion and Beauty in the Time of Asia,* edited by S. Heijin Lee, Christina H. Moon, and Thuy Linh Nguyen Tu, 154–83. New York: New York University Press, 2019.

Davis, Amira Rose. "No League of Their Own: Baseball, Black Women, and the Politics of Representation." *Radical History Review* 125 (2016): 74–96.

de Garis, Laurence. "Experiments in Pro Wrestling: Toward a Performative and Sensuous Sport Ethnography." *Sociology of Sport Journal* 16, no. 1 (1999): 65–77. https://doi.org/10.1123/ssj.16.1.65.

de la Cruz, Enrique, Jorge Emmanuel, Abe Ignacio, and Helen Toribio. *The Forbidden Book: The Philippine-American War in Political Cartoons.* San Francisco: T'Boli, 2004.

de la Cruz, Enrique, Pearlie S. Rose Baluyut, and Rico J. Reyes. *Confrontations, Crossings, and Convergence: Photographs of the Philippines and the United States, 1898–1998.* Los Angeles: UCLA Asian American Studies Center, 1998.

DeMello, Margo. *Bodies of Inscription: A Cultural History of the Modern Tattoo Community.* Durham: Duke University Press, 2000.

DeWitt, Howard. "The Watsonville Anti-Filipino Riot of 1930: A Case Study of the Great Depression and Ethnic Conflict in California." *Southern California Quarterly* 61, no. 3 (1979): 291–302. https://doi.org/10.2307/41170831.

Dhingra, Pawan. "Being American Between Black and White: Second-Generation Asian American Professionals' Racial Identities." *Journal of Asian American Studies* 6, no. 2 (2003): 117–47. https://doi.org/10.1353/jaas.2004.0004.

Diaz, Josen Masangkay. *Postcolonial Configurations Dictatorship, the Racial Cold War, and Filipino America.* Durham, NC: Duke University Press, 2023.

Diaz, Robert, Marissa Largo, and Fritz Pino, eds. *Diasporic Intimacies: Queer Filipinos and Canadian Imaginaries.* Chicago: Northwestern University Press, 2017.

Doolan, Yuri W. "Transpacific Camptowns: Korean Women, US Army Bases, and Military Prostitution in America." *Journal of American Ethnic History* 38, no. 4 (2019): 33–54. https://doi.org/10.5406/jamerethnhist.38.4.0033

Douglas, Mary. "Deciphering a Meal." *Daedalus* 101, no. 1 (Winter 1972): 61–81. https://www.jstor.org/stable/20024058.

Eisenberg, Matt. "FSU Sorority Sister Is Back with This Stunning Flag Football Highlight Reel." *espnW*, December 2, 2015. www.espn.go.com.

Empeno, Henry, "Anti-Miscegenation Laws and the Filipino." In *Letters in Exile: An Introductory Reader on the History of Pilipinos in America,* edited by Jesse Quinsaat. Los Angeles: UCLA Asian American Studies Center, 1976.

Eng, David. *Racial Castration: Managing Masculinity in America.* Durham, NC: Duke University Press, 2001.

España-Maram, Linda N. "Brown 'Hordes' in McIntosh Suits: Filipinos, Taxi Dance Halls, and the Performing Immigrant Body in Los Angeles, 1930s–1940s." In *Generations of Youth: Youth Cultures and History in Twentieth Century America*, edited by Joe Austin and Michael Nevin Willard, 118–34. New York: New York University Press, 1998.

España-Maram, Linda N. *Creating Masculinity in Los Angeles's Little Manila: Working-Class Filipinos and Popular Culture, 1920s–1950s*. New York: Columbia University Press, 2006.

Espiritu, Yen Le. *Home Bound: Filipino American Lives across Cultures, Communities, and Countries*. Berkeley: University of California Press, 2003.

Espiritu, Yen Le. "'We Don't Sleep Around like White Girls Do': The Politics of Home and Location." In *Home Bound: Filipino American Lives across Cultures, Communities, and Countries*, 157–78. Berkeley: University of California Press, 2003.

Fajardo, Kale Bantigue. *Filipino Crosscurrents: Oceanographies of Seafaring, Masculinities, and Globalization*. Minneapolis: Minnesota University Press, 2011.

Fajardo, Kale Bantigue. "Queering and Transing the Great Lakes: Filipino/a Tomboy Masculinities and Manhoods across Waters." *GLQ* 20, no. 1–2 (2014): 115–40. https://doi.org/10.1215/10642684-2370387.

Farrales, May. "Colonial, Settler Colonial Tactics and Filipino Canadian Heteronormativities at Play on the Basketball Court." In *Diasporic Intimacies: Queer Filipinos and Canadian Imaginaries*, edited by Robert Diaz, Marissa Largo, and Fritz Pino, 183–97. https://doi.org/10.2307/j.ctv47wd88.18.

Feagin, Joe. *The White Racial Frame Centuries of Racial Framing and Counter-Framing*. New York: Routledge, 2010.

Ferguson, Roderick. *Aberrations in Black: Toward a Queer of Color Critique*. Minneapolis: University of Minnesota Press, 2004.

Fidler, Merrie. *The Origins and History of the All-American Girls Professional Baseball League*. Jefferson: McFarland, 2015.

Fisher, Jill A. "Tattooing the Body, Marking Culture." *Body and Society* 8, no. 4 (2002): 91–107. https://doi.org/10.1177/1357034X02008004005.

Fleetwood, Nicole R. *On Racial Icons: Blackness and the Public Imagination*. New Brunswick: Rutgers University Press, 2015.

Foucault, Michel. *Discipline and Punish: The Birth of the Prison*. New York: Vintage Books, 1977.

Fouché, Rayvon. *Game Changer: The Techno-Scientific Revolution in Sports*. Baltimore: John Hopkins University Press, 2017.

Francisco, Luzviminda. "The First Vietnam: The U.S. Philippine War of 1899–1902." In *Letters in Exile: An Introductory Reader on the History of Pilipinos in America*, edited Jesse Quinsaat. Los Angeles: UCLA Asian American Studies Center, 1976.

Francisco-Menchavez, Valerie. *Labor of Care: Filipina Migrants and Transnational Families in the Digital Age*. Urbana: University of Illinois Press, 2019.

Fujiwara, Lynn, and Shireen Roshanravan. *Asian American Feminism and Women of Color Politics*. Seattle: University of Washington Press, 2018.

Gems, Gerald R. *The Athletic Crusade: Sport and American Cultural Imperialism.* Lincoln: University of Nebraska Press, 2006.

Gilroy, Paul. *The Black Atlantic: Modernity and Double-Consciousness.* Cambridge, MA: Harvard University Press, 1995.

Goffman, Erving. *The Presentation of Self in Everyday Life.* New York: Doubleday, 1959.

Gonzalves, Theodore S. *The Day the Dancers Stayed: Performing in the Filipino/American Diaspora.* Philadelphia: Temple University Press, 2009.

Gopinath, Gayatri. *Impossible Desires: Queer Diasporas and South Asian Public Cultures.* Durham, NC: Duke University Press, 2005.

Gopinath, Gayatri. *Unruly Visions: The Aesthetic Practices of Queer Diaspora.* Durham, NC: Duke University Press, 2018.

Green, Christine, and Laurence Chalip. "Sport Tourism as the Celebration of Subculture." *Annals of Tourism Research* 25, no. 2 (1998): 275–91. https://doi.org/10.1016/S0160-7383(97)00073-X.

Guiliano, Jennifer. *Indian Spectacle: College Mascots and the Anxiety of Modern America.* New Brunswick, NJ: Rutgers University Press, 2015.

Gupta, Akhil, and James Ferguson. "Beyond 'Culture': Space, Identity, and the Politics of Difference." *Cultural Anthropology* 7, no. 1 (1992): 6–23. https://www.jstor.org/stable/656518.

Guthrie-Shimizu, Sayuri. *Transpacific Field of Dreams: How Baseball Linked the United States and Japan in Peace and War.* Chapel Hill: University of North Carolina Press, 2012.

Halberstam, Judith. *Female Masculinity.* Durham, NC: Duke University Press, 1998.

Hall, Stuart. "Cultural Identity and Diaspora." In *Identity: Community, Culture, Difference*, edited by Jonathan Rutherford, 222–37. London: Lawrence and Wishart, 1990.

Hall, Stuart. "Encoding and Decoding in Televisual Discourse." In *Writings on Media*, edited by Charlotte Brundson, 247–66. Durham, NC: Duke University Press, 2021.

Hall, Stuart, ed. *Representation: Cultural Representations and Signifying Practices.* Thousand Oaks: SAGE, 1997.

Halvorson, Britt E., and Joshua O. Reno. *Imagining the Heartland: White Supremacy and the American Midwest.* Berkeley: University of California Press, 2022.

Harris, Cheryl I. "Whiteness as Property." *Harvard Law Review* 106, no. 8 (1993): 1701–91. https://doi.org/10.2307/1341787.

Hartmann, Douglas. *Race, Culture and the Revolt of the Black Athlete: The 1968 Olympic Protests and Their Aftermath.* Chicago: University of Chicago Press, 2003.

Herbert, Annalisa. "Growing Up Brown in America: The Filipino Mango Athletic Club of San Francisco 1938–1955." MA thesis, University of California, Los Angeles, 1996.

Ho, Jennifer Ann. *Racial Ambiguity in Asian American Culture.* New Brunswick, NJ: Rutgers University Press, 2015.

Hoganson, Kristin. *Fighting for American Manhood: How Gender Politics Provoked the Spanish-American and Philippine-American Wars.* New Haven, CT: Yale University Press, 1998.

Hoganson, *The Heartland: An American History.* New York: Penguin Books, 2020.

Hong, Grace Kyungwon. *The Ruptures of American Capital: Women of Color Feminism and the Culture of Immigrant Labor*. Minneapolis: University of Minnesota Press, 2006.

Hong, Grace Kyungwon, and Roderick A. Ferguson, eds. *Strange Affinities: The Gender and Sexual Politics of Comparative Racialization*. Durham, NC: Duke University Press, 2011.

hooks, bell. *Ain't I a Woman? Black Women and Feminism*. New York: Routledge, 2014.

Hune, Shirley. "Introduction: Through 'Our' Eyes: Asian/Pacific Islander American Women's History." In *Asian/Pacific Islander American Women: A Historical Anthology*, edited by Shirley Hune and Gail M. Nomura, 1–22. New York: New York University Press, 2003.

INCITE! Women of Color against Violence. *The Revolution Will Not Be Funded: Beyond the Non-profit Industrial Complex*. Durham, NC: Duke University Press, 2017.

Inhorn, Marcia C. *The New Arab Man: Emergent Masculinities, Technologies, and Islam in the Middle East*. Princeton, NJ: Princeton University Press, 2012.

Jacobs, Sean. "'Get Used to Me': Muhammad Ali and the Paradoxes of Third World Solidarity." *Radical History Review* 131 (2018): 199–210. https://doi.org/10.1215/01636545-4355353.

Jamero, Peter. *Growing Up Brown: Memoirs of a Filipino American*. Seattle: Washington University Press, 2006.

James, C. L. R. *Beyond a Boundary*. Durham, NC: Duke University Press, 2013.

Johnson, Javon. "Sincerely, These Hands: Mayweather, Money, and Masculinity." In *Rings of Dissent: Boxing and the Performance of Rebellion*, edited by Rudy Mondragón, Gaye Theresa Johnson, and David J. Leonard. Chapel Hill: University of North Carolina Press, forthcoming.

Joo, Rachael. *Transnational Sport: Gender, Media, and Global Korea*. Durham, NC: Duke University Press, 2012.

Joo, Rachael, and Sameer Pandya. "On the Cultural Politics of Asian American Sports." *Amerasia* 41, no. 2 (2015): ix–xix. https://doi.org/10.17953/aj.41.2.ix.

Joshi, Khyati Y. *White Christian Privilege: The Illusion of Religious Equality in America*. New York: New York University Press, 2020.

Jun, Helen Heran. *Race for Citizenship: Black Orientalism and Asian Uplift from Pre-Emancipation to Neoliberal America*. New York: New York University Press, 2011.

Kang, Dredge Byung'chu. "Idols of Development: Transnational Transgender Performance in Thai K-Pop Cover Dance." *Transgender Studies Quarterly* 1, no. 4 (2014): 559–71.

Kelley, Robin D. G. *Yo Mama's Disfunktional! Fighting the Culture Wars in Urban America*. Boston: Beacon Press, 1997.

Kim, Daniel Y. *Writing Manhood in Black and Yellow: Ralph Ellison, Frank Chin, and the Literary Politics of Identity*. Stanford, CA: Stanford University Press, 2005.

Kim, Helen Jin. *Race for Revival: How Cold War South Korea Shaped the American Evangelical Empire*. New York: Oxford University Press, 2022.

Kramer, Paul. *Blood of Government: Race, Empire, the United States, and the Philippines*. Chapel Hill: University of North Carolina Press, 2006.

Ladd, Tony, and James A. Mathisen. *Muscular Christianity: Evangelical Protestants and the Development of American Sport*. Grand Rapids, MI: Baker Books, 1999.

Lanctot, Neil. *Negro League Baseball: The Rise and Ruin of a Black Institution*. Philadelphia: University of Pennsylvania Press, 2008.

Larke-Walsh, George S. *Screening the Mafia: Masculinity, Ethnicity and Mobsters from "The Godfather" to "The Sopranos."* Jefferson, NC: McFarland & Company, 2010.

Lasco, Gideon. "'Little Brown Brothers': Height and the Philippine-American Colonial Encounter (1898–1946)." *Philippine Studies* 66, no. 3 (2018): 375–406. https://doi.org/10.1353/phs.2018.0029.

Lee, Erika. "Asian American Studies in the Midwest." *Journal of Asian American Studies* 12, no. 3 (2009): 247–73. https://doi.org/10.1353/jaas.0.0045.

Lee, Yomee. "Beyond Black and White: Chinese American Women's Experience in Sports." In *Asian American Athletes in Sport and Society*, edited by Richard King, 13–31. New York: Routledge, 2015.

Leonard, David. *Playing While White: Privilege and Power on and off the Field*. Seattle: University of Washington Press, 2017.

Lewinnek, Elaine, Gustavo Arellano, and Thuy Vo Dang. *A People's Guide to Orange County*. Berkeley: University of California Press, 2022.

Lipsitz, George. *The Possessive Investment in Whiteness: How White People Profit from Identity Politics*. Philadelphia: Temple University Press, 1998.

Litsky, Frank. "Victoria Manalo Draves, Olympic Champion Diver, Dies at 85." *New York Times*, April 29, 2010.

Lock, Margaret M., and Judith Farquhar, eds. *Beyond the Body Proper: Reading the Anthropology of Material Life*. Durham, NC: Duke University Press, 2007.

Lorde, Audre. *Sister Outsider: Essays and Speeches*. Trumansburg, NY: Crossing Press, 1984.

Lowe, Lisa. *Immigrant Acts: On Asian American Cultural Politics*. Durham, NC: Duke University Press, 1996.

Lowe, Lisa. *The Intimacies of Four Continents*. Durham, NC: Duke University Press, 2015.

Lowenstein, Jeff Kelly. "Health Industry Brings Filipinos to Champaign." CU-CitizenAccess, October 5, 2012. https://cu-citizenaccess.org/.

Mabalon, Dawn Bohulano. "As American as Jackrabbit Adobo: Cooking, Eating, and Becoming Filipina/o American before World War II." In *Eating Asian America: A Food Studies Reader*, edited by Robert Ji-Song Ku, Martin F. Manalansan, and Anita Mannur, 147–76. New York: New York University Press, 2013. https://doi.org/10.18574/nyu/9781479818952.003.0012.

Mabalon, Dawn Bohulano. *Little Manila Is in the Heart: The Making of the Filipina/o American Community in Stockton, California*. Durham, NC: Duke University Press, 2013.

Maginn, Paul, and Christine Steinmetz. *(Sub)Urban Sexscapes: Geographies and Regulation of the Sex Industry.* New York: Routledge University Press, 2015.

Majors, Richard, and Janet Mancini Billson. *Cool Pose: The Dilemmas of Black Manhood in America.* New York: Lexington, 1992.

Manalansan, Martin F., IV. "Beyond Authenticity: Rerouting the Filipino Culinary Diaspora." In *Eating Asian America: A Food Studies Reader,* edited by Robert Ji-Song Ku, Martin F. Manalansan IV, and Anita Mannur, 288–300. New York: New York University Press, 2013.

Manalansan, Martin F., IV. Introduction to *Cultural Compass: Ethnographic Explorations of Asian America,* edited by Martin F. Manalansan IV, 1–16. Philadelphia: Temple University Press, 2000.

Manalansan, Martin F., IV. *Global Divas: Gay Filipinos in the Diaspora.* Durham, NC: Duke University Press, 2003.

Manalansan, Martin F., IV. "Messing Up Sex: The Promises and Possibilities of Queer of Color Critique." *Sexualities* 21, no. 8 (2018): 1287–90. https://doi.org/10.1177/1363460718794646.

Manalansan, Martin F., IV. "The 'Stuff' of Archives: Mess, Migration, and Queer Lives." *Radical History Review* 120 (2014): 94–107. https://doi.org/10.1215/01636545-2703742.

Manalansan, Martin F., IV, and Augusto F. Espiritu, eds. *Filipino Studies: Palimpsests of Nation and Diaspora.* New York: New York University Press, 2016.

Manalansan, Martin F., IV., Chantal Nadeau, Siobhan B. Somerville, and Richard T. Rodríguez. "Queering the Middle: Race, Region, and a Queer Midwest." *GLQ: A Journal of Lesbian and Gay Studies* 20, no. 1 (2014): 1–12. https://doi.org/10.1215/10642684-2370270.

Marcus, George E. "Ethnography in/of the World System: The Emergence of Multi-sited Ethnography." *Annual Review of Anthropology* 24 (1995): 95–117. https://www.jstor.org/stable/2155931

Mariano, L. Joyce Zapanta. *Giving Back: Filipino America and the Politics of Diaspora Giving.* Philadelphia: Temple University Press, 2021.

Mazumdar, Sucheta. "General Introduction: A Woman-Centered Perspective on Asian American History." In *Making Waves: An Anthology of Writings by and About Asian American Women,* edited by Asian Women United of California, 1–22. Boston: Beacon Press, 1989.

Mendoza, Victor Román. *Metroimperial Intimacies: Fantasy, Racial-Sexual Governance, and the Philippines in U.S. Imperialism.* Durham, NC: Duke University Press, 2015.

Mills, Charles. *The Racial Contract.* Ithaca, NY: Cornell University Press, 1997.

Mitchell, Kevin. "Manny Pacquiao: 'I Changed When I Heard the Voice of God.'" *The Guardian,* October 4, 2014. www.theguardian.com.

Montez de Oca, Jeffrey. *Discipline and Indulgence: College Football, Media, and the American Way of Life during the Cold War.* New Brunswick, NJ: Rutgers University Press, 2013.

Moore, Louis. *I Fight for a Living: Boxing and the Battle for Black Manhood, 1880–1915.* Urbana: University of Illinois Press, 2017.

Moraga, Jorge E. "'Riverboat Ron': A Critical Reading of Ron Rivera, American Brownness & Latino Masculinities in the NFL." *Journal of Sport and Social Issues* 0, no. 0 (2022): 1–27.

Mossière, Géraldine, "Sharing in Ritual Effervescence: Emotions and Empathy in Fieldwork." *Anthropology Matters* 9, no. 1 (2007): 1–14.

Muñoz, Jose Esteban. *Disidentifications: Queers of Color and the Performance of Politics.* Minneapolis: University of Minnesota Press, 1999.

Murashako, Alex. "Manny Pacquiao Is a 'Bible-Quoting Maniac,' Says Rick Warren." *Christian Post*, June 4, 2012. www.christianpost.com.

Ngo, Fiona. "Punk in the Shadow of War." *Women & Performance: A Journal of Feminist Theory* 22, no. 2–3 (2012): 203–32.

Nguyen, Mimi. "The Biopower of Beauty: Humanitarian Imperialisms and Global Feminisms in an Age of Terror." *Signs: Journal of Women in Culture and Society* 36, no. 2 (2011): 359–83. https://doi.org/10.1086/655914.

Nievera-Lozano, Melissa-Ann. Introduction to *The Pilipinx Radical Imagination Reader*, edited by Melissa-Ann Nievera-Lozano and Anthony Abulencia Santa Ana, 1–5. San Francisco, CA: Philippine American Writers and Artists, 2018.

Niiya, Brian, *More than a Game: Sport in the Japanese American Community.* Los Angeles: Japanese American National Museum, 2000.

Novio, Norman A. "Why My God Won't Show Up for Mayweather-Pacquiao." *Mindoro Smorgasbord* (blog), April 19, 2015. http://nanovio.blogspot.com.

Ocampo, Anthony Christian. *The Latinos of Asia: How Filipino Americans Break the Rules of Race.* Stanford, CA: Stanford University Press, 2016.

Okamura, Jonathan Y. *Imagining the Filipino American Diaspora: Transnational Relations, Identities, and Communities.* New York: Routledge, 2013.

Omi, Michael, and Howard Winant. *Racial Formation in the United States.* 3rd ed. New York: Routledge, 2014.

Oriard, Michael. *Reading Football: How the Popular Press Created an American Spectacle.* Chapel Hill: University of North Carolina Press, 1993.

Orquiza, Rene. *Taste of Control: Food and the Filipino Colonial Mentality Under American Rule.* New Brunswick: Rutgers University Press, 2013.

Osborne, Laurence. "Boxer, Godfather, Politician. Can Manny Pacquiao Do Everything?" *Newsweek*, October 30, 2011. www.newsweek.com.

Padoongpatt, Mark. *Flavors of Empire: Food and the Making of Thai America.* Berkeley: University of California Press, 2017.

Parezo, Nancy. "A 'Special Olympics': Testing Racial Strength and Endurance at the 1904 Louisiana Purchase Exposition." In *The 1904 Anthropology Days and Olympic Games Sport, Race, and American Imperialism*, edited by Susan Brownell, 59–126. Lincoln: University of Nebraska Press, 2008.

Parreñas, Rhacel Salazar. *Servants of Globalization: Migration and Domestic Work.* 2nd ed. Stanford, CA: Stanford University Press, 2015.

Parreñas, Rhacel Salazar. "'White Trash' Meets the 'Little Brown Monkeys': The Taxi Dance Hall as a Site of Interracial and Gender Alliances between White Working

Class Women and Filipino Immigrant Men in the 1920s and 30s." *Amerasia Journal* 24, no. 2 (1998): 115–34. https://doi.org/10.17953/amer.24.2.76oh5w0863oql643.

Perillo, Lorenzo. *Choreographing in Color: Filipinos, Hip-Hop, and the Cultural Politics of Euphemism*. New York: Oxford University Press, 2020.

The Philippine Souvenir Booklet. 1904. Accessed April 9, 2019. https://humanzoos.net.

Pilapil, Virgilio R. "Dogtown U.S.A.: An Igorot Legacy in the Midwest." *Journal of Filipino American National Historical Society* 2 (1992): 45–49.

Poblete, Joanna. *Islanders in the Empire: Filipino and Puerto Rican Laborers in Hawaiʻi*. Urbana: University of Illinois Press, 2014.

Posadas, Barbara M. "The Hierarchy of Color and Psychological Adjustment in an Industrial Environment: Filipinos, the Pullman Company, and the Brotherhood of Sleeping Car Porters." *Labor History* 23, no. 3 (1982): 349–73. https://doi.org/10.1080/00236568208584662.

Posadas, Barbara M., and Roland L. Guyotte. "Unintentional Immigrants: Chicago's Filipino Foreign Students Become Settlers, 1900–1941." *Journal of American Ethnic History* 9, no. 2 (1990): 26–48.

Prashad, Vijay. *The Karma of Brown Folk*. Minneapolis: University of Minnesota Press, 2000.

Pronger, Brian. *Arena of Masculinity: Sports, Homosexuality, and the Meaning of Sex*. New York: St. Martin's Press, 1990.

Puar, Jasbir K., and Amit Rai. "Monster, Terrorist, Fag: The War on Terrorism and the Production of Docile Patriots." *Social Text* 20, no. 3 (2002): 117–48.

Public Broadcasting Service. *Asian Americans: Breaking Ground, Episode 1*. Video, 00:54:11, May 11, 2020. www.pbs.org.

Putney, Clifford. *Muscular Christianity: Manhood and Sports in Protestant America, 1880–1920*. Cambridge: Harvard University Press, 2003.

Puwar, Nirmal. *Space Invaders: Race, Gender and Bodies out of Place*. Oxford: Berg Publishers, 2004.

Rafael, Vicente L. *White Love and Other Events in Filipino History*. Durham, NC: Duke University Press, 2000.

Ratna, Aarti. "Not Just Merely Different: Travelling Theories, Post-feminism and the Racialized Politics of Women of Color." *Sociology of Sport Journal* 35 (2018): 197–206. https://doi.org/10.1123/ssj.2017-0192.

Reddy, Chandan. *Freedom with Violence: Race, Sexuality, and the US State*. Durham, NC: Duke University Press, 2011.

Reddy, Vanita. *Fashioning Diaspora: Beauty, Femininity, and South Asian American Culture*. Philadelphia: Temple University Press, 2016.

Reft, Ryan. "From Perpetual Foreigner to Pacific Rim Entrepreneur: The U.S. Military, Asian Americans, and the Circuitous Path of Sport." In *Asian American Sporting Cultures*, edited by Stanley I. Thangaraj, Constancio R. Arnaldo, Jr., and Christina B. Chin, 23–52. New York: New York University Press, 2016.

Regalado, Samuel O. *Nikkei Baseball: Japanese American Players from Immigration and Internment to the Major Leagues*. Urbana: University of Illinois Press, 2013.

Remollino, Bernard James. "'Scrapping into a Knot': Pinoy Boxers, Transpacific Fans, and the Troubling of Interwar California's Regimes." *Alon: Journal for Filipinx American and Diasporic Studies* 1, no. 2 (2021): 149–78. https://doi.org/10.5070/ln41251006.

Reyes, Angela. "Image into Sequence: Colonial Photography and the Invention of Filipino Evolution." *Semiotic Review* 9 (January 2021). www.semioticreview.com.

Rios, Bernardo R. *Transnational Sport in the American West: Oaxaca California Basketball.* Lanham, MD: Lexington, 2019.

Rodriguez, Robyn. *Migrants for Export: How the Philippine State Brokers Labor to the World.* Minneapolis: University of Minnesota Press, 2010.

Ruanto-Ramirez, J. A. "Why I Don't (Really) Consider Myself a Filipinx: Complicating 'Filipinxness' from a Katutubo Intervention." In *Filipinx American Studies: Reckoning, Reclamation, Transformation*, edited by Rick Bonus and Antonio T. Tiongson, Jr., 298–307. New York: Fordham University Press, 2022. https://doi.org/10.1515/9780823299607-028.

Rumbaut, Ruben G. "Ages, Life Stages, and Generational Cohorts: Decomposing the Immigrant First and Second Generations in the United States." *International Migration Review* 38 (2004): 1160–205.

Rutherford, Dudley. "Nearly 200 Evangelical Leaders Slam Christianity Today." *Christian Post*, December 22, 2019. www.christianpost.com.

Samie, Samaya Farooq. "Hetero-Sexy Self/Body Work and Basketball: The Invisible Sporting Women of British Pakistani Muslim Heritage." *South Asian Popular Culture* 11, no. 3 (2013): 257–70. https://doi.org/10.1080/14746689.2013.820480.

San Juan, E., Jr. "Overseas Filipino Workers: The Making of an Asian-Pacific Diaspora." *Global South*, 3, no. 2, (2009): 99–129.

Sands, Robert R. *Sport Ethnography.* Urbana: Human Kinetics, 2001.

Sarmiento, Thomas Xavier. "To Return to Saint Louis: Reading the Intimacies of the Heartland of U.S. Empire through 'The Dogeater.'" *Amerasia Journal* 46, no. 2 (2020): 218–35. https://doi.org/10.1080/00447471.2020.1852701.

Scheper-Hughes, Nancy, and Margaret M. Lock. "The Mindful Body: A Prolegomenon to Future Work in Medical Anthropology." *Medical Anthropology Quarterly* 1, no. 1 (1987): 6–41. https://www.jstor.org/stable/648769Sheppard.

Schultz, Jaime. "Reading the Catsuit: Serena Williams and the Production of Blackness at the 2002 U.S. Open." *Journal of Sport & Social Issues* 29, no. 3 (2005): 338–57. https://doi.org/10.1177/0193723505276230.

Shah, Nayan. *Contagious Divides: Epidemics and Race in San Francisco's Chinatown.* Berkeley: California University Press, 2001.

Shah, Sonia, ed. *Dragon Ladies: Asian American Feminists Breathe Fire.* Boston: South End Press, 1997.

Shankar, Shalini. *Advertising Diversity: Producing Language and Ethnicity in American Advertising.* Durham, NC: Duke University Press, 2015.

Sheehan, Rebecca. "'Little Giants of the Ring': Fighting Race and Making Men on the Australia-Philippines Boxing Circuit, 1919–1923." *Sport in Society* 15, no. 4 (2012): 447–61. https://doi.org/10.1080/17430437.2012.672232.

Sheppard, Samantha. *Sporting Blackness: Race, Embodiment, and Critical Muscle Memory on Screen.* Berkeley: University of California Press, 2020.

Shimizu, Celine Parreñas. *The Hypersexuality of Race: Performing Asian/American Women on Screen and Scene.* Durham, NC: Duke University Press, 2007.

Shimizu, Celine Parreñas. *Straitjacket Sexualities: Unbinding Asian American Manhoods in the Movies.* Stanford, CA: Stanford University Press, 2012.

Siu, Lok. "Queen of the Chinese Colony: Gender, Nation, and Belonging in Diaspora." *Anthropological Quarterly,* vol. 78, no. 3 (Summer 2005): 511–542.

Smith, Yevonne R. "Women of Color in Society and Sport." *Quest* 44, no. 2 (1992): 228–50. https://doi.org/10.1080/00336297.1992.10484052.

Sobchack, Vivian. "Baseball in the Post-American Cinema, or Life in the Minor Leagues." *East-West Film Journal* 7, no. 1 (1993): 1–23.

Strobel, Leny Mendoza. "Born Again Filipino: Filipino American Identity and Asian Panethnicity." *Amerasia Journal* 22, no. 2 (1996): 31–53. https://doi.org/10.17953/amer.22.2.v7841w4h7881hko4.

Stuckey, Sterling. *Slave Culture: Nationalist Theory and the Foundations of Black America.* New York: Oxford University Press, 1987.

Suarez, Theresa C. "Militarized Filipino Masculinity and the Language of Citizenship in San Diego." In *Militarized Currents: Toward a Decolonized Future in Asia and the Pacific,* edited by Setsu Shigematsu and Keith L. Camacho, 181–201. Minneapolis: University of Minnesota Press, 2010.

Sugrue, Thomas. *The Origins of the Urban Crisis: Race and Inequality in Postwar Detroit.* Princeton, NJ: Princeton University Press, 2014.

Sullivan-Blum, Constance R. "'It's Adam and Eve, Not Adam and Steve': What's at Stake in the Construction of Contemporary American Christian Homophobia." In *Homophobias: Lust and Loathing Across Time and Space,* edited by David A. B. Murray, 48–63. Durham, NC: Duke University Press, 2009. https://doi.org/10.1515/9780822391395-005.

Sumida, Stephen H. "East of California: Points of Origin in Asian American Studies." *Journal of Asian American Studies* 1, no. 1 (1998): 83–100. https://doi.org/10.1353/jaas.1998.0012.

Svinth, Joseph R. "The Origins of Philippines Boxing, 1899–1929." *Journal of Combative Sport* (2001): 1–8.

Szto, Courtney. *Changing on the Fly: Hockey through the Voices of South Asian Canadians.* New Brunswick, NJ: Rutgers University Press, 2020.

Tadiar, Neferti Xina M. *Fantasy Production: Sexual Economies and Other Philippine Consequences for the New World Order.* Hong Kong: Hong Kong University Press, 2004.

Thaman, Katie "Wydown Middle School's Mascot Takes Sixth-Graders Back to 1904." *Saint Louis Post-Dispatch,* April 20, 2000.

Thangaraj, Stanley Ilango. "Ballin' Indo-Pak Style: Pleasures, Desires, and Expressive Practices of South Asian American Masculinities." *International Review for the Sociology of Sport* 45, no. 3 (2010): 372–89. https://doi.org/10.1177/1012690210371047.

Thangaraj, Stanley I. *Desi Hoop Dreams: Pickup Basketball and the Making of Asian American Masculinity*. New York: New York University Press, 2015.

Thangaraj, Stanley I. "'I Was Raised Buddhist': Tiger Woods, Race, and Asian-ness." *Sociology of Sport Journal* 37, no. 1 (2020): 27–35. https://doi.org/10.1123/SSJ.2019-0067.

Thangaraj, Stanley I. "Masculinities." *Feminist Anthropology* 3, no. 2 (2022): 254–62. https://doi.org/10.1002/fea2.12104.

Thangaraj, Stanley I. "Playing through Differences: Black–White Racial Logic and Interrogating South Asian American Identity." *Ethnic and Racial Studies* 35, no. 6 (2012): 988–1006. https://doi.org/10.1080/01419870.2012.661868.

Thangaraj, Stanley I. "'We Share the Same Ancestry': US Kurdish Diasporas and the Aspirational and Ascriptive Practices of Race." *American Anthropologist* 124, no. 1 (2022): 104–17. https://doi.org/10.1111/aman.13698.

Thangaraj, Stanley I., Constancio R. Arnaldo, Jr., and Christina B. Chin, eds. *Asian American Sporting Cultures*. New York: New York University Press, 2016.

Thangaraj, Stanley I., Aarti Ratna, Daniel Burdsey, and Erica Rand. "Leisure and the Racing of National Populism." *Leisure Studies*, 37, no. 6 (2018): 1–14. https://doi.org/10.1080/02614367.2018.1541473.

Theberge, Nancy. "Gender and Sport." In *Handbook of Sports Studies*, edited by Jay Coakley and Eric Dunning, 322–33. Thousand Oaks, CA: SAGE, 2000.

Theberge, Nancy. "Toward a Feminist Alternative to Sport as a Male Preserve." *Quest* 37, no. 2 (1987): 193–202. https://doi.org/10.1080/00336297.1985.10483834.

Tiongson, Antonio T., Jr. *Filipinos Represent: DJs, Racial Authenticity, and the Hip-hop Nation*. Minneapolis: Minnesota University Press, 2013.

Toffoletti, Kim, and Peter Mewett, eds. *Sport and Its Female Fans*. New York: Routledge, 2012.

Tsing, Anna Lowenhaupt. *Friction: An Ethnography of Global Connection*. Princeton, NJ: Princeton University Press, 2004.

Tuan, Mia. *Forever Foreigners or Honorary Whites? The Asian Ethnic Experience Today*. New Brunswick, NJ: Rutgers University Press, 1998.

Tuan, Mia. "On Asian American Ice Queens and Multigeneration Asian Eth-nics." *Amerasia Journal* 25, no. 1 (1999): 181–86. https://doi.org/10.17953/amer.25.1.q0v817986t6h67q2.

US Census Bureau. "Filipino Alone; Filipino Alone or in Any Combination; United States; 2020." Accessed February 3, 2020. https://data.census.gov.

US Census Bureau. "Quick Facts: Champaign City, IL; Population Estimates, July 1, 2020." Accessed September 5, 2020. www.census.gov.

Uperesa, Lisa. *Gridiron Capital: How American Football Became a Samoan Game*. Durham, NC: Duke University Press, 2022.

Vang, Chia. "Hmong Youth, American Football, and the Cultural Politics of Ethnic Sports Tournaments." In *Asian American Sporting Cultures*, edited by Stanley I. Thangaraj, Constancio R. Arnaldo, Jr., and Christina B. Chin, 199–220. New York: New York University Press, 2016.

Vega, Sujey. *Latino Heartland: Of Borders and Belonging in the Midwest*. New York: New York University Press, 2015.

Velasco, Gina. "Performing the Filipina 'Mail-Order Bride': Queer Neoliberalism, Affective Labor, and Homonationalism." *Women & Performance: A Journal of Feminist Theory* 23, no. 3 (2013): 350–72. https://doi.org/10.1080/0740770X.2013.849064.

Velasco, Gina. *Queering the Global Filipina Body: Contested Nationalisms in the Filipina/o Diaspora*. Urbana: University of Illinois Press, 2020.

Vergara, Benito M., Jr. *Displaying Filipinos: Photography and Colonialism in Early 20th-Century Philippines*. Quezon City, Philippines: University of the Philippines Press, 1995.

Vergara, Benito M., Jr. *Pinoy Capital: The Filipino Nation in Daly City*. Philadelphia: Temple University Press, 2009.

Villegas, Mark. *Manifest Technique: Hip Hop, Empire, and Visionary Filipino American Culture*. Urbana: University of Illinois Press, 2021.

Volpp, Leti. "American Mestizo: Filipinos and Antimiscegenation Laws in California." *U.C. Davis L. Review* 33, no. 4 (2000): 795–835.

Walker, Vanessa Siddle. *Their Highest Potential: An African American School Community in the Segregated South*. Chapel Hill: University of North Carolina Press, 1996.

Wang, Oliver. "Everybody Loves an Underdog: Learning from Linsanity." In *Asian American Sporting Cultures*, edited by Stanley I. Thangaraj, Constancio R. Arnaldo, Jr., and Christina Chin, 75–101. New York: New York University Press, 2016.

Wang, Oliver. *Legions of Boom: Filipino American Mobile DJ Crews in the San Francisco Bay Area*. Durham, NC: Duke University Press, 2015.

Wang, Oliver. "Living with Linsanity." *Los Angeles Review of Books*, March 6, 2012. https://lareviewofbooks.org.

Willms, Nicole. *When Women Rule the Court: Gender, Race, and Japanese American Basketball*. New Brunswick, NJ: Rutgers University Press, 2017.

Winkelmann, Tessa. *Dangerous Intercourse: Gender and Interracial Relations in the American Colonial Philippines, 1898–1946*. Ithaca, NY: Cornell University Press, 2023.

Wong, Deborah. *Louder and Faster: Pain, Joy, and the Body Politic in Asian American Taiko*. Berkeley: University of California Press, 2019.

Woodward, Ian. "Material Culture and Narrative: Fusing Myth, Materiality, and Meaning." In *Material Culture and Technology in Everyday Life: Ethnographic Approaches*, edited by Phillip Vannini, 59–72. New York: Peter Lang, 2009.

Yamada, Mitsuye. "Asian Pacific American Women and Feminism." In *This Bridge Called My Back: Writings by Radical Women of Color*, edited by Cherríe Moraga and Gloria Anzaldúa, 71–75. Albany: SUNY Press, 1981.

Yamada, Mitsuye. "Invisibility Is an Unnatural Disaster: Reflections of an Asian American Woman." In *This Bridge Called My Back: Writings by Radical Women of Color*, edited by Cherríe Moraga and Gloria Anzaldúa, 30–35. Albany: SUNY Press, 2015.

Yep, Kathleen. "Linsanity and Centering Sport in Asian American Studies and Pacific Islander Studies." *Amerasia Journal* 38, no. 3 (2012): 133–37. https://doi.org/10.17953/amer.38.3.c6423501kt30oljp.

Yep, Kathleen. *Outside the Paint: When Basketball Ruled at the Chinese Playground.* Philadelphia: Temple University Press, 2009.

Yep, Kathleen. "Peddling Sport: Liberal Multiculturalism and the Racial Triangulation of Blackness, Chineseness and Native American-ness in Professional Basketball." *Ethnic and Racial Studies* 35, no. 6 (2012): 971–87. https://doi.org/10.1080/01419870.2012.661867.

INDEX

Page numbers in *italics* indicate figures

ABA. *See* Asian Basketball Association
Abdurraqib, Hanif, 139
ability. *See* athletic abilities and skills
AB Syndicate. *See* Asian Ballers (AB)
  Syndicate
Adidas, 92–94
African Americans: Asian Americans'
  emulation of, 162n5; basketball skills
  displayed by, 2, 103; and call-and-
  response, 81; cool associated with,
  93–94, 97, 129; cultural styles associated
  with, 90, 93–94, 106–8, 162n5; Filipina/
  os' emulation of, 106–8, 129; Filipina/
  os likened to, 16; heterosexual framing
  of, 106–7; hypermasculinity associated
  with, 50, 53; at Mayweather-Pacquiao
  fight, 49; negative attitudes toward, 52–
  53; swagger associated with, 106; violence against, 161n60; women athletes,
  119, 126–27. *See also* anti-Blackness
Aguilar-San Juan, Karín, 48, 165n16
Ahmed, Sara, 79
Alger, Horatio, 39
Ali, Muhammad, 36, 44
American studies, 8, 142
anthropology of sport, 143
anti-Blackness, 27, 52–53
anti-miscegenation laws, 18–19
Appadurai, Arjun, 23
Aquino, Kristine, 8–9
Asian Americans: heterogeneity of, 11;
  Lin as favorite of, 112; racial experi-

ences of, 11, 95; US sports marketed
  to, 5. *See also* Filipina/os; South Asian
  Americans
Asian and Asian American men: basketball leagues for, 24–25, 28, 94–97; stereotypes of, 42, 106. *See also* Filipina/
  os; South Asian American men
Asian and Asian American women: in
  flag football, 115–38; identity formation of, 115–19; racialization of, 29,
  116–21, 125–29, 131–38; stereotypes of,
  4, 12, 115, 117–18, 120–21, 128–29, 164n9,
  166n40. *See also* Filipina athletes;
  Filipina/os
Asian Ballers (AB) Syndicate, 89–113,
  140–41
Asian Ballers Network, 96
Asian Basketball Association (ABA),
  95–96
Asian Hoops, 96
assimilation, as goal of US colonialism,
  13–17, 41, 72, 90, 106, 113, 139, 140
athletic abilities and skills: of African
  Americans, 103; of Asian Americans,
  112–13; of Filipino basketball players,
  82, 100–106; flag football players, 115–
  18; racial preconceptions/prejudices
  in judgments of, 4, 67–68, 103, 112–13,
  115–18, 125–29, 131–37; white superiority
  claimed for, 67–68; women's, 1–4, 41,
  115–18, 125–29, 131–37, 139
Australia, 8–9

as tool for analyzing, 5; Filipina/os and, 4, 37, 57, 58; and the Louisiana Purchase Exposition, 67–70; pensionado program and, 17, 72; persistent remnants of, 39, 53, 57, 85–86, 144; and race, 53; Spanish, 13; sport as means of, 4, 8, 12–17; US, 13–14, 39–41, 57, 58, 70, 85; YMCA and, 40–41

Communion (Christian sacrament), 33–34, 36

consumption: middle-class Filipino basketball players and, 28, 90, 93–94, 97–99, 101–3, 106, 108–9, 113; representations and, 44

cool, 92–94, 97–98, 103, 110, 129–31

Costner, Kevin, 66

crossovers (basketball), 1–4, 88, 139

crossovers (culture): analytical/theoretical uses of, 5–9, 12, 141, 143–44; Filipina/os and, 3, 5, 8, 29; gender, 2–4, 6, 7; labor migration as, 8; in language, 79–80; racial, 3–4, 6, 9–13. *See also* transnationalism

Cruz, Denise, 99, 162n2

Curry, Stephen, 103

Davis, Amira Rose, 142

De La Hoya, Oscar "Golden Boy," 21, 36, 46

De Leon, Adrian, 85

DeRozan, DeMar, 112

diaspora: Christianity and, 46; Filipina/o identity and, 5–6, 9–10, 22–23, 45, 86, 113; Marcos's influence on, 26; masculine norms of, 3–4, 7, 9, 29; Pacquiao and, 9, 22, 27–28, 35, 37, 39, 45, 47, 53, 58–59; sexual norms and practices in, 54–59; sport's role in identity formation of, 5, 8–9, 22–23, 143

Draves, Victoria Manalo, 19–20

dunking, 103

Easter Sunday (film), 45–47

emasculation. *See* feminization

Eng, David, 28

Entertainment and Sports Programming Network (ESPN), 101–2, 115–16

España-Maram, Linda, 41

ethnic studies, 141–42

ethno-nationalism: boodle fights and, 84–86; in the diaspora, 3; heteronormative/heteropatriarchal character of, 45, 57–58; Pacquiao and, 9, 24, 32, 36, 37, 39, 44–45; in the Philippines, 13; tattoos as expression of, 108–11; team uniforms as expression of, 28

eugenics, 68

Fabolous, 137

Facebook, 23, 43, 50, 76, 81, 100–102

fair play, 22, 40, 134

Farhood, Steve, 51

Farrales, May, 8–9

Farrell, Will, 158n39

Feagin, Joe, 53

feminization: of Filipina/os, 106–7; of Filipinos, 31, 35, 55; of male labor, 28, 35, 85; of the Philippine nation, 37, 59; Protestantism blamed for, 41; of volleyball, 76–77

Ferguson, Roderick, 7, 16

Fidler, Merrie, 142

Field of Dreams, 66

Filipina athletes: in basketball, 77; experiences of, 1–4, 45; and familial expectations, 29; in flag football, 29, 115–38; identity formation of, 115–19; racialization of, 29, 116–21, 125–29, 131–38. *See also* Asian and Asian American women

Filipina/os: class differences among, 73; crossovers performed by, 8; dehumanization of, 57, 58; discrimination against, 18–20; labor migration of, 8, 17–19, 28, 31, 35, 65, 72–74; opposition to immigration of, 18; and race, 9–14, 18–21, 27, 71–72, 103, 106–8, 142;

Filipina/os (*cont.*)
sexuality of, 18, 71; stereotypes of, 10, 18, 106–7; US immigration of, 17–19, 25–27, 156n71; US sports marketed to, 5; value of studying, 8; violence against, 18, 71. *See also* Asian Americans; diaspora; ethno-nationalism; identity formation
Filipina/o sporting cultures: and colonialism, 4, 8, 12–17; consumption in, 28; gendered expectations in, 2–4; history of, 5; and identity formation, 4–5, 8–9, 19–23; methodology of studying, 23–25; racial contours of, 9–13, 20–21; significance of, 29–30; transnational and transhistorical contexts of, 12–13, 21, 22–23; uniforms of, 89–94; and US norms and expectations, 4. *See also* sport; sporting cultures
Filipino Mango Athletic Club (FMAC), 20–21
Filipino Repatriation Act (1935), 19
Filipino Student Bulletin (newspaper), 17, 156n71
Filipino Students Christian Movement, 17
first-generation immigrants, 24
flag football, 25, 115–38; heterosexual framing of, 117, 121, 124, 130; history of, 120; motivations for and gains from playing, 120, 122–24; physical and bodily aspects of, 116–18, 120–24, 126, 129–30; popularity of, 166n42; principles of, 164n2; racial dynamics in, 29, 115–21, 125–29, 131–38, 141; sexual stereotypes and expectations challenged in, 115–38
FMAC. *See* Filipino Mango Athletic Club
food, 78–79
football, 15, 117, 120, 130. *See also* flag football

Garcia, Ceferino, 10, 14, 42
gender: boodle fights and, 84, 86–87; crossovers concerning, 1–4, 6, 7; Filipino American basketball and, 76–77; and food preparation, 87; in sporting cultures, 2–3, 119. *See also* feminization; masculinity; women; women athletes
Godfather trilogy (films), 97
Goodfellas (film), 97
Graham, Billy, 157n4
Great Depression, 18, 71

Halberstam, J. Jack, 7
Hall, Stuart, 43
Halvorson, Britt E., 64
Hardaway, Tim, 88
Harris, Cheryl, 29, 118, 136
Hatton, Ricky "the Hitman," 56
heartland. *See* Midwest
Hernandez, Leyla, 45
heteronormativity: in Canada, 8; in the Midwest, 66, 72; Pacquiao and, 48, 54–57; of sporting cultures, 22
heteropatriarchy: diaspora and, 7, 9–10, 107; nationalism and, 39, 45, 58, 86; Pacquiao and, 37, 39
heterosexual framing: of African American men, 106–7; of female spectatorship, 114; of Filipinos, 106–7, 113–14; of flag football, 117, 121, 124, 130; of masculinity, 80, 107, 113–14
Hmong community, 129, 166n42
Hoganson, Kristen, 67
homosociality: arm wrestling and, 52; boodle fights and, 84–87; in Filipino American basketball, 28, 64, 76, 79–80, 83, 100–101
Hong, Grace, 7, 16
Hoosiers (film), 65

identity formation: of Asian American women, 115–19; basketball and, 64, 81, 90; diaspora and, 5–6, 9–10, 22–23, 45, 86, 113; of Filipina athletes, 115–19; of Filipina/os, 4–5, 8–9, 19–21, 81,

ABOUT THE AUTHOR

Constancio R. Arnaldo Jr. is a Sociocultural Anthropologist who examines the cultural politics of sports, pleasure, and identity formation at the nexus of race, class, gender, and sexuality in the Filipinx American community. He is co-editor of *Asian American Sporting Cultures*.